CREATIVE ENCOUNTER

UNIVERSITY OF NORTH CAROLINA
STUDIES IN THE GERMANIC LANGUAGES
AND LITERATURES

Initiated by RICHARD JENTE (1949–1952), established by F. E. COENEN (1952–1968)

SIEGFRIED MEWS, EDITOR
Publication Committee: Department of Germanic Languages

For other volumes in the "Studies" see pages 181–82.

Send orders to: (U.S. and Canada)
The University of North Carolina Press, P.O. Box 2288
Chapel Hill, N.C. 27514
(All other countries) Feffer and Simons, Inc., 31 Union Square, New York, N.Y. 10003

NUMBER NINETY-ONE

UNIVERSITY
OF NORTH CAROLINA
STUDIES IN
THE GERMANIC LANGUAGES
AND LITERATURES

Creative Encounter
Festschrift for Herman Salinger

Edited by
Leland R. Phelps
with the Assistance of
A. Tilo Alt

CHAPEL HILL
THE UNIVERSITY OF NORTH CAROLINA PRESS
1978

© University of North Carolina

Studies in the Germanic Languages

and Literatures 1978

Library of Congress Cataloging in Publication Data

Main entry under title:

Creative encounter.

(University of North Carolina studies in the
Germanic languages and literatures)
English or German.
"The publications of Herman Salinger": pp. 171–79.
1. German literature—History and criticism—
Addresses, essays, lectures.   2. Literature, Compara-
tive—Addresses, essays, lectures.   3. Salinger,
Herman, 1905–   I. Salinger, Herman, 1905–
II. Phelps, Leland R.   III. Alt, Arthur Tilo,
1931–   IV. Series: Studies in the Germanic
languages and literatures (Chapel Hill, N.C.); no. 91.

PT36.S24C7   830   77-27603
ISBN 0-8078-8091-4

Manufactured in the U.S.A.

Contents

ESSAYS IN COMPARATIVE LITERATURE

ESSAYS IN GERMAN LITERATURE

Contents

Dedication

Herman Salinger's academic career has been a creative encounter in the very best sense. A poet, translator and scholar-teacher, he has brought to the disciplines of German and Comparative Literature an unusual constellation of insights, sensitivity and understanding. The distinguished caliber of his own poetic works, *Angel of our Thirst* and *A Sigh is the Sword*, as well as his perceptive artistic translations from the German make it most fitting that this *Festschrift* open with poems written especially for the occasion by Rudolf Hagelstange and Karl Krolow, two major German poets whose works Professor Salinger introduced to the English-speaking world.

A group of scholars joined these two distinguished poets to present their colleague and personal friend of long standing with a token of their professional esteem and friendship. The wide range of interests represented by their contributions from the fields of German and Comparative Literature is indicative of Herman Salinger's own breadth as a scholar-teacher. Although he was trained as a Germanist, he never restricted himself to the literature of that one language. His catholic interests led him early in his academic life into the field of Comparative Literature which he tirelessly advocated throughout his teaching career. Herman Salinger's life-long concern for literature both as a creative act and as a scholarly pursuit is reflected in this volume, and the editors and contributors join in honoring him by dedicating this *Festschrift* to him as he leaves the profession to which he devoted his energies as a poet, scholar and teacher.

L. R. P.

Der Alchimist

In meiner aufgestauten Trauer
spare ich mir fliehendes Entzücken.
Das übersehene Lächeln wecke ich auf.
Blind verwundet bersten ich vor Gelächter
verwandle fehlend die Stürze in Sprung oder Flug.
Ich will mich satt trinken an meinen Mängeln.

Salz wird mir süß, Entzücken kehrt sich in Kummer
Aus jeder heimlichen Liebschaft
wächst mir offener Haß, aus meinen
Niederlagen kaufe ich meinen Triumph
taumele von unverhoffter Auferstehung
zu sanfter Verwesung, von Nacht und Vernichtung
zu mächtigem Morgen.

Hölle und Himmel Tugend und Laster –
ich hege den Verdacht daß mir
asketisch altmodischer Gott nicht
ohne seinen gemütlichen Teufel Sancho Panza
und dieser nicht ohne seinen närrischen Ritter
Don Quichote die Arena betritt in der die
Spiegelfechter ihre überlebten Turniere austragen.
Fernab, auf den offenen Feldern,
im Takelwerk der Ideen und Ideologien
den Irrgängen des Blutes streiten sich
die Dämonen um meinesgleichen und mich.

Falls sie mich fressen sollten,
lasse ich sie auf meiner Zunge zergehen
wie Götter.

Rudolf Hagelstange
für
Hermann Sahlinger

30. VII.
1975

The Alchemist

Rudolf Hagelstange for Herman Salinger

Into my stored-up sadness
I hoard your fleeting ecstasy.
The overlooked smile I reassess.
Fatally wounded, I am bursting with laughter,
falling I transform the plunges into leap, into flight.
I will drink myself full of my own shortcomings.
Salt becomes sweet to me, delight is turned to sorrow.
From every clandestine love
luxuriates open hate, out of my
defeats I pile high my triumph,
stagger from unhoped-for resurrection
to gentle decay, from night and annihilation
to mightier morning.

Hell and heaven, virtue and vice—
I harbor a hidden suspicion that your
ascetic, old-fashioned God does not—
without his congenial devil Sancho Panza
and the latter not without his foolish knight
Don Quixote—enter the arena in which the
shadow-fencers execute their outmoded tournaments.
Far off, on the open fields,
in the tug of war of ideas and ideologies,
in the labyrinths of the blood,
the demons are fighting over me and the likes of me.

If they should start to devour me,
I shall let them dissolve on my tongue
like gods.

30 July 1975   (translated by H. S.)

xi

KARL KROLOW

61 Darmstadt, Park Rosenhöhe 5
Telefon 75680

Das sagt dir nichts

für Hermann Salinger

Das sagt dir nichts — Hören, sehen
durch Fenster, die einfachste Geschichte
der Welt wie Kanuwalten, in der man
kam. Hast du gelebt? Wen geht
das etwas an? Sie fühltest manchmal
Dich beobachtet wie jemand,
der sein Polizeibild kennt.
Dein Ende hilft das nichts.
Die Fortsetzung der Biographie
ist schon das andere Leben.

Karl Krolow

Darmstadt, 2. XI. 75

That Tells You Nothing

Karl Krolow

That tells you nothing—Something overheard
through the window, the simplest story
in the world like manhood into which you
entered. Have you lived? Whose business
is that anyway? You sometimes felt
yourself observed like somebody
who knows his own passport picture.
The ending is not important.
The continuation of the biography
is already the *other* life.

2 November 1975   (translated by H. S.)

Tabula Gratulatoria

Beda Allemann
Universität Bonn
Bonn, Germany

A. Tilo Alt
Duke University
Durham, North Carolina

Maria P. Alter
Villanova University
Villanova, Pennsylvania

Hellmut Hermann Ammerlahn
University of Washington
Seattle

W. Banks Anderson, Jr.
Duke University
Durham, North Carolina

Anne F. Baecker
University of North Carolina
Greensboro

Harry Bergholz
University of North Carolina
Chapel Hill

Leonidas Betts
North Carolina State University
Raleigh

Norman H. Binger
University of Kentucky
Lexington

Haskell M. Block
State University of New York
Binghamton

Elaine E. Boney
San Diego State University
San Diego, California

Frank L. Borchardt
Duke University
Durham, North Carolina

Charles Kilgo Bradsher
Duke University
Durham, North Carolina

Ralph and Lucy Braibanti
Durham, North Carolina

Luise H. Bronner
University of Massachusetts
Boston

George Crawford Buck
University of Washington
Seattle

William H. and Elaine M. Cartwright
Duke University
Durham, North Carolina

Mary Church
Santa Monica, California

R. Taylor Cole
and Mrs. Cole
Durham, North Carolina

Mary Anne Collins-Stauffer
Princeton Theological Seminary
Princeton, New Jersey

Herbert and Waltraud Deinert
Cornell University
Ithaca, New York

Ingeborg M. B. Dent
Methodist College
Fayetteville, North Carolina

Harriet Grooters Dishman
Boston, Massachusetts

Carol J. Drowota
Baptist College at Charleston
Charleston, South Carolina

Sadik T. Duda
St. Augustine's College
Raleigh, North Carolina

Martin Dyck
Massachusetts Institute of Technology
Cambridge

Eugene H. Falk
University of North Carolina
Chapel Hill

Evelyn Scherabon Firchow
University of Minnesota
Minneapolis

John Fitzell
Rutgers University
New Brunswick, New Jersey

Werner P. Friederich
University of North Carolina
Chapel Hill

Marion A. Gleason
New Canaan, Connecticut

Valerie D. Greenberg
Chapel Hill, North Carolina

Hildegard Kopf Greene
Springfield, Virginia

Diether H. Haenicke
Wayne State University
Detroit, Michigan

Rudolf Hagelstange
Erbach im Odenwald, Germany

Walther L. Hahn
University of Oregon
Eugene

Gerald W. Hartwig
Duke University
Durham, North Carolina

Einar and Eva L. Haugen
Harvard University
Cambridge, Massachusetts

Henry Conrad Helmke
Auburn University
Auburn, Alabama

Eloise Alexander Henderson
Hamilton College
Clinton, New York

Gunter H. Hertling
University of Washington
Seattle

Charles W. Hoffmann
Ohio State University
Columbus

Frederic B. M. Hollyday
Duke University
Durham, North Carolina

V. C. Hubbs
University of Michigan
Ann Arbor

Linda Lee Jacobs
Lexington, Kentucky

Christa and Sheridan Johns
Durham, North Carolina

Roger Dick Johns
Huntingdon College
Montgomery, Alabama

Klaus W. Jonas
University of Pittsburgh
Pittsburgh, Pennsylvania

Terry Gregory-Patrick Kane
Ravenna, Ohio

Patrick D. Kenan
Duke University
Durham, North Carolina

Gerd Kiper
Technische Universität Hannover
Hannover, Germany

Günter Klabes
Vassar College
Poughkeepsie, New York

Erika-Anette Koeppel
Duke University
Durham, North Carolina

Karl Krolow
Darmstadt, Germany

Barbara Christine Marie Kuck
Fairfield, Connecticut

John G. Kunstmann
University of North Carolina
Chapel Hill

Jill Salinger Lamkin
Norfolk, Virginia

George S. Lane
University of North Carolina
Chapel Hill

John Hamilton Langley
Regents Press of Kansas
Lawrence

Waltraud Lauf
Duke University
Durham, North Carolina

Paul Lawson
The Charioteer Press
Washington, District of Columbia

Richard H. Lawson
University of North Carolina
Chapel Hill

Luise A. Lenel
Montclair, New Jersey

Kathryn Crommelin Lieb
Wayne, Pennsylvania

John L. Lievsay
Bethesda, Maryland

Sara Gearhart Lightner
New Wilmington, Pennsylvania

Hans Lowenbach
Durham, North Carolina

Charles Whitsett Lyle
Havre de Grace, Maryland

Ernst and Marianne Manasse
North Carolina Central University
Durham, North Carolina

Alan K. Manchester
Durham, North Carolina

Harry T. McPherson
Duke University
Durham, North Carolina

Siegfried Mews
University of North Carolina
Chapel Hill

A. McA. ("Mac") Miller
New College
University of South Florida
Sarasota

Sterling Arthur Minor
Nashville, Tennessee

Helmut W. Motekat
Universität München
Munich, Germany

Thomas Andrew Neville
Yorktown High School
Falls Church, Virginia

Robert Judson Niess
Duke University
Durham, North Carolina

James C. O'Flaherty
Wake Forest University
Winston-Salem, North Carolina

Lewis Patton
Duke University
Durham, North Carolina

Heinrich Pfeiffer
Alexander von Humboldt Foundation
Bonn-Bad Godesberg, Germany

Leland R. and Ruth S. Phelps
Duke University
Durham, North Carolina

Thomas C. Pollock
and Mrs. Pollock
New York University
New York

Richard A. Preston
Duke University
Durham, North Carolina

Angelika Langen von Ramm
Durham, North Carolina

Helmut Rehder †
University of Texas
Austin

Herbert and Irene Reichert
University of North Carolina
Chapel Hill

William H. Rey
University of Washington
Seattle

Phillip H. Rhein
Vanderbilt University
Nashville, Tennessee

Sieghardt M. Riegel
University of Wisconsin
Madison

Kindred Aaron Ritchie
Durham, North Carolina

Philip W. Roberts
and Mrs. Roberts
Glastonbury, Connecticut

James Lancelot Rolleston
Duke University
Durham, North Carolina

Donald and Frieda Rosenberg
Duke University
Durham, North Carolina

Tabula Gratulatoria   xix

David Louis and Sylvia Salinger
Glenview, Illinois

Jennifer W. Salinger
Washington, District of Columbia

Wendy L. Salinger
Folly Beach, South Carolina

Jeffrey L. Sammons
Yale University
New Haven, Connecticut

Helmut Schanze
Rheinisch-Westfälische
Technische Hochschule
Aachen, Germany

Ann Salinger Scheid
Troy, New Hampshire

Marvin and Roslyn Schindler
Wayne State University
Detroit, Michigan

Heinrich Schnitzler
Vienna, Austria

George Schoolfield
Yale University
New Haven, Connecticut

Ernst I. Schürer
University of Florida
Gainesville

George Carl Schwarz
Hope Haven Children's Hospital
Jacksonville, Florida

Christoph E. Schweitzer
University of North Carolina
Chapel Hill

Lester W. J. Seifert
University of Wisconsin
Madison

R. Baird Shuman
University of Illinois
Urbana/Champaign

William Merritt Singer
Durham, North Carolina

Robert M. Sitton
Portland, Oregon

Samuel D. Soule
St. Louis, Missouri

W. M. Spackman
Princeton, New Jersey

Marcel Tetel
Duke University
Durham, North Carolina

Royal L. Tinsley, Jr.
University of Arizona
Tucson

Don C. Travis, Jr.
University of Texas
Austin

Vladimir G. Treml
Duke University
Durham, North Carolina

Bruno J. Urban
Durham, North Carolina

Lydia Helen Vollmer
Monterey, California

Bruce W. Wardropper
Duke University
Durham, North Carolina

Nancy Palmer Wardropper
North Carolina Central University
Durham, North Carolina

Hermann Weigand
Yale University
New Haven, Connecticut

Gerhard H. Weiss
University of Minnesota
Minneapolis

Homer Covode Welsh
Kutztown State College
Kutztown, Pennsylvania

Ulrich K. Wesche
University of Denver
Denver, Colorado

Paul Knowlton Whitaker
University of Kentucky
Lexington

A. Leslie Willson
University of Texas
Austin

Mrs. Wayne Wonderley
Lexington, Kentucky

Dewey Kiper Ziegler
University of Kansas
Lawrence

Theodore Ziolkowski
Princeton University
Princeton, New Jersey

Swirbul Library
Adelphi University
Garden City, New York

Department of Modern Languages and Literatures
Carnegie-Mellon University
Pittsburgh, Pennsylvania

Department of Germanic Languages and Literature
Duke University
Durham, North Carolina

Department of Germanic Languages and Literatures
State University of New York
Albany

Department of Germanic Languages
University of North Carolina
Chapel Hill

University of North Carolina
Studies in the Germanic Languages and Literatures
Chapel Hill

New College
University of South Florida
Sarasota

Department of German Studies
Stanford University
Stanford, California

Department of Modern Languages
Trinity College
Hartford, Connecticut

Department of Romance and Germanic Languages and Literatures
Wayne State University
Detroit, Michigan

Junior Year in Germany, Munich and Freiburg
Wayne State University
Detroit, Michigan

ESSAYS IN COMPARATIVE LITERATURE

Some Concepts of The Tragic in Versions of Electra

Eugene H. Falk

It was George Boas[1] who once wrote that he was "not going to play that ancient game of trying to define the indefinable." He did not believe that satisfactory definitions of such terms as "tragedy" or "comedy" could be given. It is, however, a different matter, I believe, to seek to fathom the phenomenon of *the tragic*. Max Scheler[2] rightly rejected the inductive method by which some critics—to this day—seek to isolate the tragic on the basis of literary works, without seeming to realize that one would already have to know what the tragic is in order to identify it in the works. He likewise rejected the notion of relying on an identification of the tragic based on emotional reactions, a procedure that is bound to tell us more about ourselves than about the tragic. According to Scheler, the tragic is an essential element of the universe itself.

In this paper, I do not propose to arrive at a definition of tragedy or become involved in arguments about the merits of various views of the tragic. Instead, I should like to examine a few versions of the *Electra*, in the hope of catching at least a glimpse of some aspects of what we may agree to consider as components of the tragic. The spirit of the time may of course at any given period determine what is perceived as a "tragedy," but the sense of *the tragic* must be timeless and immutable, for only thus could it be an "essential element of the universe."

Let us first consider some of the salient features of the Sophoclean *Electra*. Almost at the outset, we learn from the old servant who looked after Orestes as a boy that it was Electra who had the courage to act resolutely and to hand over her young brother to the servant after the murder of their father Agamemnon. Orestes, affirming the justice of his cause, recalls Apollo's words according to which he is to win just revenge, but with stealth. The old servant consequently gives the false account of a chariot race in which Orestes was killed, and Orestes himself brings the urn that supposedly contains his ashes. All this is to mislead the murderous mother Clytemnestra and her husband Aegisthus, the usurping king.

Orestes establishes not only his justification for what he is about to do, but also his superior right to carry out his revenge in a manner that may be repugnant to an objective observer, for the means are made to justify the end, which he foresees will make him glare on his foes "like a blazing star." In his appeal to the gods he prays for success so that he may win what appears as his own glory of coming as a "purifier," justly sent by the Gods.

As soon as Orestes withdraws, Electra emerges, and it is almost unthinkable that we could be oblivious to the dimension of time as soon as we are made to realize that her wailing fills not only the space before the royal palace, but also the years that have elapsed since the murder of her father when Orestes had barely reached his teens. Her first words are a forceful reminder of the duration of her woes, and at the same time of the fact that for her the past is ever present, so much so that we are led to imagine that the murder has just occurred. This is an important device because the intensity of her emotions is thereby made plausible and their justification convincing. Sophocles thus makes her rise above common humanity to a height where she indeed stands alone as an exceptional example of enduring suffering and inconsolable grief.

We hear her, still ignorant of her brother's arrival, repeat again and again the vow never to cease her sorrowful laments, her accusations against her murderous mother and stepfather, and her insistent calls for revenge. By the closing in of the past upon the present, and by the drawing of the impending future into the present, our sense of time, having first been impressed upon us, is obliterated. Thereby the timelessness and the validity of the values that Electra defends are effectively impressed upon us. Moreover, she does not condemn the consolations of the noble women of the Chorus; she merely finds their efforts useless and pleads with them to suffer what she knows may appear as monomaniacal madness, for she is not blind to the judgment she elicits from those whose values shift under the stress of fear and of a reasonable urge for self-preservation. In vain does the Chorus point to the uselessness of Electra's ceaseless sorrow and lament, vain are the exhortations not to pass the bounds of common sense and to allow her sisters and her brother to help carry the burden of her grief; and finally, vain are the encouragements whereby the Chorus hopes to rekindle Electra's faith in the power and justice of Zeus. Although Electra recognizes the validity of reasonableness common to man and even feels ashamed of her lack of moderation, she herself cannot espouse the values of those who consider the common measure of restraint natural. Quite aware of being driven by the same sort of evil which she sees in her foes, she is, in view of her values and the conditions which she is forced to face, far from recognizing therein any guilt. On the contrary, she sees her excessive grief and her unquenchable thirst for revenge not only as justified but as unavoidable as long as her obligation to justice, to honor, and to nobility remains alive.

A similar theme of self-justification occurs again in Electra's encounter with her timid sister Chrysothemis. Electra finds herself reproached for her inordinate and ineffectual anger. Chrysothemis sees no purpose in empty threats that may lead to her being persecuted and suffering in utter helplessness. Prudence is therefore her guide to behavior, and pride or honor does not compensate for the loss of whatever little joy and happiness life may still have to offer her. She is quite willing to indulge in the hope of even modest satisfactions if the price she has to pay is merely that of yielding to authority. Chrysothemis knows that justice is not on her side but on Electra's, yet she prefers to be sensible, rather than foolishly honorable. She would, she claims, speak her mind, were it not for her weakness and her fear of reprisals. Electra's response is intended to establish not only her superior values but also the commitment imposed by superior values. For Electra they impose a choice between expediency and righteousness, between rationalization and facing up squarely to the demands of one's value judgments. We may readily detect an element of existentialist ethics in Electra's need of a clean conscience and in her challenge to Chrysothemis to make a resolute choice between sensible self-interest and seemingly foolish commitments to loyalty, and between integrity and shameful expediency.

That flattery is not her way becomes evident in the confrontation with her mother. Electra shows once more that she has no choice but to be evil, surrounded as she is by evil, and that she has become possessed by blind hatred and incapable of seeing her mother's point of view. Sophocles has marked Clytemnestra's attitudes towards Electra and Orestes with striking ambivalence, an ambivalence born of motherly affection and of resentment bred by fear and threats. This realistic psychological portrayal of "love in hate" precludes an unequivocal judgment of Clytemnestra. If her case against Agamemnon were nothing but a pretext to justify the murder of her husband, who in her mind had no right to sacrifice her daughter Iphigenia, Electra might appear completely justified, and the righteous would be seen to triumph over the wicked. Electra's murderous intentions with regard to her mother might then appear as the result of madness, and the punishment of the guilty would appear painful only because of its occurrence within a family. This *pathos* clearly depends on placing blood relations above any other —relations we can hardly claim have remained unchallenged in the past or in more recent times. None of these considerations could be brought to bear positively on any conception of the tragic.

Clytemnestra, then, is not presented as a wicked murderer who killed her husband in cold blood: she has a motivation, and it weakens Electra's case against her mother; for Electra, who plans a murder "with justice" and is ready to carry it out by herself, at least while she believes Orestes dead, is as "guilty" as her mother: she condemns Clytemnestra for the deed, just or unjust. Electra repudiates murderous revenge, yet she herself appears to be guided by no other principle. To all appearances, Electra is blinded to the point of approving her own planned misdeeds while condemning her mother's act determined by similar, equally strong motivations. However, that is not so, for she knows that she is possessed with hatred, and she is ashamed of having to act against her will. However blinded by provocations and by her rage Electra may be, even at the height of resentment and frenzy she is capable of reflection and of knowing that she is wrong, as well as capable of self-judgment and of knowing that she is not guilty.

It may appear that the play ends favorably for Electra. Under divine orders Orestes accomplishes Electra's purposes and brings retributive justice to bear on those who are guilty in the eyes of Agamemnon's children. In the Sophoclean play there is not a hint of retribution against the avengers themselves. When Orestes emerges after he has killed his mother, not even the Chorus finds words of blame. Finally, Electra's last words are cruel demands for the disposal of Aegisthus' body, almost as cruel as those she uttered when she heard her mother's outcry at the moment of her death. This is where the sequence of *events* ends.

On the level of incidents, Electra gains everything she has hoped for; on the level of themes, she incurs of necessity, without guilt but also without innocence, a grave loss that is the price she knew she had to pay, namely, to become evil in destroying evil, to become what she despises. Since I am not concerned here with *Electra* as a "tragedy," but with the *tragic* as it exists in the universe and finds a reflection in some tragedies, I wish to point out that Scheler's conception of the destruction of a higher value by a lesser one, or by one that is equal to that which is destroyed, may well have its merits as one aspect of the tragic. In the Sophoclean *Electra*, however, I do not see this aspect developed. A passage in Martin Buber's *Good and Evil* is far more revealing.[3] I shall limit myself here to what I consider essential for the purposes of this inquiry. Though Buber deals with the problem in an entirely different context and with ramifications that are at best tangential to our theme, I find that his distinction between "the chaos of possibilities of being" and "self-unification" places Electra in a more significant perspective than our habitual criteria for tragic action could do.

In her unbending determination to seek revenge, Electra actually denies honor, loyalty, justice though they seem to guide her. At the same time, however, she knows that she is helplessly drawn into evil acts by the evil that surrounds her. In her encounters with the Chorus, her sister, and her mother, she is confronted with problems that demand an answer based on a purpose, a *chosen* purpose. Instead, she is either helplessly torn between *sophrosyne* (temperance, prudence, moderation) and an impelling act she knows is bound to lead to self-abomination; or, aware of her own evil purposes, she extols her virtuous loyalty and self-denial in opposition to her sister's clinging to a few of life's pleasures cheapened by cowardice; or else, in her confrontation with her mother, she indulges in self-righteous sophistry. As Buber might say, her soul is driven round in a dizzy whirl, in a "swirling chaos" in which it "does what it wills not to do, what is preposterous to it, the alien, the evil . . . ." Her soul is overcome by chaotic appetites and never achieves direction. "To the extent," says Buber, "to which the soul achieves unification it becomes aware of itself as sent in quest of it. It comes into the service of good or into service for good." The impossibility of Electra's "becoming a whole, becoming a form, of crystallization of the soul . . ." presents, to my mind, a universal aspect of the tragic. It is part of human nature, of living within the chaos of our contradictions and of letting that chaos of emotions, with all its alluring potentialities, distract us from committing ourselves by decisions for wholeness and goodness. As Buber says:

Everything in the nature of inclinations, of indolence, of habits, of fondness for possibilities which has been swashbuckling within us, must be overcome, and overcome, not by elimination, by suppression, for genuine wholeness can never be achieved like that, never a wholeness where downtrodden appetites lurk in the corners. Rather must all these mobile or static forces, seized by the soul's rapture, plunge of their own accord, as it were, into the mightiness of decision and dissolve within it. Until the soul as form has such great power over the soul as matter, until chaos is subdued and shaped into cosmos, what an immense resistance!

Hofmannsthal is known to have admitted that his *Electra* reveals the delight he felt in the contrast between his play and the "devilishly humane atmosphere" of Goethe's *Iphigenia*. In fact, only the barest traces of humanity can be detected in Hofmannsthal's play. True, Orestes is moved by Electra's suffering, but apart from that, there are only a couple of humane references made by two of the servants who cannot hear without commiseration the abusive, cruel comments the other servants make about frenzied, ferocious Electra.

But even their pity for the princess, who is made to eat with the dogs and is beaten by Aegisthus, is less the result of commiseration of one human being with another than of indignation at the merciless ill-treatment of a person of high rank.

At times Electra wallows in suffering. At a certain hour of the day—the hour when her father's murder occurred—she withdraws to feed her memory and her visions on the murder she witnessed long ago. During her hallucinations she believes that she perceives her father's shade, and in her self-gratifying prophecies she sees streams of sacrificial blood of the victims of her revenge gush upon her father's grave.

At no time is Electra made to justify her cause before a Chorus of noble women, before her sister, or before her mother. Instead of the Chorus, we find at the beginning of the play only the women who serve in the palace, and we gather that most of them are in no other relationship with her than that of hurling insults at each other. Much the same holds true for Electra's relationship with her mother, but here the mutual threats and affronts are exacerbated by the virulence of their hostility, which leaves no occasion for either mother or daughter to triumph on the strength of decorum, high-mindedness, and righteousness. And Chrysothemis is so obsessed with fear and instinctive drives that all she elicits is Electra's repugnance. Chrysothemis is made frantic by her fear of her mother, of Aegisthus, and of Electra's ceaseless provocations that bring reprisals against both of them, but Electra does not show the slightest pity for her sister's yearning for peace, marriage, and motherhood. Electra has nothing but brutal contempt and derision for her sister's womanly hopes and for her all-too-human desire to flee terror and to forget. Later, after the message that makes her believe that Orestes is dead, Electra seeks her sister's help to kill Clytemnestra and Aegisthus. However, instead of trying to win over Chrysothemis by convincing her of the righteousness of their cause, Electra actually seeks to exploit her sister's weakness, and to tempt and ensnare her by flattery and bribery, by visions of rapturous womanhood and blissful motherhood.

Hofmannsthal's Clytemnestra does not even mention her daughter Iphigenia in self-justification. The closest she comes to even suggesting a mere semblance of self-defense is when she remarks, in a helpless sort of reflection, that Agamemnon made the mistake of returning at the wrong time and that his death was a matter of chance with no one left to blame. She can even imagine that if they were to meet, she could face him with the tenderness of old friends. She is a sick woman who feels exhausted from sleepless nights or from nightmares engendered by the fear of retribution from the absent but living Orestes and by the ever-present recriminations of Electra's undying hatred. She clings superstitiously to the belief that some as yet unknown ritual or sacrifice, human if necessary, may rid her of debilitating dreams so that she may regain her strength. She suspects Electra of knowing the secret remedy, and she cajoles and threatens in turn. But all she gains is at first only tantalizing revelations and finally Electra's frequently repeated visions of the slaughter of Agamemnon's murderers and of her own raging triumph over her oppressors.

In this play, so obviously tinged with Freudian notions, Electra provides the most significant self-revelation in the scene in which Orestes discloses his identity. She tells him that when she became aware of her body and of her desires, she heard the sighs and the groans of her father and out of his grave he betrothed her to hatred. Wedded to hatred, she sacrificed the "sweet shudders" of love to her father.

Orestes, so different from the Orestes of Sophocles, has to overcome his hesitation to kill his mother, and seeks strength in the divine command he has received and in threats of divine punishment should he fail. Electra, however, persists in the description of her degradation and reminds him of what she has had to give up and to endure. Here, and here alone, Hofmannsthal seems to perceive a glimmer of the Sophoclean concept of renunciation. Hofmannsthal succeeds in fusing his notion of Electra's marriage to hatred with the Sophoclean Electra's lament for having had to espouse cruelty, and so his Electra sacrifices generous restraint and gives birth to curses and to despair, her children begotten by hatred.

The play ends with the murder of Clytemnestra, Aegisthus, and their followers. The populace has joined the victorious Orestes, and during the jubilation within the palace Electra is rendered speechless by the burden of happiness. Out in the courtyard she bids her sister follow her example, be silent and dance, for in happiness only silence and dance are fitting. Her frenzied dance is an acting out of her chaotic frame of mind which can find no other outlet than bodily action. Then at the height of her triumph she collapses. On seeing Electra's rigid body on the ground, Chrysothemis, whom we know to be easily terrified, runs to the palace, beats her hands against the portal and calls for Orestes, yet silence is the only response.

In spite of the fact that Electra is depicted as a character possessed with hatred, who makes one wonder at times if she can maintain in the chaos of her emotions the precarious balance between lucidity and insanity, Hofmannsthal has made the balance tip in favor of lucid self-awareness. Only because Electra is aware of the loss of her soul can we recognize in her a predisposition for tragic action; we can at least comprehend why, when confronted with an almost demented mother and a grievously depressed sister, she finds no occasion to extol the merits of her cause. Consequently we must wonder whether the destruction of

unmitigated wickedness by implacable revenge is an appropriate constellation of forces for the achievement of a tragic action. The world of
Hofmannsthal's *Electra* is very largely a world without values, and the
chaos of instinctive drives is no substitute for values, decisions, and
commitments.

Although Hofmannsthal is supposed to have based his *Electra* on
the Sophoclean model, it becomes clear that he was by no means entirely oblivious to that other very different *Electra* by Euripides, nor was
the more ancient Aeschylean concept of the character of Orestes without
effect on him.

From the point of view of the concept of the tragic that is emerging
in this paper, the character of Electra in Euripides is in large measure
bereft of the qualities of the tragic we find in Sophocles. This Electra's
intense grief is due less to the death of her father than to the hardships
she has to endure because she cannot enjoy all the advantages Agamemnon's protection would have afforded her. Her lamentations over
his death are weighed down by ostentatious self-pity. She displays her
wretchedness primarily to expose the unjust harshness of Aegisthus.
Her constant diatribes are intended to awaken the wrath of the gods
against Aegisthus and her mother. In this play Aegisthus is known to
have tried to have Electra killed, but it was Clytemnestra who saved her
daughter's life by having her marry a farmer and thereby appeasing
Aegisthus, who was afraid lest Electra give birth to a noble and poten-
tially dangerous progeny. Clytemnestra was not motivated by magna-
nimity, but by her fear of being hated by the people for an inexcusable
crime. She believed that her murder of Agamemnon was seen as justified
on the grounds that he had killed Iphigenia and had brought Cassandra
to share his affection with his wedded wife. But Electra knows that her
mother's self-justifications were spurious and that her indifference to
moral restraint coincided with Agamemnon's departure for Troy. When
Electra reveals this insight while refuting her mother's self-defense, Clytemnestra seeks refuge in belated, vain regrets. Clearly, Clytemnestra
has no authentic cause, and Electra's sense of justice is based on little
else than deprivation, injured pride, jealousy, envy, and a grief that
lacks authenticity. These are not decisive characters facing each other
with opposing unassailable values and commitments. Both are blinded
by cruel selfishness and cunning, and the destruction of either might
well elicit the Shakespearean comment that "there's small choice in
rotten apples." Both feel some guilt, but this is not the guiltless guilt of
Oedipus whose every move was intended to avoid guilt, nor that of
Creon whose personal sense of justice ensnared him in the web of
compelling doom. Orestes alone is faced with the anguish of deciding
whether he should take upon himself the sin of killing his mother or that

other sin of leaving his father's death unavenged. Yet in his decision he is stripped of any opportunity to make a real choice because he slavishly obeys—with pain and without moral approval—Apollo's brutal, ignorant oracle. Orestes, the man, is thereby reduced to a mere tool. It appears, then, that in Euripides' *Electra* elemental, chaotic selfishness on the one hand and thoughtless yielding on the other lead to events without that elevated state of awareness from which alone purposeful deeds of great consequence can be conceived and carried out, within a relentless clash of conflicting values whose immanent justification stems from absolute good, and with that sense of guiltless guilt a tragic character experiences in face of inevitable loss, of the inevitable price he is made to pay for being what he has chosen and decided to be in his supreme effort to step out of chaos, which commits one to nothing, into wholeness, which necessarily asserts itself in attitude and action. When instinct or mere yielding leads from fatal acts to remorse, the pitiful, and not the tragic, in the human condition is revealed to us.

So far we have seen variations of much the same materials yielding different concepts of characters with consequently different effects upon the tragic, or the lack of it, in the plays. As we approach Giraudoux's *Electra*, not only do the materials and characters change, but even the tone. Giraudoux grasped that aspect of the tragic of which Scheler is the proponent. Given the materials of his subject matter, that was nothing less than a feat of imagination and of critical insight. He understood with keen awareness that the conflicting values that are pitted against each other must be superior values, held as absolute by the protagonists, that they must inevitably collide because of their essential, active opposition, that one or both values must be destroyed because of the relentlessness with which the protagonists adhere to them. Giraudoux also understood that the protagonists cannot show a sense of guilt, convinced as they must necessarily be of the righteousness of their particular cause and thus of the unassailable quality of their values. And finally Giraudoux recognized that the conclusion of the conflict must carry with it a sense of loss; not a loss that one would not be willing to incur again if one had to, however painful it might be, but a loss that measures the authenticity of one's allegiances. He dispensed with many traditional features of the materials of the myth. Electra does not even know with any certainty whether her mother and Aegisthus have actually murdered her father Agamemnon. She has suspicions, but does not achieve certainty until, at the end of the play, she forces her mother to confess her hatred for Agamemnon, and Aegisthus to suggest his own part in the crime. Although she is almost made to marry the palace gardener, she is not ill-treated nor does she exhibit any self-pity. She is the resolute seeker of truth, of certainty, of authenticity, of justice; she is the conscience that does not permit the covering up of defects; she is the implacable enemy of palliation, she is a soul that strives for crystalline wholeness.

The entire first act of Giraudoux's two-act play carries the theme of palliation. Agamemnon is dead and buried; let murder fade into oblivion, or, better still, let the assumption prevail that the king slipped, fell on his sword, and died. Let old crimes be forgotten, let the state prosper in peace and happiness, and above all leave well enough alone. Humanity being full of defects and inadequacies, happiness and peace demand that these remain "stifled under a triple layer of forgetfulness, death, and ordinary human justice." Implacable righters of wrongs, those restless few who, like Electra, are possessed with a sense of righteousness, and whose justice and duty endow them with an irreconcilable fervor for truth, must be rendered harmless lest they "ruin the state, the individual, and the best families." Against this background of self-righteous affirmations of meretricious virtues, Electra emerges as the very incarnation of the Kantian categorical imperative, and we are not surprised to find her in the end advocating the idea that it would be better for the whole world to be destroyed than to see it saved by a single lie. Giraudoux is not content to seek the tragic on the bloodstained hands of compulsive avengers whose souls may thereafter have to endure the torment of remorseful anguish for having had to serve as agents of a fate bent on horrible retribution. He perceives the tragic in the inevitable clash of equally committed and equally justified forces. One stands for life, for living, however basely, but always contains at least the potential, however remote, of emerging from the chaos in which, as Buber would say, "it can clutch at any object, past which the vortex happens to carry it, and cast its passion upon it . . . ." and yet at some moment it may become directed and purposeful so that "it can set about the audacious work of self-unification." The other, to use once more Buber's words, is the force of the soul that has already "given up undirected plenitude in favour of the one taut string, the one stretched beam of direction," an achievement through which it "comes into service of good or into service for good." This force, personified by Giraudoux's Electra, cannot tolerate any compromise even with well-intentioned expedience. From this point of view of absolute commitment, any lack of an equally absolute determination, or any sign of prevarication or even of temporization, is despicable and intolerable.

Giraudoux, who likes the image of scales, weighs survival against virtuous death. The problem that faces the world of Aegisthus and that of Electra may be briefly stated thus: When life is at stake, when Argos is invaded and threatened with abominable cruelty and savage extinction, what is the value of rigid virtue that glories in destruction, and how weighty is the infamy of a lie if by it alone life can be made to endure and perhaps to be fashioned ultimately by repentance in the mold of virtue? These worlds are irreconcilable, and the mutual distrust that separates them inevitably leads to destruction. Both sides are right and yet both sides are wrong; neither is guilty for they cannot be what they are not, and the tragic is due to their insistence on being implacably and irremediably what they are.

Like Giraudoux, Sartre has adopted in *Les Mouches* very few of the material components of the ancient versions, and we may also assume that Giraudoux's treatment of Aegisthus probably made an impression on him. I am thinking of that surprising turn of events where Aegisthus, in Giraudoux's second act, suddenly repudiates his past by publicly proclaiming his change of heart in order to win Electra's respect and become worthy of the throne for at least as long as his presence may be needed to repel the invasion of the Corinthians and to save Argos. Sartre's Aegisthus, however, is clearly motivated by political cunning, and he goes so far as to repent. His repentance is initially a stratagem designed to keep the people of Argos in abject subservience to Zeus and to himself. After the murder of Agamemnon, in fear of the people's reprisals, he proclaims his guilt and persuades the people of Argos to join him and Clytemnestra, on the anniversary of Agamemnon's death, in a national exercise of public penitence for the sins each and every one has committed against his dead. The dead are believed to rejoin their families in their homes, at their tables, in their beds, and to cause children and adults, all of whom are guilty in the omniscient minds of the dead, to endure the most harrowing experiences. Publicly confessed sins keep the people humble, submissive, and as much enslaved to the will of their ruler as they are to the ever-present threats of retribution by Zeus. On the fifteenth anniversary of Agamemnon's death, Aegisthus, who has never felt any remorse, now realizes that in all these years of guile and deception he has sacrificed to Zeus love, hope, and even lust, for the sake of keeping his crown. He now sees himself ensnared by his own fraud to the point of actually falling into the trap of the superstitious belief he devised for the others. He recognizes the vanity of his power, which has been nothing but a shadow of the presumed power of Zeus himself. He realizes that he was unable to fashion his life because he knowingly yet blindly agreed to have its course determined by expediency and falsehood. He is ready to die at the hands of Orestes, who happens to arrive in time to witness the height of indignity inflicted upon his people. This Aegisthus is merely pitiful in his recognition of having wasted his life and reduced it to nothing by yielding its direction to a cheap impulse to cling to his spoils, and of having thereby dispossessed his own soul of the power to determine the course of his life. He is a prime example of the victims caught in the vortex of which Buber speaks. His sense of loss is the very reverse of the tragic sense of loss experienced by the Sophoclean Electra, for she had to take evil upon herself in a cause she believed was righteous, whereas this Aegisthus espouses evil only to find that it has led to the surrender of his freedom in self-direction and wholeness. For this reason he plays a crucial part in placing Electra and Orestes in perspective.

For Sartre's Electra the public remorse is of no concern; her conscience is clear; she feels free of sin or guilt. She ridicules the general propensity to display one's guilt, and the hypocrisy by which her mother and others proclaim certain sins in order the better to conceal the sins that may bring them into greater disrepute. She is rebellious and provocative in the presence of Orestes while his identity is still unknown to her. She appears in a white dress instead of the black dress of mourning at the frightening ceremony during which the ghosts of the dead are supposed to emerge from their cave. She dances in front of the cave seemingly to lay bare the king's deception and to prove that the dead are not angry at her joy. Though the context in which the dance occurs differs from that found in Hofmannsthal, here it foreshadows—while in Hofmannsthal it reveals in retrospect—what Buber meant when he said: "The soul driven round in the dizzy whirl cannot remain fixed within it; it strives to escape."

Electra seems to wish to prove to the people that their fear is without foundation, but her main concern is not a decisively positive purpose of freeing them, but rather an almost instinctual desire to expose Aegisthus' fraudulent power, for she does not love the people of Argos, she merely despises her mother and hates Aegisthus. She dreams of a strong, brutal Orestes who will destroy her enemies. The kind, tender young man who reveals his identity appeals to her humanity, but disappoints her dreams of the hero who will act instead of her. What a contrast to the Electra of Sophocles! When he does act like the brother of her dreams and kills Aegisthus, she awakens to the horror of the reality of which she liked to dream as a possibility, and wants to avert the murder of Clytemnestra. When Orestes does kill his mother, Electra reacts with dismay. Confronted by Zeus, who is ready to strike the same bargain with Orestes and Electra as he did with Aegisthus and Clytemnestra, if they merely agree to repent, Electra's rebellious spirit is broken and, overcome with fear, she regresses into a state of immaturity that breeds illusions, and then repents. Her railing and bombast, her bold dreams, her defiance, all crumble in the face of the dead whose weight she cannot endure. She thus displays the unrealized potential of the tragic, for she lacks the strength to withstand the crushing burden of living with the responsibility of realized intentions and of being what the deeds of resolution make her. Instead of purposeful direction, she follows mere delusions. She can perceive the goal, but only as a possibility —for she lacks the courage to carry out the task of "self-unification." She thus remains arrested at the stage of possibilities, and easily falls victim to previously set, and thus ingrained, patterns of attitude and action. Her flirtation with purpose and commitment is ended.

It is not surprising that Sartre should have chosen Orestes to fill the role of the tragic hero, for Orestes is the man of decisive action. He was brought up by his tutor as a man without local identity. When he learns who he is, he comes to the palace of his ancestors, to the land of his people, he, the stranger everywhere. He comes uncommitted, and finds his people plagued by pangs of conscience that suck, in the shape of enormous parasitical flies, the sap of their lives, thoughts, and determination. Although he comes with a yearning for the comforting warmth of belonging and of submerging himself in the tender fellowship that smooths out the ruggedness of the path on which the solitary individual struggles toward self-definition and self-determined identity, although he seeks to find the home of which he was deprived by fate, repelled as he is by the evidence of his people's otherness, he decides to leave and asks Electra to join him. But he is captivated by his sister's apparent mission to recapture freedom for the Argives, and he embraces her cause, commits himself, and stays. In contrast to Electra, he does so less for the sake of retributive justice than to restore his people's sense of human dignity. He is not motivated by hatred but by love. He wants to open his people's eyes and free them from the abject fear and guilt that dominate their lives. When he is warned by Zeus that his action would deprive his people of the comforts their faith offers, that he would reveal to them life as it is, "foul and feeble, a barren boon," Orestes insists on offering them his gift of awareness, a necessary part of which is despair. For Orestes, "human life begins on the far side of despair." It begins where the responsibility of one's own conscience begins. He knows also, and this is the tragic aspect of his resolution, that for his most precious gift he will be rewarded by the hatred of the people who resent being deprived of accustomed comforts, and that he will have to leave his newfound homeland as a hated man, under the threats of his own people and pursued by the wrath of Zeus, whom he has dispossessed of the minds of men. Orestes pays the price of his own happiness and accepts his return to the lonely road to exile, the solitude of the man cursed by the vulgar crowd who are still unable to perceive what he really meant: that he really set them free by taking their sins and guilt upon himself. Not as a Christian Redeemer, to be sure, but as the loving son who dispersed the darkness of superstition by the light of the mind. He knows that he is crushed by what is still human matter, and that is the tragic aspect of his fate. He also knows that however insignificant his gift may appear to be—the gift of untrammeled thought—it is the greatest gift he can offer. Sartre's Orestes is after all an heir to that lasting tradition which in Pascal's words has fixed the measure to man:

Man is but a reed, the most feeble thing in nature; but he is a thinking reed. The entire universe need not arm itself to crush him. A vapour, a drop of water suffices to kill him. But, if the universe were to crush him, man would still be more noble than that which kills him, because he knows that he dies and the universe knows nothing of the advantage it has over him. All our dignity consists, then, in thought. On that we must found our claims, not on space and time which we cannot fill. Let us endeavour, then, to think well; this is the principle of morality. (*Pensées*, No. 347)

I wish to submit that these words of Pascal also reflect the basic premise without which that quality of the tragic I have tried to emphasize here is unattainable.

NOTES

[1] George Boas, "The Evolution of the Tragic Hero," *The Carleton Drama Review*, I (1955–56), 5–21.
[2] Max Scheler, *Vom Umsturz der Werte* (Bern, 1955), pp. 149–69. All other Max Scheler quotations in this paper are from this source.
[3] Martin Buber, *Good and Evil* (New York, 1953), pp. 125–32. All other Martin Buber quotations in this paper are from this source.

Goethe's Adaptation of Romeo and Juliet

Leland R. Phelps

Goethe's controversial version of Shakespeare's *Romeo and Juliet* was begun and completed in just over three weeks, between 7 and 31 December 1811. Rehearsals under Goethe's direction started in early January, and the first performance was on 1 February 1812 in honor of Duchess Luise's birthday. From his earliest days in Weimar Goethe had given unstintingly of his time and talent to help make a special occasion of Luise's birthday. After he had assumed the directorship of the Weimar theater in 1791, his contributions to the annual celebration were often premieres of unusual theatrical productions. A number of plays performed for the first time for Luise, for example, were German versions of foreign masterpieces. Among these were, in addition to the adaptation of *Romeo and Juliet*, Voltaire's *Mahomet* (1800) and *Tancred* (1801) translated by Goethe, Schiller's translations of Gozzi's *Turandot* (1803) and Racine's *Phädra* (1805), and *Der standhafte Prinz* (1811), which August Wilhelm Schlegel had translated from the Spanish of Calderon. *Romeo und Julia*, unlike the other works just mentioned, was not a translation but an adaptation of a German translation of Shakespeare's tragedy. The review of the first performance in the *Journal des Luxus und der Moden* referred to the drama as "*Romeo und Julia* nach Shakespeare und Schlegel von Goethe."[1] Approximately three-quarters of the lines are from August Wilhelm Schlegel's translation, many modified by Goethe, and the remaining quarter of the tragedy consists of entirely new lines composed by Goethe.[2] The poet used only such words as "bearbeiten,"[3] "concentrieren,"[4] and "Redaktion"[5] in referring to his *Romeo und Julia*. He did not consider the adaptation suitable for publication,[6] in fact no copy of the work was found among his unpublished papers after his death. Two manuscripts were eventually discovered in theater archives, and the first publication was in the *Nachträge zu Goethes sämtlichen Werken*, Volume II (1841).

Goethe had hoped that his *Romeo und Julia*, though unpublished, would be a welcome addition to what he considered to be the limited repertoire of the German theater of his day. On 21 February 1812 he wrote to Cotta: "Der einzige Gewinn ist, daß wir ein Stück auf dem

Repertorio mehr haben, welches jährlich einige Male wiederholt werden kann, und dies ist jetzt für ein deutsches Theater schon ein Großes, da alles täglich ephemerer zu werden scheint."[7]

Nine performances were given while Goethe was director of the Weimar theater, the last on 23 March 1816 when Pius Alexander Wolff and his wife, who had created the roles of Romeo and Julia in 1812, appeared on the stage in Weimar for the last time. Attempts to introduce the adaptation to a wider theatrical public did not meet with general acceptance. Goethe had a copy of the play made for Franz Kirms in Berlin where it was performed in 1812 but was not well received by the public or critics. *Romeo und Julia* was also staged at the Burgtheater in Vienna (1816), in Braunschweig and Dresden (1823), and in Frankfurt am Main (1831) but never with any particular success.

Scholars have tended to disregard the adaptation or, if they have commented on it, have often condemned it as an anomaly, a mistake by a genius. Ernst Leopold Stahl labels it "eine Fehlgeburt," "eine einzige schier unbegreifliche Verirrung" which completely destroys the uniqueness of Shakespeare's creation.[8] Horst Oppel characterizes it as irresponsible ("rücksichtslos"),[9] and August Sauer maintains that at the time Goethe was working on *Romeo und Julia* his concern with Shakespeare was at its lowest point ("auf dem Gefrierpunkt").[10] Goethe himself, however, was very satisfied with what he had done. The performance for Luise's birthday was, according to Goethe, well received ("gut aufgenommen"),[11] and he had, as mentioned above, hopes that his adaptation would become a part of the standard repertoire of the day. In a letter to Reinhard dated 13 February 1812 he referred to making the adaptation as a great study and maintained that he had never gained a deeper insight into Shakespeare's talent than during the time he was working on *Romeo and Juliet*.[12]

In view of what Goethe had to say about his experience with *Romeo and Juliet*, terms such as "Fehlgeburt," "Verirrung" and "rücksichtslos" would certainly seem to misrepresent the poet's attitude both toward Shakespeare and his own intention in adapting, not translating, the tragedy. August Wilhelm Schlegel had made an excellent poetic translation of *Romeo and Juliet* in 1796, and there was, therefore, no reason for Goethe to repeat the task. Actually, Goethe had originally intended to produce Schlegel's translation in 1797 with Christiana Neumann as Juliet, the only actress at the time in whom he had complete confidence.[13] Her unexpected death in September 1797 resulted in the cancellation of the plan. There is no indication whether the proposed 1797 production would have involved basic changes in the tragedy or not. Diary entries dated 8 and 10 June 1797 indicate that Goethe and Schlegel had discussed the latter's essay on *Romeo and Juliet* that had appeared that same year in *Die Horen*. In it Schlegel stressed such points as the importance of the enmity between the two families ("der Angel um welchen sich alles dreht"),[14] Romeo's love for Rosaline ("die Ouvertüre zu der musikalischen Folge von Momenten, die sich alle aus dem ersten entwickeln, wo Romeo Julien erblickt"),[15] the importance of Mercutio ("eine große Nebenfigur")[16] and the deletion of questionable and playful puns,[17] all aspects of the tragedy that were either modified or eliminated in Goethe's 1811 adaptation. We certainly can assume that Schlegel, in these discussions, must have made his position clear as far as the basic text was concerned.

Adapting *Romeo and Juliet* in December 1811 was not a rash decision on Goethe's part made on the spur of the moment. The diary entry for 1 March 1811 ("*Romeo und Julia* nach Tisch") indicates renewed interest in the play months before work on the adaptation began. In addition, Pius Alexander Wolff, the actor who created the role of Romeo in 1812, wrote to a friend in a letter dated 26 December 1811: "Er [Goethe] hat nämlich die ganz aufgegebene Idee mit *Romeo und Julia* wiederergriffen, und um sich uns gefällig zu zeigen, das Stück selbst bearbeitet."[18] Wolff, who had deen having problems with Goethe, had requested on 5 December 1811 that he and his wife be released from the Weimar theater. As can be seen from the above letter, the Wolffs changed their plans, and the roles of Romeo and Juliet were instrumental in keeping them in the Weimar theater troupe. Wolff's use of the expressions "Idee mit *Romeo und Julia*" and "das Stück selbst bearbeitet" indicate clearly that this production was not envisioned simply as the staging of a German translation of the tragedy.

When Goethe decided to adapt *Romeo and Juliet*, he was following a well-known English tradition. For over a century English directors, actors, and dramatists had been preparing and producing adaptations of Shakespeare's plays. When the theaters in London were reopened by Charles II in 1660, the plays that had been banned by the Puritans were revived and played before audiences with new standards and tastes. The unaltered *Romeo and Juliet* was revived on 1 March 1662 and the renowned diarist, Samuel Pepys, attended the performance. In his diary he records that he "saw *Romeo and Juliet* the first time it was ever acted; but it is a play of itself the worst that ever I heard in my life." Soon thereafter James Howard adapted it as a tragicomedy and for a time the London audiences had the choice of Shakespeare's masterpiece on alternate evenings with a tragic or a happy ending.[19]

In *The History and Fall of Caius Marius* (1679) Thomas Otway transplanted the love story of Romeo and Juliet from Renaissance Italy to ancient Rome and joined it to a plot involving a political feud between two families, each of which was intent on determining the selection of the next consul of Rome. This outlandish adaptation of Shakespeare's tragedy proved such a great success that it replaced *Romeo and Juliet* on the London stage for over half a century.[20] Otway discarded the entire first act of Shakespeare's text except for an abridged version of Mercutio's Queen Mab speech. In the following four acts the original scenes and speeches as well as the sequence of scenes were frequently changed and much new material was added. The major innovation of this adaptation that attracted the attention of other adapters was allowing Lavinia (Juliet) to awaken in the tomb before the death of Young Marius (Romeo), a device that permitted the adapter to write a scene full of high pathos before the final tragedy.

Theophilus Cibber returned to Shakespeare's original setting for his 1744 version of the play, *Romeo and Juliet, a Tragedy, Revised and Altered from Shakespeare*. This adaptation contains lines from Shakespeare, from Otway's *The History and Fall of Caius Marius* and by Cibber himself. The most drastic changes were made in Act I. Not only did Cibber give the play a new beginning, a scene in which Old Capulet and Paris discuss Juliet, but he also deleted the entire ball scene. Throughout the play speeches and scenes were altered, new material added, and the roles of such characters as Mercutio, Friar Laurence and the Prince were greatly reduced in importance. In the final scene Cibber followed Otway and allowed Juliet to awaken in the tomb before Romeo died. This was one of the popular acting versions of *Romeo and Juliet* just before the middle of the eighteenth century.

David Garrick, the great actor, director and adapter of Shakespeare, created the version of *Romeo and Juliet* that dominated the English stage during the second half of the eighteenth and the first decades of the nineteenth centuries. It was first published in 1748 as *Romeo and Juliet. By Shakespeare, with Alterations and an additional Scene, as it is performed at the Theater-Royal in Drury Lane*. By 1793 Garrick's adaptation had gone through fifteen editions to become the most widely used acting text in England.

The major changes that Garrick made in the tragedy involve the elimination of characters and passages and the composing of additional material. He deleted Lady Montague and Lady Capulet and all references to Rosaline as well as the prologues to Acts I and II. All puns deemed unacceptable to an eighteenth-century audience were eliminated. He rearranged the sequence of scenes in Act I and introduced a new scene in Act V, Juliet's funeral procession accompanied by a dirge that he wrote. Following Otway's lead, he permitted Juliet to awaken in the tomb before Romeo's death. He deleted about ninety lines from the end of the final scene and wrote a new, short conclusion.

Special attention has been given to the English adaptations just discussed not only because they were important for the stage history of *Romeo and Juliet* but also because J. J. Eschenburg lists these specific versions in his book *Über Shakespeare* (1787) under the heading of adaptations and imitations of *Romeo and Juliet*.[21] Eschenburg also discussed these four adaptations in the notes appended to his translation of *Romeo and Juliet* in volume 12 of his Shakespeare translations (1777), a book that Goethe used while working on his adaptation in December 1811.

Goethe was particularly aware of Garrick's importance both for the English stage and for Shakespeare. A copy of the report of Garrick's Shakespeare festival at Stratford-on-Avon from 6 to 8 September 1769 is to be found attached to the first volume of the Wieland Shakespeare translation in the library of Goethe's father. A note on the report in Goethe's own hand reads: "tiré du Mercure de France du mois Decembre 1769." In 1797 Goethe had also discussed August Wilhelm Schlegel's essay on *Romeo and Juliet* with him. In it Schlegel went into detail criticizing the deletions and alterations that Garrick had made in the tragedy.

The major changes which Goethe made in adapting the tragedy were to restructure Act I, beginning the action with the masked ball scene and to end the play with Juliet's death. In addition, he eliminated all references to Rosaline and reduced the number of characters and the importance of the nurse and Mercutio. Many of the puns and expressions that he did not consider in good taste were deleted, and the element of humor was greatly reduced. He excluded less important sections such as Juliet's childhood and Mercutio's Queen Mab speech in order to concentrate on the main action. In general he made his version conform more completely to the unities of time and place.[22]

When Goethe made his adaptation of *Romeo and Juliet*, he was working within a tradition that began with the reopening of the theaters in London in the seventeenth century, a tradition that distinguished clearly between the artistic poetic value of Shakespeare's dramas and the demands that the practical needs of the theater made on those same works. This same distinction was made in Goethe's day in Germany and was taken up by Ferdinand Hand, the reviewer of the first performance of Goethe's *Romeo und Julia*. Referring to the opening scene between the quarrelling servants, a scene that Goethe had deleted, Hand wrote: "Nur in Shakespeare können sie unbedingt geduldet werden, und dies heißt für unsere Zeit, in dessen gedruckten Werken, so lange nicht von theatralischer Darstellung die Rede war."[23] The issue concerns not the ultimate stature of Shakespeare as a poet but rather the demands that the theater made on his works at any particular time. Goethe formulated the problem in a slightly different way in the third part of his essay "Shakespeare und kein Ende" (1816) when he distinguished between two Shakespeares, the great creative poet and the poet who wrote for the stage of his own day: "Shakespeares Name und Verdienst gehören in die Geschichte der Poesie; aber es ist eine Ungerechtigkeit gegen alle Theaterdichter früherer und späterer Zeiten, sein ganzes Verdienst in der Geschichte des Theaters aufzuführen . . . So gehört Shakespeare notwendig in die Geschichte der Poesie; in der Geschichte des Theaters tritt er nur zufällig auf."[24]

There is no question concerning the validity of Shakespeare's dramas as literary works of art of the highest order. When, however, such a drama is to be realized on the stage in a given era, the director responsible for the realization forms a conception of it based on the taste and demands of the theater of his day as well as on the facilities and techniques at his disposal, all often at variance with those that existed at the time the particular drama was written. Goethe as a poet and as director of the theater in Weimar was involved with both aspects of the problem, which he discussed in "Shakespeare und kein Ende." It should not be forgotten that he was confronted with the problem of adapting some of his own dramatic works to the practical needs of the theater of his day. In the case of *Egmont* he left to Schiller the task of preparing it for the stage. He himself undertook the project of adapting *Götz*. Many years before he had reworked his first dramatic work *Geschichte Gottfriedens von Berlichingen mit der eisernen Hand. Dramatisiert* (1771) as *Götz von Berlichingen mit der eisernen Hand. Ein Schauspiel* (1773). Although he now called it a *Schauspiel*, he was aware that as a drama it still was not a viable vehicle for the stage in Weimar. It was too long, too diffuse, and too complicated as far as number of scenes and scene changes were concerned. In 1803–4 he made a stage adaptation of the work to satisfy the needs of the theater as he saw them. Like his adaptation of *Romeo und Julia*, it was never published during his lifetime. The rationale behind the adaptation of *Götz* was formulated by Goethe in an essay on the German theater that he wrote in 1813 and is similar to that which he applied to *Romeo and Juliet*: "Die Maximen der frühern Redaktionen wurden auch hier abermals verwendet. Man verminderte die Szenenveränderungen, gewann mehr Raum zu Entwicklung der Charaktere, sammelte das Darzustellende in größere Massen und näherte mit vielen Aufopferungen das Stück einer echten Theatergestalt."[25] As in the case of *Romeo und Julia*, Goethe had tried to produce a stage version of a literary work of high merit. The fact that these adaptations were not published would seem to indicate that they were, for Goethe, of a different nature from the originals. They were made for the German theater at a certain point in its history and were not meant to have timeless quality. There could be a difference between a dramatic work approached by a reader as a printed literary work and that same dramatic work presented to an audience in a theater. Goethe stated this difference in a striking manner when he wrote that "der Leser sich vom Zuschauer und Zuhörer trennen müsse; jeder hat seine Rechte, und keiner darf sie dem andern verkümmern."[26]

Goethe no doubt became more fully aware of the transitory aspect of the dramatic vehicle on the stage over against the printed drama as a literary work after assuming the directorship of the Weimar theater in 1791. With six years of practical experience behind him, he wrote to von Moll on 2 July 1797 summarizing his thoughts on this matter in clear and unambiguous terms:

> Leider ist alle theatralische Wirkung nur für den Augenblick; und so ist, ich darf es wohl aus langer Erfahrung sagen, auch alles übrige was sich auf's Theater bezieht; selbst die nächstkünftige Zeit darf uns kaum beschäftigen, und kein Plan gelingt der einigermaßen in die Ferne geht. Wem die Aufsicht über eine solche Anstalt aufgetragen ist, der muß wohl nach Grundsätzen und im Ganzen in einer Folge handeln; aber er gewöhnt sich doch nach und nach, so wie die Schauspieler selbst, von einem Tage zum andern, von einem Monate zum andern zu leben.[27]

Goethe's adaptation of *Romeo and Juliet* was not an incomprehensible error or the result of irresponsibility on his part. It was an attempt to come to terms with a great literary work of art and adapt it to the demands of the theater of his day as he saw them. Meant for the moment and never intended as an artistic statement with timeless validity, it must be considered in the light of the tradition out of which it came, a tradition that ended when the unaltered texts of Shakespeare's plays became sacrosanct later in the nineteenth century.

NOTES

[1] Ferdinand Hand, "Romeo und Julia nach Shakespeare von Goethe auf dem Weimarischen Hoftheater," *Journal des Luxus und der Moden*, XXVII (März, 1812), 142.

[2] Hans Georg Heun, *Romeo und Julia in Goethes Bearbeitung* (Berlin, 1965), p. 10.

[3] Johann Wolfgang von Goethe, *Werke* (Weimar, 1887 ff.), Sec. 4, XXII, 246. (Hereafter referred to as *WA*).

[4] Ibid., pp. 320, 328.

[5] Ibid., p. 286.

[6] Ibid.

7 Ibid.

8 Ernst Leopold Stahl, *Shakespeare und das deutsche Theater* (Stuttgart, 1947), p. 202.

9 Horst Oppel, *Englisch-deutsche Literaturbeziehungen* (Berlin, 1971), I, 106.

10 Sauer as quoted by Werner Deetjen, "Shakespeare-Aufführungen unter Goethes Leitung," *Shakespeare Jahrbuch*, LXVIII (1932), 30.

11 *WA*, Sec. 4, XXII, 320.

12 Ibid., p. 270.

13 Heinrich Husemann, *Shakespeare Inszenierungen unter Goethe in Weimar* (Wien, 1968), p. 153.

14 August Wilhelm Schlegel, "Über Shakespeares *Romeo und Julia*," *Die Horen*, IX, Part 6 (1797), 25.

15 Ibid.

16 Ibid., p. 35.

17 Ibid., p. 42.

18 Julius Wahle, *Das Weimarer Hoftheater unter Goethes Leitung* (Weimar, 1892), p. 242.

19 Hazelton Spencer, *Shakespeare Improved* (Cambridge, Mass., 1927), pp. 73–74.

20 Ibid., p. 100. See also Charles Beecher Hogan, *Shakespeare in the Theater, 1701–1800* (Oxford, 1952), I, 461.

21 J. J. Eschenburg, *Über Shakespeare* (Zürich, 1787), p. 457.

22 For a detailed discussion of Goethe's adaptation of *Romeo and Juliet* see Hans Georg Heun, *Romeo und Julia in Goethes Bearbeitung* (Berlin, 1965). Heun has discussed the changes that Goethe made in Shakespeare's tragedy in more general terms in "Goethes Kritik an Shakespeares *Romeo und Julia*," *Shakespeare Jahrbuch*, XCVIII (1962), 201–15.

23 Hand, "Romeo und Julia nach Shakespeare," pp. 155–56.

24 *WA*, Sec. 1, XLI, Part 1, 65.

25 Ibid., Sec. 1, XL, 104.

26 Ibid., Sec. 1, XL, 105.

27 Ibid., Sec. 4, XII, 180.

Heine and the French Symbolists

Haskell M. Block

Heinrich Heine has been rightly proclaimed as one of the major forces in the development of French poetics and poetry in the middle and later years of the nineteenth century.[1] He lived for the last twenty-five years of his life, from 1831 to 1856, in Paris, and, both during his lifetime and afterwards, he enjoyed immense popularity among the French reading public. It has been estimated that more collections of Heine's poetry were published in French translation in the second half of the nineteenth century than of all other German poets combined.[2] Unquestionably, his personal relations with such French friends and admirers as Nerval and Gautier played a large role in the diffusion of his work. Younger contemporaries, such as Baudelaire and Banville, drew on Heine's thought and art, and helped to direct and sustain an interest in Heine on the part of their symbolist followers. Mallarmé and Villiers de l'Isle-Adam, Verlaine and Laforgue, these and others responded in different ways to the appeal of Heine's poetry and, to at least some extent, incorporated his themes and processes into their own art.

It would be excessive to see Heine as a symbolist poet. His early and best-known lyrics are squarely part of the Romantic tradition: direct and poignant expressions of deeply felt personal emotion. His late poems, especially those of his very last years, are more religious and philosophical in theme and implication, and to this extent point to an affinity with some of the poetry of the symbolists; but the intensely personal note is ever present, and the complex interiorization of experience characteristic of the symbolists is quite removed from Heine's more concrete and objective rendering of reality. Nevertheless, the French symbolists and their predecessors elaborated an image of Heine in many ways akin to the norms and values they set forth for their own poetry and indeed for poetry generally. This selective appropriation was possible because of real and important anticipations of symbolist doctrines and styles in Heine's work, but these exist along with other elements and preoccupations that are poles apart from those of the symbolists. In examining Heine in a symbolist perspective, we must not lose sight of the many-sidedness of his art.

25

Gérard de Nerval's interest in translating Heine's poetry extended for over two decades. As a letter of 1840 from Nerval to Heine indicates, the process of translation was marked by a close and warm personal collaboration.[3] Nerval's command of German was uneven; perforce, his translations tended to stress those themes and experiences in Heine's poetry most in accord with his own sensibility. The result is a somewhat symbolist version of Heine.[4] Nerval's translations tend to reduce Heine's ironic and satiric edge in favor of an assertion of dream, nostalgia, and reverie.

Nerval's translations of Heine were first published, with an elaborate introductory essay, in two parts in the *Revue des Deux Mondes* for 15 July and 15 September 1848. Recent study has shown that large sections of the introduction and commentary were actually written by Gautier and were then subjected to minor alteration by Nerval.[5] This collaboration makes the introductory essay all the more interesting in the light of Gautier's importance for Baudelaire and his followers. Nerval is aware of the rich variety of themes in Heine's poetry, but emphasizes the legendary and supernatural elements rather than the satiric and political: "Nous préférons vous offrir un simple bouquet de fleurs de fantaisie, aux parfums pénétrants, aux couleurs éclatantes."[6] Gautier, on the other hand, stresses the mixture of antithetical attitudes and styles in Heine, and his miraculous plastic powers of expression: "Heine est naturelle-ment sensible, idéal, plastique, et avant tout spirituel." Above all, for Gautier, Heine's is a poetry of suggestiveness, mystery, and magic: "Les mots chez lui ne désignent pas les objets, ils les évoquent."[7] Gautier's account of Heine's art provides a striking example of a symbolist view of Heine *avant la lettre*; the opposition of naming and evoking in Gautier's formulation came to be elaborated by Baudelaire and Mallarmé as a distinguishing element of symbolist aesthetics.

While Gautier and Nerval accentuated qualities that were in fact present in Heine's art, Nerval's French translation tended to expand Heine's diction at the expense of the metaphorical compression of the original text. In part, this elaboration may reflect Nerval's replacement of Heine's verse by a highly charged poetic prose, but it may also indi-cate a particular way of viewing Heine's poetry. As an illustration, we may compare Heine's "Abenddämmerung" from the cycle *Die Nordsee* with Nerval's translation. The French text reads very much like a sym-bolist *poème en prose*:

Abenddämmerung

Am blassen Meeresstrande
Saß ich gedankenbekümmert und einsam.
Die Sonne neigte sich tiefer und warf
Glührote Streifen auf das Wasser,
Und die weißen, weiten Wellen,
Von der Flut gedrängt,
Schäumten und rauschten näher und näher—
Ein seltsam Geräusch, ein Flüstern und Pfeifen,
Ein Lachen und Murmeln, Seufzen und Sausen,
Dazwischen ein wiegenliedheimliches Singen—
Mir war, als hört' ich verschollne Sagen,
Uralte, liebliche Märchen,
Die ich einst als Knabe
Von Nachbarskindern vernahm,
Wenn wir am Sommerabend
Auf den Treppensteinen der Hausthür
Zum stillen Erzählen niederkauerten,
Mit kleinen, horchenden Herzen
Und neugierklugen Augen;
Während die großen Mädchen
Neben duftenden Blumentöpfen
Gegenüber am Fenster saßen,
Rosengesichter,
Lächelnd und mondbeglänzt.

Le Crépuscule

Sur le pâle rivage de la mer je m'assis rêveur et solitaire. Le soleil déclinait et jetait des rayons ardents sur l'eau, et les blanches, larges vagues, poussées par le reflux, s'avançaient écumeuses et mugissantes. C'était un fracas étrange, un chuchotement et un sifflement, des rires et des murmures, des soupirs et des râles, entremêlés de sons caressants comme des chants de berceuses.—Il me semblait ouïr les récits du vieux temps, les charmants contes des féeries qu'autrefois, tout petit encore, j'entendais raconter aux enfants du voisinage alors que, par une soirée d'été, accroupis sur les degrés de pierre de la porte, nous écoutions en silence le narrateur, avec nos jeunes coeurs attentifs et nos yeux tout ouverts par la curiosité, pendant que les grandes filles, assises à la fenêtre au-dessus de nous, près des pots de fleurs odorantes, et semblables à des roses, souriaient aux lueurs du clair de lune.

It will be recognized that "Abenddämmerung" is in fact a mingling of sensations and memories in an aura of dream-like nostalgia. The poem expresses three distinct phases of time: the vantage point of the present; the retrospective account of events in the past; and the suggestion by these past events of a still more remote past, in the poet's childhood. A similar movement may be noted in Mallarmé's "Apparition," all due allowance made for the more concrete and sensuous quality of Heine's imagery. Nerval is not able to retain in French the vigorous power of compound words in German. Thus, Heine's "wiegenlied-heimliches Singen" (l. 10) is rendered by Nerval as "de sons caressants comme des chants de berceuses"; similarly, in the last line of the poem, "Lächelnd und mondbeglänzt" becomes "souriaient aux lueurs du clair de lune." The active predication of Heine's final lines is converted into a state or mode of being. Nerval's static rendering of the poem reflects a more symbolist style than the original text would support.

It should be noted that while Heine was aware of Nerval's inadequacies as a translator, he genuinely admired his renditions. In the preface to his collection, *Poëmes et Légendes*, penned shortly after Nerval's death, Heine paid a moving tribute to his late friend and collaborator: "sans comprendre beaucoup la langue allemande, Gérard devinait mieux le sens d'une poésie écrite en allemand, que ceux qui avaient fait de cet idiome l'étude de toute leur vie."[8] It was Heine's good fortune to attract the admiration and friendship of generous as well as gifted French poets.

Gautier was probably Heine's most kindred spirit among his French friends, and more than once, over a period of several decades, he defended Heine as both man and poet against the calumny of detractors.[9] In an essay published soon after Heine's death, Gautier declared: "Nul écrivain n'eut à la fois tant de poésie et tant d'esprit."[10] He had read and reread Heine's poetry and found that, even in prose translation, it moved and disturbed him in its mingling of love and death, nostalgia and suffering, the voluptuous and the exotic. Allusions to Heine's poetry in essays on other poets make it clear that Gautier knew Heine's work very well. Gautier's special importance for the symbolists is attested to in many ways, in Baudelaire's dedication of *Les Fleurs du Mal*, in his special praise of Gautier's gift of correspondences, in Mallarmé's noble tribute to Gautier in "Toast funèbre,"—"Magnifique, total et solitaire"—to cite only a few indications. His impact on the symbolists deserves more detailed study.[11] Gautier's role as champion of Heine in France is summed up eloquently by an account of Banville of a conversation with Gautier shortly before the latter's death:

—Enfin, dis-je à Gautier, . . . quel rang donnez-vous à Henri Heine, parmi les poètes contemporains?
—Mais le premier! me répondit sans hésitation le divin Théo . . .[12]

It is noteworthy that Banville, one of the formative influences on Mallarmé and his contemporaries, shared the enthusiasm of Nerval and Gautier for Heine. Unlike them, he never met the German poet; yet he felt impelled to compose an elegy, "A Henri Heine," published a week after Heine's death.[13] Banville sees death for Heine as a liberation and a transformation, the end of the poet's suffering and his rejuvenation in the realm of pure music: "Tu montes dans l'azur en chantant des louanges!" For Banville, Heine is the greatest poet of the century after Victor Hugo:

La première fois que je lus *L'Intermezzo*, le plus beau poème d'amour qui ait jamais été écrit, il me sembla qu'un voile se déchirait devant mes yeux et que je voyais pour la première fois une chose longtemps rêvée et cherchée. Quoi! ce n'était pas un impossible désir! cela se pouvait donc, un poème exempt de toute convention et de toute rhétorique, où le chanteur est si sincère que, lorsqu'il me montre son coeur déchiré et saignant, je me sens en même temps inondé par le sang qui coule de mon coeur![14]

Banville's appreciation of the sincerity and directness of Heine's personal expression is characteristic of the response of French poets generally. Like his contemporaries, Banville prefers the *Lyrisches Intermezzo* to Heine's other work. Again, Nerval's translation played a decisive role in shaping French response. It is interesting to note that Banville saw Heine much as Baudelaire would view himself, as the poet of modern life. Heine, Banville insists, is "en même temps le plus parisien et le plus moderne des hommes." His image of Heine is marked by a deep sense of the martyrdom of the modern poet in a society hostile or indifferent to his art. Heine's physical infirmity in his last years as well as his exile from his native land served for Banville to invest him with exemplary significance. In a commemorative essay on Banville, Mallarmé raises the question: "Qui, des modernes, à côté ou comparable" and answers: "Je nomme Heine, sa lecture préférée, si autre!"[15] For Mallarmé, only Poe among all other modern poets can be placed alongside Heine in relation to Banville.

These preferences clearly indicate that the symbolist poets and their predecessors looked on Heine as a fellow "poète maudit." Heine himself was acutely conscious of the wretched lot of the modern German poet, doomed for the most part to a tragic fate. The conjunction of poetry and suffering, along with the figure of the poet as victim of exile, made Heine particularly sympathetic to the symbolists and helped to invest him with broad representative significance.

During the 1850s and 1860s it would have been virtually impossible for any reader in France concerned with poetry to escape the presence of Heine. Largely owing to the labors of Saint-René Taillandier, substantial selections of both poetry and prose appeared in several issues of the *Revue des Deux Mondes*. All during the 1860s Michel Lévy was publishing volumes of Heine in French translation, so that in 1867 Sainte-Beuve could write of him: "Il est fort à la mode en ce moment chez nous."[16] Heine provided the French reading public with an abundance and variety of both poetry and prose in harmonious accord with the emerging literary values of the later nineteenth century.

The response of Baudelaire to Heine is more ambivalent than that of his predecessors and also more intricate, for it is in Baudelaire's critical statements that Heine emerges as a major force in the assimilation of the symbolist aesthetics of German Romanticism.[17] Baudelaire was familiar with Heine's poetry and had read much of Heine's prose, in translation. The similarities and parallels between Baudelaire and Heine are striking,[18] and Baudelaire late in life may have been aware of them: a common irony, ambiguity, and alienation; a preoccupation with the themes of unfulfillment, death, and decay; and a consequent melancholy and brooding pessimism. Yet, despite these affinities, Heine is not a major force in shaping Baudelaire's poetics or poetry. His art and thought have none of the seminal importance for Baudelaire of Hugo, Poe, or Gautier, to cite only a few. The similarities of Heine and Baudelaire are far more impressive than any conscious affiliation or influence in their relationship. For Baudelaire, Heine was but one of many figures on the literary scene, not always of immediate or central interest, but striking and worthy of attention.

Among Heine's first journalistic activities in Paris were chronicles for German newspapers, subsequently collected in the volume, *De la France* (Paris, 1833). These essays included an account of the *Salon* of 1831, which Baudelaire read with care by way of preparing himself to write his *Salons* of 1845 and 1846. In the first of these, Heine is quoted only briefly, but in the second, he is cited at great length by way of illustrating and clarifying Baudelaire's aesthetic premises and Delacroix's method. The crucial passage, taken from Heine's essay on Decamps in the *Salon* of 1831, reads as follows:

Voici quelques lignes de M. Henri Heine qui expliquent assez bien la méthode de Delacroix, méthode qui est, comme chez tous les hommes vigoureusement constitués, le résultat de son tempérament: "En fait d'art, je suis surnaturaliste. Je crois que l'artiste ne peut trouver dans la nature tous ses types, mais que les plus remarquables lui sont révélés dans son âme, comme la symbolique innée d'idées innées, et au même instant."[19]

It is interesting to note that in his review of *De la France* in 1833, Sainte-Beuve praised Heine for his magical and symbolizing power and cited the very passage alluded to by Baudelaire;[20] however, Sainte-Beuve quotes Heine incompletely in a way that Baudelaire does not.[21] Clearly, Baudelaire read the French text of Heine's *Salon*, and we may assume that he gave careful attention to the whole of Heine's discussion of artistic creativity and judgment.

Much of what Heine asserts in his essay on Decamps must have served to confirm concepts that Baudelaire derived from Diderot, Sainte-Beuve, or Poe, among a variety of sources, or that he developed for himself. Thus, Heine insists on the supreme role of the imagination in artistic creation.[22] Works must be judged in relation to the artist's aims and imagination, rather than according to abstract rules. Each truly great artist, Heine declares, creates his own aesthetic; his artistry must therefore be viewed in relation to the adequacy of his artistic means.

It is in elaborating the artist's means that Heine sets forth a symbolist aesthetic that was by then commonplace in German Romanticism but was only beginning to gain ground in France: "Sons et paroles, couleurs et formes, le visible surtout, ne sont pourtant que des symboles de l'idée, symboles qui naissent dans l'âme de l'artiste quand il est agité par le saint-esprit du monde; ses œuvres ne sont que des symboles à l'aide desquels il communique aux autres âmes ses propres idées."[23] It is shortly after this general account of artistic works as symbols that Heine asserts, in the passage cited by Baudelaire, that the artist's models are revealed in his soul "comme la symbolique innée d'idées innées, et au même instant."

We should look more closely at Heine's vocabulary and his concept of the symbolic character of artistic expression in order to appreciate the importance of Baudelaire's appropriation of Heine's thought. Not only is Heine arguing for the artist's complete imaginative freedom; he is also asserting, in this essay, the essential spirituality of art in the language of transcendental idealism. This is perhaps evident in the German text of the passage cited above in French: "Töne und Worte, Farben und Formen, das Erscheinende überhaupt, sind jedoch nur Symbole der Idee, Symbole, die in dem Gemüthe des Künstlers aufsteigen, wenn es der heilige Weltgeist bewegt. . . ."[24] Underlying Heine's aesthetic is the Neo-Kantian concept of the autonomy of the symbol. More precisely, the cosmic origin of works of art as "Symbole der Idee" is strikingly suggestive of Schelling's philosophy of art, despite Heine's denigration of Schelling in *Zur Geschichte der Religion und Philosophie in Deutschland*.

For Schelling, an Idea is an objective reflection of the Absolute. This reflection must perforce be symbolic. Art, which Schelling defines as the finite representation of the infinite, reveals Absolute form only in symbols. Art in the modern world fulfills the function of mythology in the ancient world. As Schelling points out in his *Vorlesungen über die Methode des akademischen Studiums* (1803), "Die Mythologie der Griechen war eine geschlossene Welt von Symbolen der Ideen."[25] Similarly, in the essay, "Philosophie und Religion" (1804), Schelling declares: "Wahre Mythologie ist eine Symbolik der Ideen. . . ."[26] Schelling's definition of the relationship of symbol and myth was taken over by Friedrich Creuzer in his *Symbolik und Mythologie der alten Völker, besonders der Griechen* (1810), wherein the symbol is defined as the visible representation of the Idea or, as Creuzer puts it, "der verkörperten Idee."[27] The translation into French of Creuzer's work by J. D. Guigniaut, published as *Religions de l'antiquité* in 1825 and 1829 with extensive commentary by the translator, is of central importance in the development of the aesthetic of French symbolism.[28] For Creuzer, the symbol is distinct from allegory in being self-constitutive: "le symbole est l'idée même, rendue sensible et personnifiée."[29] The same notion of the autonomy of the symbol, "die Existenz der Idee selbst," again probably derived from Schelling, occurs in Solger's *Vorlesungen über Ästhetik* (1829), in a philosophical context more appealing to Heine than that of Schelling.[30] That Baudelaire was aware of the historical and philosophical background of the passage he cited from Heine may be doubted, but there can be no question of Heine's reflection of currents of transcendental idealism in his assertion of the autonomy of the symbol and the spirituality of art. These concepts confirmed and supported an aesthetic that Baudelaire developed from a wide variety of philosophical, religious, and literary sources. Heine's "supernaturalism" in his essay on Decamps is at a far remove from the Swedenborgian mysticism that Baudelaire also appropriated and used for his own ends, for Heine is concerned essentially with the relationship of art to nature in the process of artistic creation. It is significant that Baudelaire could adopt Heine's views without in any way repudiating his own reliance on a mystical theory of the nature and function of poetic creation. Apart from Novalis, German Romantic symbolism is generally philosophical rather than mystical, viewing symbols as expressions of mental processes rather than as magical signs or hieroglyphs. In Baudelaire, in part through the mediation of Heine, a Neo-Platonic and mystical tradition of symbolic speculation is reinforced by the formulations of Neo-Kantian idealism. The fact that Neo-Platonic concepts dominated symbolist aesthetics in France does not diminish the importance of German Romantic symbolism as part of the groundwork of modern French poetry.

Baudelaire's subsequent attitudes toward Heine are quite varied. In an essay of 1852, "L'Ecole païenne," Baudelaire sharply attacked the divorce between literature and religion, which he saw as increasingly dominant in the modern world. The celebration of antique beauty and pagan sensuality, which he decries in this essay, is not wholly absent in Baudelaire's earlier writings,[31] but here he strikes out vigorously at contemporary notions of *l'art pour l'art*. It is altogether likely that this attack was aimed at Nerval and Banville, as well as other contemporaries, but the chief object of condemnation is Heine, and the empty paganism of the day "est le fait d'un homme qui a trop lu et mal lu Henri Heine et sa littérature pourrie de sentimentalisme matérialiste."[32] This is not Baudelaire at his critical best. Clearly, Heine's anti-clericalism infuriated him. Despite his praise for Voltaire over Heine, Baudelaire had no sympathy with the Voltairean and libertarian aspects of Heine's art. Heine's spacious conception of the poet combined social and political functions with the notion of the poet as prophet and seer. Baudelaire could accept the poet as "mage" far more readily than the poet as revolutionary, yet his subsequent writings make it clear that he admired Heine as a poet even while rejecting his critique of religion. In his "Exposition Universelle 1855," Baudelaire draws on Heine in deriding doctrinaire aestheticians and refers to Heine as "ce charmant esprit, qui serait un génie s'il se tournait plus souvent vers le divin."[33] We do not know if Baudelaire and Heine ever met, but they had many friends and literary relationships in common, and it is reasonable to suppose that Baudelaire was aware of Heine, not only through the efforts of Nerval and Gautier and the pages of the *Revue des Deux Mondes*, but also in the translation of *Intermezzo* by Paul Ristelhuber, published by Poulet-Malassis in 1857. A sense of kinship with Heine must have grown on Baudelaire during the last years of his life, for among his last projected writings was a response to an essay by Jules Janin on Heine, drafted by Baudelaire in February 1865. Baudelaire decries Janin's attack on Heine as both man and poet, and the critic's condemnation of Heine's preoccupation with death, suffering, and the transience of human existence. For Baudelaire, Heine's difficult personality is part of his character as a poet. France, he insists, has very few poets; "elle n'en a pas un seul à opposer à Henri Heine."[34] This final judgment of Baudelaire reflects the growing awareness in France, in the years immediately preceding and following Heine's death, of the originality and richness of his achievement. Baudelaire defends Heine's character with the same justification he had employed for Poe:

"*genus irritabile vatum*."[35] For Baudelaire as for Mallarmé, Heine and Poe are conjoined as representatives of the modern poet.

Mallarmé's response to Heine illustrates the continuing fascination with the author of *Intermezzo* of the generation of poets that followed Baudelaire. The young Mallarmé was an avid reader of the poetry of his day, English and German as well as French, and he seems to have read and reread translations of Heine around 1860.[36] Mallarmé alludes to Heine briefly in a letter of April 1864, and more extensively in a letter of May of the following year in acknowledging poems of his friend, Henri Cazalis: "Je ne t'ai rien dit de charmants poèmes amoureux que tu m'as envoyés en avril, je les adore dans leur brièveté, à l'égal des délicieux soupirs de Heine."[37] These remarks would suggest that Mallarmé, like other French poets, responded most fully in Heine's work to the *Lyrisches Intermezzo*. He owned a copy of translations of Heine's poetry, probably *Poëmes et Légendes* (1855), which he lent to his friend Des Essarts, and presumably to other young poets as well. In a letter to Mallarmé of October 1864, Des Essarts alludes to Heine's appealing mixture of humor and melancholy.[38] Heine for Mallarmé and his confrères was essentially a lyric poet of simple and tender feeling, although there is evidence that Mallarmé knew his satirical work from an allusion to *Atta Troll* in "Un spectacle interrompu," written perhaps several years before its publication in 1875.[39] In later years, Mallarmé does not seem to have reread Heine frequently, but it is evident that Heine was a continuing part of his literary experience and came to be viewed by him as a classic poet. This is apparent from a letter to Dr. Thomas W. Evans, friend of Mallarmé's admired Méry Laurent and translator of Heine's memoirs into English. In thanking Dr. Evans for a copy of the Heine volume, Mallarmé declares: "l'homme et le poëte que fut Heine s'entourent de notre sympathie à ce point que toute page retrouvée prend, pour nous, l'importance exquise d'une relique."[40] Dr. Evans's translation included a long and detailed introductory essay, illuminating Heine by way of a sustained comparison with Byron that Mallarmé especially praised, and describing the gothic and macabre elements in Heine's work as "manifested in a like manner only perhaps in some of the poems of Edgar A. Poe."[41] Mallarmé himself conjoined Heine and Poe in his essay of 1892 on Banville. Evans's account of Heine's life in France, his role in the French literary scene, and his stature as "the greatest poet of modern Germany" cannot have failed to arrest Mallarmé's attention. For Mallarmé, "cet admirable lyrique," like Poe, is an enduring part of the pantheon of letters.

While Mallarmé came to view Heine as an exemplary poet, Mallarmé's poetry does not seem to be profoundly marked by Heine's art. Mallarmé's best-known early poems are strikingly Baudelairean in theme and style, but Heine's ironic and parodistic vein may be seen in early occasional poems, such as "Contre un poëte parisien."[42] Mallarmé's later poetry with its intricate syntax and complex interiorization of experience is stylistically quite apart from Heine's work, but there may be underlying similarities between Mallarmé's probing examination of philosophical ultimates in his magnificent *tombeaux*, and Heine's anguished interrogation into the meaning of existence in the poetry written near the very end of his life. It may well be that Mallarmé compared Banville to Heine because he had heard Banville speak of Heine as among his favorite poets. For Mallarmé, Heine and Banville, like Hugo and Poe and indeed all great poets, testify to man's spirituality and transforming power: "La *divine transposition*, pour l'accomplissement de quoi existe l'homme, *va du fait à l'idéal*."[43] This idealization is the poet's office, a celebration of the mystery and grandeur of existence. Heine for Mallarmé is unmistakably a descendent of "notre aïeul Orphée," a permanent part of man's poetic endeavor and achievement.

We should note in passing the limited but real impact of Heine on members of Mallarmé's poetic circle. During the early 1860s Catulle Mendès translated Heine's dramatic works and imitated his love poems.[44] Mallarmé's lifelong friend, Villiers de l'Isle-Adam, emulated Heine's Romantic manner in many of his ealy poems, with their themes of martyrdom, exile, and unfulfilled love. Villiers's early poetry is simple and transparent, closer in manner to Hugo or Musset than to Mallarmé. The last poem in the series, "Les Préludes," begins with an epigraph from Heine's *Intermezzo,* but the fascination of vice and the abyss, as well as the poet's acute sense of the flight of time and his consciousness of his own damnation, all point more immediately to Baudelaire as the dominant source of inspiration. Heine is but one of many examples animating the young Villiers, a model of genuine but partial and transient import.

The relationship of Verlaine to Heine is more complex. Not only through the poetry of Mendès, but directly, as part of voluminous reading in his youth, Verlaine acquired a familiarity with Heine's poetry.[45] A good deal of the writing of both poets is in the vein of popular poetry. Many of their poems share a naive simplicity, tenderness, and charm. The frank assertion of passion, the direct expression of the poet's longings and sufferings, the feelings of nostalgia and regret for a vanished moment of delight, all point to a deep affinity between Heine and Verlaine.[46] Camille Mauclair has insisted that Verlaine's essential role in France is as a continuator of Heine in a poetry of open subjectivity and musicality, combining the resources of folk poetry and the lyric of personal artistry.[47] It is reasonable to suppose that Heine's example helped significantly to shape Verlaine's art at the beginning of the latter's career, although Verlaine's first volume, *Les Poèmes saturniens* (1866), seems on the whole less personal than Heine's love lyrics. Verlaine's later work is more consciously concerned with delicate nuances of feeling and mood creation in a manner that only partially resembles Heine's more direct mode of utterance. Verlaine seems to have viewed Heine in the same way as did many of his elder contemporaries, as a *poète maudit*. In an essay on Baudelaire of 1865, Verlaine declares that in his extreme sensitivity and nervousness, Baudelaire exceeds even Heine.[48] For the young Verlaine, both poets incarnate the turbulent and anguished spirit of modernity, in a society in which dream and art are separated and in which the poet must pursue pure beauty in the realm of the ideal. Verlaine's conception of the poet's nature and function is more restricted than that of Heine, yet quite apart from any question of imitation or influence, both poets share common themes and processes to a markedly significant degree.

Most of the symbolist poets read Heine solely in translation, and most of them regarded Heine largely as the poet of the *Lyrisches Intermezzo*. The most striking exception to this tendency is Jules Laforgue. Not only did Laforgue read and cite Heine in German; he drew consciously on the ironic, satiric, and parodistic manner of Heine, which is on the whole more typical of his art than the early poetry in the Romantic sentimental mode. The lively conversational and colloquial idiom of Laforgue, along with his spirited irony and deft humor, is in no way representative of the poetry of the young symbolists who followed Mallarmé. Laforgue's participation in the symbolist enterprise is more apparent in his personal relationships and in his aesthetic speculations than in his poetic style. The distance between Laforgue and the more conventional symbolists is indicated in part by their very different appreciations of Heine. In an early poem, "Epicuréisme," published in the Toulouse weekly, *La Guêpe* in 1879, Laforgue describes the lighthearted vagabondage of a *flâneur* in Paris, whose preferred reading includes Heine:

> "Ce buffon de génie" a dit Schopenhauer
> Qui sanglote et sourit, mais d'un sourire amer![49]

Laforgue's early image of Heine is in part that of a buffoon or a *pierrot*, akin perhaps to Laforgue's image of himself or of the poet generally. In both Paris and Berlin, Laforgue was an admiring and impassioned reader of Heine. In closing a letter of December 1880 to Gustave Kahn, he declares: "Je vous quitte pour relire mon ami H. Heine,"[50] and in a letter from Berlin to Charles Henry in December 1881, Laforgue quotes in German from three of the poems in the *Lyrisches Intermezzo*, all expressive of the longing for love, and speaks of his heart as "Pourri, pourri de tristesse."[51] The mockery, irreverence, playfulness, and whimsy of Laforgue's *Complaintes* led reviewers of his poetry and prose poems to compare him to Heine.[52] Mauclair subsequently declared categorically: "l'ironie de Jules Laforgue est issue de celle de Heine, et Laforgue, s'il eût vécu plus longtemps, eût été le Heine français."[53] Whether Laforgue thought of himself as "the French Heine" may be doubted. Warren Ramsey has concluded, more cautiously: "It is impossible to say whether years of development, filling in youthfully spare outlines, would have given to Laforgue's works the substance of Heine's; but at least he was of the same race of poets."[54] While Laforgue is essentially more personal, less political or social in his satiric poetry than Heine, their similarities in tone and style are real and pervasive.[55] It is not surprising to find the French poet's sympathy for Heine embracing the man as well as his work. In notes for an unwritten essay on Baudelaire, Laforgue contends that the poet of *Les Fleurs du Mal* created a manner in keeping with the ideal of Poe and literary martyrdom, while Heine endured his martyrdom intensely and fully, without Baudelaire's obsessive self-consciousness: "pour bien le comprendre songez un instant au pôle opposé, à l'enfant malade et christ—point créole—mais ayant vraiment sondé la pensée philosophique humaine—obéissant à ses crises, pas de pose, pas maître de lui-même—Heine."[56] It is striking to note that for Laforgue, Heine and Baudelaire are at opposite extremes as men and as poets, the one yielding to the crises and pain of existence, the other imposing a manner as a shield to mitigate the harshness of reality. Laforgue's admiration of Heine for having plumbed the depths of human philosophic thought may well refer to the Heine of the *Romanzero* and *Das Buch Lazarus*, to the poet's heroic confrontation of the meaning of life and death at the ultimate margin of existence, wherein perhaps his greatest literary achievement is to be found.

We do wrong to both Heine and ourselves to view him simply as a French symbolist *avant la lettre*. Despite abundant parallels in themes and styles, Heine is in important ways quite different from the French symbolists. In particular, he does not seem to have shared the recurrent mystical and esoteric view of poetry pervading the symbolist tradition. To be sure, Heine was aware of the role of mystery, suggestiveness, and musicality as poetic techniques, but nowhere does he seem to elaborate an account of these processes as part of a formulated credo or program. Heine's awareness of spiritual themes and implications in poetry is quite independent of the Neo-Platonic mysticism that symbolist aesthetics reflects. On the other hand, the fascination of Heine for the French symbolists and their genuine admiration of his art point to the profoundly human commitment of both Heine and the symbolists. Contrary to fashionable misconceptions of the French symbolists, they did not reject the claims of perceptible reality or the here and now, any more than did Heine reject universal values in the name of an obsessive preoccupation with political and social issues of his day. The symbolists and their predecessors may have selected and absorbed those values of Heine's art that corresponded most closely to their own needs and predilections, but this selectivity is a necessary part of the way in which all literature is assimilated and transformed. It is in large measure through the efforts of a gifted line of French poets, from Nerval to Laforgue and beyond, that Heine has become not only a German but also a European poet, calling on us to participate in the great tradition of European and world literature. This tradition Heine enriched and ennobled magnificently.

NOTES

¹ See Louis P. Betz, *Heine in Frankreich* (Zürich, 1895); Kurt Weinberg, *Henri Heine: "Romantique défroqué," héraut du symbolisme français* (New Haven and Paris, 1954); Oliver Boeck, *Heines Nachwirkung und Heine-Parallelen in der französischen Dichtung* (Göppingen, 1972).
² For discussion of translations of Heine's poetry in nineteenth-century France, see Edmond Duméril, *Lieds et ballades germaniques* (Paris, 1934), pp. 233–64.
³ See Heine, *Briefe*, ed. F. Hirth (Mainz, 1951), V, 315–16.
⁴ Cf. Daniel-A. de Graaf, "Gérard de Nerval traducteur de Henri Heine," *Les Langues modernes*, XLIX (1955), 126.
⁵ Jean Richer, "Une Collaboration Gautier-Gérard: L'Etude sur Henri Heine signée de Nerval," *Revue d'Histoire Littéraire de la France*, LV (1955), 206–9.
⁶ *Revue des Deux Mondes*, Nouvelle série, XXIII (1848), 224.
⁷ Ibid., p. 226.
⁸ Heine, *Poëmes et Légendes* (Paris, 1859), p. vii.
⁹ Cf. Edmond et Jules de Goncourt, *Journal* (Monaco, 1956), VI, 218.
¹⁰ Gautier, *Souvenirs romantiques* (Paris, 1929), p. 254.
¹¹ See Nicolae Babuts, "Une réexamination de la dette de Baudelaire envers Théophile Gautier," *Revue des Sciences Humaines*, fasc. 127 (juillet-septembre 1967), 351–80.
¹² Banville, *Mes Souvenirs* (Paris, 1882), p. 444.
¹³ See Eileen Souffrin, "Banville et le mort de Heine," *Revue de littérature comparée*, XL (1966), 187–211.
¹⁴ Banville, p. 440.
¹⁵ Mallarmé, *Oeuvres complètes* (Paris, 1956), p. 522.
¹⁶ Cited in Joseph Dresch, *Heine à Paris (1831–1856)* (Paris, 1956), p. 145.
¹⁷ For backgrounds, see especially Albert Béguin, *L'Ame romantique et le rêve* (Paris, 1946); Lloyd James Austin, *L'Univers poétique de Baudelaire* (Paris, 1956); Bengt Algot Søren-

sen, *Symbol und Symbolismus* (Kopenhagen, 1963); Liselotte Dieckmann, *Hieroglyphics: The History of a Literary Symbol* (St. Louis, 1970).

[18] See Weinberg, *Henri Heine* and also "Heine, Baudelaire, Mallarmé: Atavism and Urbanity," *Western Review*, XXI (1957), 119–35; Herman Salinger, "Heinrich Heine's Stature after a Century," *Monatshefte*, LXVIII (1956), 312–13.

[19] Baudelaire, *Critique d'art* (Paris, 1965), I, 106.

[20] Sainte-Beuve, "Henri Heine," *Premiers Lundis* (Paris, 1874), II, 256–57.

[21] Cf. Weinberg, *Henri Heine*, p. 218, n. 1.

[22] Heine, *De la France* (Paris, 1833), p. 305.

[23] Ibid., p. 307.

[24] Heine, "Decamps," in Michael Mann, ed., *Heine: Zeitungsberichte über Musik und Malerei* (Frankfurt/Main, 1964), p. 42.

[25] Schelling, *Sämmtliche Werke*, Erste Abtheilung (Stuttgart, 1859), V, 287–88.

[26] Ibid., VI, 67.

[27] Creuzer, *Symbolik* (Leipzig, 1810), I, 153.

[28] See Pierre Moreau, "Le symbolisme de Baudelaire," *Symposium*, V (1951), 89–102; "Symbole, Symbolique, Symbolisme," *Cahiers de l'Association Internationale des Etudes Françaises*, VI (1954), 123–29; "De la symbolique religieuse à la poésie symboliste," *Comparative Literature Studies*, IV (1967), 5–16.

[29] Creuzer, *Religions de l'antiquité* (Paris, 1825), I, 30.

[30] See René Wellek, *A History of Modern Criticism* (New Haven, 1965), III, 198; also, Wolfgang Kuttenkeuler, *Heinrich Heine: Theorie und Kritik der Literatur* (Stuttgart, 1972), p. 91. For Solger's conception of the symbol, see Sørensen, pp. 277–88.

[31] See F. W. Leakey, *Baudelaire and Nature* (Manchester, 1969), pp. 24 ff.

[32] Baudelaire, *Critique littéraire et musicale* (Paris, 1961), p. 90.

[33] Baudelaire, *Critique d'art*, I, 187–88.

[34] Baudelaire, *Critique littéraire et musicale*, p. 436.

[35] Ibid., p. 205.

[36] Henri Mondor, *Vie de Mallarmé* (Paris, 1941), p. 23.

[37] Mallarmé, *Correspondance: 1862–1871* (Paris, 1959), p. 165.

[38] Ibid., p. 138, n. 1.

[39] See Mallarmé, *Oeuvres complètes*, p. 276 and pp. 1549–50.

[40] Mallarmé, *Correspondance: 1890–1891* (Paris, 1973), p. 473.

[41] *The Memoirs of Heinrich Heine . . . with an introductory essay by Thomas W. Evans, M.D.* (London, 1884), p. 24.

[42] Cf. Kurt Wais, *Mallarmé* (München, 1952), pp. 73–76; Weinberg, *Henri Heine*, p. 278, n. 1.

[43] Mallarmé, *Oeuvres complètes*, p. 522.

[44] Cf. Luc Badesco, *La Génération poétique de 1860* (Paris, 1971), pp. 808 and 961–62.

[45] Georges Zayed, *La Formation littéraire de Verlaine* (Genève et Paris, 1962), p. 47.

[46] Cf. Edmond Duméril, *Le Lied Allemand et ses traductions poétiques en France* (Paris, 1933), pp. 263–66.

[47] Camille Mauclair, *La religion de la musique* (Paris, 1919), pp. 112–13.

[48] Verlaine, *Oeuvres posthumes* (Paris, 1913), II, 9.

[49] Jules Laforgue, *Les pages de la Guêpe* (Paris, 1969), p. 92.

[50] Laforgue, *Lettres à un ami* (Paris, 1941), p. 23.

[51] Laforgue, *Oeuvres complètes* (Paris, 1925), IV, 77–78.

[52] Cf. J. L. Debauve, *Laforgue en son temps* (Neuchâtel, 1972), pp. 202, 220.

[53] Camille Mauclair, *La vie humiliée de Henri Heine* (Paris, 1930), p. 290.

[54] Warren Ramsey, *Jules Laforgue and the Ironic Inheritance* (New York, 1953), p. 100.

[55] See Boeck, pp. 204–23.

[56] Jules Laforgue, "Notes inédites sur Baudelaire," *Entretiens politiques et littéraires*, II (avril 1891), 98.

Verwandlung des Lyrischen:
Mörike und Shakespeare

Helmut Rehder †

Eduard Mörike: *Gesang zu zweien in der Nacht*

Sie   Wie süß der Nachtwind nun die Wiese streift
Und klingend jetzt den jungen Hain durchläuft!
Da noch der freche Tag verstummt,
Hört man der Erdenkräfte flüsterndes Gedränge,
Das aufwärts in die zärtlichen Gesänge
Der reingestimmten Lüfte summt.

Er   Vernehm ich doch die wunderbarsten Stimmen,
Vom lauen Wind wollüstig hingeschleift,
Indes, mit ungewissem Licht gestreift,
Der Himmel selber scheinet hinzuschwimmen.

Sie   Wie ein Gewebe zuckt die Luft manchmal,
Durchsichtiger und heller aufzuwehen;
Dazwischen hört man weiche Töne gehen
Von sel'gen Feen, die im blauen Saal
Zum Sphärenklang,
Und fleißig mit Gesang,
Silberne Spindeln hin und wieder drehen.

Er   O holde Nacht, du gehst mit leisem Tritt
Auf schwarzem Samt, der nur am Tage grünet,
Und luftig schwirrender Musik bedienet
Sich nun dein Fuß zum leichten Schritt,
Womit du Stund um Stunde missest,
Dich lieblich in dir selbst vergissest—
Du schwärmst, es schwärmt der Schöpfung Seele mit!

I

Unter Mörikes Gedichten ist der "Gesang zu zweien in der Nacht" eines der ältesten, wärmsten, sinnlichsten Stücke,—nicht gerade "schlicht," wie man es sonst bei dichterischen Anfängen erwarten dürfte, aber doch wahr und glaubhaft. Stoff und Struktur sind sorgfältig miteinander balanziert und erinnern an das melodisch-feierliche Spiel mit der Sprache, wie es zuweilen die Lyrik des Rokoko und der Romantik auszeichnet. Wie bei einem lange gewachsenen und schon etwas abgeschliffenen Kristall hat sich hier viel von früher Seinsweise und vorpoetischer Form erhalten—mythischer Glaube an die Wirklichkeit des Natürlichen; erste Ahnung von der Schöpferkraft des Geschlechtlichen; blitzhafte Erkenntnis der menschlichen Verflochtenheit in die Widersprüche des Daseins. Aber der Schreck der Erkenntnis ist in lyrische Lust umgeschlagen und hat im Wechselgesang Gestalt angenommen. Was dabei herausgekommen, ist nicht ein "Lied" mit bestimmtem Anfang und Schluß, mit einzelnen Strophen und wiederholbarer Melodie, wie etwa in der "Lorelei," sondern ein "Gesang" aus dem Irgendwo, zu dem sich stets neue Töne und Worte finden ließen, neue Zeitmaße, neue Stimmlagen und Stimmhöhen. Ein Lied schließt sich ans menschliche Leben an, klärend und deutend; Gesang weist darüber hinaus, in ein zweites, neues, unsinniges Ordnungsgefüge. Die Substanz eines lyrischen Gedichts ist einmalig, unwiederholbar, und doch ist es wie ein menschliches Lebewesen nur in wiederholter Begegnung zu erfassen und zu verwirklichen, und nur in dieser Wiederholung des Einmaligen in der *Zeit* ist zu erfahren was den wesentlichen Gehalt eines Gedichts ausmacht. "Gesang zu zweien in der Nacht" ist eine stets sich wieder vollziehende und erneuernde menschliche Ursituation —die Steigerung hörbarer und sehbarer Empfindungsgehalte der Nacht unter dem Zauber des Erotischen; die gegenseitige Verflechtung weiblicher und männlicher Sinnlichkeit, die sich vor dem kosmischen Horizont abspielt. Diesen Reichtum dichterischer Bildkraft hat man immer wieder gerne gelesen, bewundert, belauscht.

II

Auch wer das Gedicht nur ein einziges Mal gelesen haben sollte, verbindet dessen eigentümliche Wirkung mit der Weise der Kommunikation, die sich unter zwei Liebenden in der Form von Echo, Wieder-

holung, Steigerung vollzieht. Der akustische Effekt der ersten Strophe
wird in der zweiten durch einen visuellen Effekt ersetzt, der sich in der
dritten Strophe zum Hörbaren zurückfindet, um dann in der vierten
Strophe in einer Durchdringung beider Medien zu kulminieren. Solche
Aufteilung, logisch und etwas pedantisch, läßt sich im Gedicht nicht
immer aufrecht erhalten. An ihrer Stelle erscheint vielmehr ein überaus
zarter und harmonischer Wandel zwischen dominantem und rezessivem
Modus der Sinnlichkeit, sobald man in der ersten und dritten Strophe
das weibliche Temperament mit vorwiegend akustischer Erlebnisweise,
in der zweiten und vierten Strophe das männliche Temperament mit
der Tendenz zur Anschaulichkeit identifizieren will. Aber kaum hat man
die Möglichkeit einer solchen Differenzierung auch nur erwogen, als sie
im Gedicht auch schon unterbrochen und aufgehoben wird, sodaß SIE
die Sprache des Mannes, ER die Sprache des Weibes zum Ausdruck
zu bringen scheinen. In solchen Augenblicken mutet das Gedicht wie
ein kosmisch-gestimmtes Ballspiel an—wie es später die neapolita-
nische Nacht in der Mozartnovelle ziert—ein spielerisches Hin- und
Herschwingen eines Pendels, das den Rhythmus der Welt in sich aufgenommen hat. Nun käme auch die heitere Wirkung des Gesangs nicht
zustande, dies Auffangen und Weiterspielen und Steigern, ohne die
Monumentalität der Anfangszeile des Gedichts, die plötzlich, rätsel-
haft, fertig und vollendet dasteht: "Wie süß der Nachtwind nun die
Wiese streift."

In Blankvers gegossen, enthält dieser Anfang ein sanft-gleitendes
Tonbild, das ganz von ferne an den uralten Mythus von der Hochzeit
von Himmel und Erde, Uranos und Gäa, erinnert. Aber aus der Wucht
des Elementaren löst sich die Süßigkeit des Sentiments und hebt sich
aus der irdischen Dumpfheit in die Reinheit des Höheren:

> Wie süß der Nachtwind nun die Wiese streift
> und klingend jetzt den jungen Hain durchläuft!
> Da noch der freche Tag verstummt,
> hört man der Erdenkräfte flüsterndes Gedränge,
> das aufwärts in die zärtlichen Gesänge
> der rein-gestimmten Lüfte summt.

Dies aber klingt wie ein fernes, fernes Echo aus einer elegischen Nacht-
szene aus Shakespeare:

> Wie süß das Mondlicht auf dem Hügel schläft!
> Hier sitzen wir und lassen die Musik
> zum Ohre schlüpfen, sanfte Still und Nacht,
> sie werden Tasten süßer Harmonie.
>
> *Der Kaufmann von Venedig*, 5. Akt, 1. Szene

Die Ähnlichkeit der Textstellen ist überraschend, trotz aller Verschiedenheit in Gegenstand, Landschaft und Metaphorik. Bis hinab zu Rhythmus und Assonanz will ein solcher Parallelismus gewiß nicht mehr besagen, als daß sich Mörikes Ohr oder Imagination (oder welche Sensitivität auch immer bei solcher Begegnung in Betracht kommt) an einer "poetischen Stelle" in Shakespeare festgesogen haben muß, die Gestalt annahm, ehe das Einschmeichelnde des Eindrucks sich in ein bildloses Gefühl verflüchtigte. Daß es eher A. W. Schlegels poetische Diktion war als die fundamentale Bildkraft der Shakespeareschen Dichtersprache, die solche Wirkung ausstrahlte, wird aus einer Betrachtung des englischen Grundtextes deutlich, der von der Sentimentalität der Übersetzung noch nicht berührt ist:

> How sweet the moonlight sleeps upon the bank!
> (Here will we sit and let the sound of music
> Creep in our ears; soft stillness and the night
> Become the touches of sweet harmony.)

Indessen war es kaum mehr als die Magie des unendlichen Raumes der Mondnacht, dieser beglückenden Entdeckung der Romantik, die auch Mörike in ihren Bann zog und zum Gebrauch vertrauter romantischer Ausdrucksformen verlockte.

III

Was der zarten lyrischen Zeile aus Shakespeare besondere Bedeutung gibt, ist ihr Ursprung aus dem *Kaufmann von Venedig*, jenem lebenstrotzenden Spiel fundamentaler Widersprüche, worin Gastmähler, Werbungen, Handel, Geschäfte, Intrigen, Shylock, Porzia und schließlich auch das berüchtigte Pfund Fleisch eine verwirrende Rolle spielen. In all dieser Verwirrung und Leidenschaft ist es Jessica—eine "moderne," fast neutestamentliche Gestalt, die ihrem unmenschlichen Vater Shylock entsprungen ist—und für die ihr Geliebter Lorenzo—Dichter, Musiker, Weltvertrauter—die lösende poetische Formel findet: "Wie süß das Mondlicht auf dem Hügel schläft!"

Wenig ist bekannt über Mörikes Vertrautheit mit Shakespeare. Wo ein Charakter wie Larkens, der Schauspieler, im Mittelpunkt der Handlung steht wie im *Maler Nolten*, kann Shakespeare nicht weit entfernt sein. Schließlich war es ja Shakespeare, der die dichterische Regeneration der deutschen Literatur im 18. und 19. Jahrhundert inspirierte!

Seltsamerweise erscheint das Gedicht, bald als Dialog auseinander gelegt, bald in mehr-strophiger Strukturform zusammengefaßt, an mehreren Stellen in Mörikes Werken. Aber nie erscheint es gänzlich in seiner endgültigen Gestaltung, die seinem lyrischen Anfang—denn es hat einen wirklich großen, einmaligen, monumentalen Anfang!—gerecht würde. Immer wieder versucht Mörike, den "Gesang" in seiner Dichtung unterzubringen—eine Auszeichnung, die keinem anderen Gedicht widerfährt. Im *Maler Nolten* gelingt es ihm, in der phantasmagorischen Märchendichtung "Der letzte König von Orplid" der seelischen Mitteilung zwischen dem König und der Fee Thereile einen solch innigen Ausdruck zu geben, daß man glauben könnte, der "Gesang" sei zu diesem Zweck geschrieben. Aber dann entstehen auch wieder Bedenken an der Echtheit wegen der Nachbarschaft des sentimentalischen Märchen-Klischees. Der "Gesang" erscheint ebenso im Anfangsmonolog des "Spillner," wobei die lyrische Substanz des Gedichts zu einem objektiv-geschilderten Erlebnis eines individuellen Ich verzerrt wird und dadurch an dichterischem Gehalt verliert.

Eben diesem Gehalt nach ist der "Gesang" mannigfaltigen Wandlungen unterworfen. Als mögliches Erlebnis ist er jedem Leser in seiner Form nahe. Angesichts der Shakespeare-Stelle glaubt man, allmählich dem dichterischen Prozeß auf die Spur zu kommen, der ihm seine endgültige Gestaltung verleiht. Man fragt sich vielleicht sogar, warum Mörike sich nicht den ganzen Anfang der Shakespeare-Szene zu eigen gemacht, worin Shakespeare in großartiger Steigerung "in solcher Nacht" die berühmten legendären Fälle von Liebenden aufzählt, die dann in Lorenzo und Jessica gipfeln. Doch solches Fragen führt zu Mutmaßungen, die dem Dichter vorgreifen, anstatt ihm nachzufühlen und sich seiner dichterischen Magie hinzugeben.

Rilke als Europäer

Beda Allemann

In den Aufzeichnungen des Malte Laurids Brigge steht der Satz: "Er war ein Dichter und haßte das Ungefähre."[1] Rilke liebte die sichtbaren Dinge. Alte Städte, Bauwerke, Statuen, die Gestalt eines Hirten, Bettlers oder eines Pferdes sprachen ihn an. Der Kulturkreis war ihm in solchen Anschauungen gegenwärtig. Eins seiner mit Recht berühmtesten Gedichte ist einem archaischen Torso Apolls im Louvre gewidmet. Er beschwor Venedig, den Pont du Caroussel und die flandrischen Städte. Die Erinnerung an die Ebenen Rußlands verdichtete sich ihm 20 Jahre später im Bild eines Schimmels auf nächtlicher Weide. Die Kathedrale von Chartres und ihre Portalfiguren inspirierten ihn gleichermaßen wie ein altägyptisches Relief in Karnak. Er kannte und liebte die Schwermut heller nordischer Nächte, und er hat in Nordafrika die Begegnung mit der Einsamkeit der Wüste gesucht. Die harte und ekstatische Landschaft Spaniens prägte sich ihm unauslöschlich ein, und das schweizerische Wallis entzückte ihn mit Feldwegen, Weinbergen und seinen Carillon-Klängen. In der Abgeschiedenheit der kargen adriatischen Felsküste begann er auf Schloß Duino die Arbeit an den Elegien, und er liebte die französische Provence mit ihren antiken und mittelalterlichen Denkmälern.

Es gibt bei Rilke ganz unmittelbare poetische Antworten auf das, was er schauend und reisend erfährt. Aber typischer für ihn ist der andere Vorgang: daß er das Gesehene lange in sich herumträgt, bis es sich schließlich in dichterische Gestalt umsetzt. Zwischen seiner Reise durch die flandrischen Städte und der Niederschrift der entsprechenden Stücke der "Neuen Gedichte" liegt ein volles Jahr: sie erfolgt erst im Sommer 1907 in Paris. Es ist angemessen, Rilkes Europa so sinnlich und so konkret wie möglich zu verstehen. Europa ist für Rilke kein abstrakter politischer oder geographischer Begriff, sondern erfahrene Wirklichkeit: die Summe der wahrgenommenen Städte, Landschaften und Kunstwerke. Staatsgrenzen spielen dabei, jedenfalls bis 1914, keine Rolle. Der Kontinent ist eine Einheit. Das gilt auch für seine Geschichte und seine Literatur. Der junge Rilke nimmt aus ihr mit großer Selbstverständlichkeit auf, was seinem eigenen Empfinden und seiner Denkweise entgegenkommt. Er erkennt seine Lebensstimmung unmittelbar im Werke des Dänen Jens Peter Jacobsen wieder. Nicht weniger stark beeindruckt ihn Maeterlinck: seine frühen Dramen stehen im Banne dieses symbolistischen Vorbilds. Mit Verhaeren verbindet ihn in den Pariser Jahren eine persönliche Freundschaft. Literarisch bedeutsamer noch ist die Beziehung zu André Gide. Später wird Rilke zu einem der frühesten Bewunderer von Marcel Proust. Im Malte spiegelt sich der Einfluß Dostojewskis wie der Kierkegaards. Als Übersetzer nimmt Rilke aus mehreren europäischen Sprachen auf, was ihn besonders anspricht: von Baudelaire, Mallarmé und Verlaine bis zu den Sonetten Michelangelos.

Das alles ist nicht die Folge eines gelehrten Interesses an der europäischen Literatur oder auch nur einer bestimmten kulturpolitischen Absicht; es ergibt sich für Rilke wie von selbst, daß er Anregungen und künstlerische Verwandtschaften in der ganzen Breite und Tiefe der europäischen Überlieferung sucht. Man kann diese Offenheit des Dichters nach allen Seiten auch nicht aus seiner Prager Herkunft oder seiner Erziehung erklären. Eher ist sie das Ergebnis der frühen Assimilation an eine europäische Bildungsschicht, in der eben diese Offenheit eine natürliche Konvention war. (Die Gastfreundschaft großbürgerlicher und adliger Mäzene war nicht nur für die Sicherung von Rilkes äußerer Existenz wichtig.)

Wie sehr Rilke seiner ganzen künstlerischen Ausrichtung nach *Europäer* war, ist ihm selbst vielleicht erst zur Zeit des Ersten Weltkrieges voll bewußt geworden. Von den Reisen ins Ausland abgeschnitten, jeder Kommunikation mit Paris, seiner Wahlheimat beraubt, umgeben von den Parolen eines großsprecherischen Nationalismus, betont er, auf die Grundlagen seiner Existenz angesprochen: "daß ich nicht 'deutsch' empfinde,—in keiner Weise."[2] Er weiß, daß ihm das deutsche Wesen nicht fremd sein kann, da er doch ein Dichter deutscher Sprache ist. Um so befremdlicher und kränkender war ihm dieses Wesens "gegenwärtige Anwendung und sein jetziges aufbegehrliches Bewußtsein,"[3] der wildgewordene Nationalismus. Und da er seiner verbrieften Nationalität nach Österreicher war, fügt er gleich noch eine bitterböse Bemerkung über die Donaumonarchie hinzu, bringt sie auf die Formel, "die Unaufrichtigkeit als Staat": " . . . im Österreichischen ein Zuhause zu haben, ist mir rein unausdenkbar und unausfühlbar! Wie soll ich da, ich, dem Rußland, Frankreich, Italien, Spanien, die Wüste und die Bibel das Herz ausgebildet haben, wie soll ich einen Anklang haben zu denen, die hier um mich großsprechen! Genug."[4]

Es bedurfte wohl der besonders bedrängten Zeitumstände des Ersten Weltkriegs, um Rilke zu einer so rigorosen Äußerung zu bringen, die schlecht ins immer noch verbreitete Bild des Dottore serafico paßt. Rilke war kein Europäer der kulturpolitischen Manifeste und gutgemeinten Bekenntnisse, die er nicht nötig hatte. Aber die nationalistischen Hetzreden seiner Zeitgenossen zwangen ihm die Richtigstellung ab.

Rilke war nicht einmal Kriegsgegner, jedenfalls nicht im August 1914. Mit derselben Anfälligkeit für den vermeintlichen Glanz der Stunde, die wir bei so vielen und nicht immer den schlechtesten Schriftstellern seiner Generation wahrnehmen, ließ er sich von der falschen Begeisterung des Kriegsausbruchs beeinflussen und rühmte in einem bekannten Gedicht-Zyklus den wiedererstehenden Kriegsgott. Hinterher ist man klüger, und uns will das wie Ahnungslosigkeit erscheinen. Hatte Rilke wirklich geglaubt, hier komme noch einmal das antike Muster zur Geltung, gewebt aus Heroentum und Mythologie? Verwechselte er die modernen Massenheere mit den Griechen vor Troja und den Marathon-Kämpfern? Immerhin: die beiden letzten der "Fünf Gesänge" wenden sich bereits gegen die unreflektierte Kampflust, fordern die Klage und die Rühmung des Schmerzes.

Rilke mußte sehr bald einsehen, was hier wirklich ausgebrochen war, die Borniertheit und der Haß, das sinnlos Zerstörerische, der europäische Bürgerkrieg. Dieser Krieg war nicht, wie es ein paar Tage lang scheinen konnte, Befreiung und Wiedergewinn einer archaischen Daseinsform, sondern schließlich für Rilke nur noch eine merkwürdige äußere Bestätigung seiner ausgehöhlten inneren Verfassung—jener Krise seiner poetischen Produktivität, die ihn seit dem Abschluß der Arbeit an den *Aufzeichnungen des Malte Laurids Brigge* im Jahre 1910 gefangen hielt und erst mit der Vollendung der *Duineser Elegien* und den *Sonetten an Orpheus* im Februar 1922 endete.

Zuvor hatte Rilke noch einmal auf die Geburt einer neuen Gesellschaft gehofft: was der Kriegsausbruch mit Siegeszuversicht und Massenenthusiasmus nicht gebracht hatte, erwartete er vier Jahre später von der Niederlage und der sich anbahnenden deutschen Revolution. Er bewunderte die einfachen Arbeiter, die vor politischen Versammlungen in Münchner Brauhäusern das Wort ergriffen und unbeholfen genug ihre Auffassung von Friede und Zukunft aussprachen. Der nationale Größenwahn und die kurzsichtige Interessenpolitik schienen endgültig überwunden. Das einfache Volk, auf das schon einmal der ganz junge Rilke seine Hoffnungen gesetzt hatte, als er ihm seine "Wegwarten" widmete, die "Lieder, dem Volke geschenkt," von 1895—das Volk würde in einem revolutionären Aufschwung gutmachen, was die Machthaber verdorben hatten. Nicht nur die Anfänge der Münchner Räterepublik, die Rilke aus der Nähe beobachtete, weckten in ihm solche Zuversicht. Auch was seine Mutter aus Prag ihm schrieb über den neuen tschechoslowakischen Staat, klang beruhigend. Einen österreichischen Orden, der ihm damals angeboten wurde, hat Rilke abgelehnt.

Wieweit er an seine neuen Hoffnungen auf eine menschlichere Nachkriegs-Gesellschaft selber wirklich zu glauben wagte, ist nicht leicht zu beurteilen. Die Enttäuschung folgte den Erwartungen auf dem Fuß. Im Sommer 1919 reiste Rilke in die Schweiz. Er hat sie in den letzten sieben Jahren seines Lebens, außer für Aufenthalte in Paris und Venedig und einen Ausflug nach Mailand, nicht mehr verlassen.

Die unversehrte Schweiz gewährte ihm, was nach Kriegsende als dringendste Aufgabe vor ihm stand—den Anschluß wiederzufinden an seine frühere Existenz, und die Bruchstellen, die der Krieg geschlagen hatte, zu heilen. In einem scherzhaften Brief an seinen jungen Freund Balthusz Klossowski schreibt Rilke ein halbes Jahr vor seinem Tod, im Juni 1926, er sei nicht mehr "l'homme qui voyage," trotz der Visa in seinem Reisepaß, und die Expreßzüge mit all ihren Aufschriften könnten ihn nicht mehr verführen: "tout m'arrête. . . . Je finirai par avoir des petites racines barbues, et il faudra venir m'arroser de temps en temps . . ." (Balthusz, 943). Die etwas forcierte Lustigkeit des Bildes ist kennzeichnend. Im Ernst hätte Rilke niemals zugegeben, Wurzeln geschlagen zu haben. Er hat seine Bewunderung für die Landschaft des Canton du Valais nicht verhehlt und auch nicht den Einfluß, den diese Landschaft auf seine späte Dichtung gewonnen hat. Die "Quatrains Valaisans" sind ganz unmittelbare Zeugnisse dafür. Aber als eine zweite Heimat hat er das Wallis, hat er die Schweiz nicht empfunden. Was ihn an dieser fast heroischen Landschaft faszinierte, war, daß ihr Licht ihn an die Ile de France erinnerte und ihre Tektonik ihm Spanien wieder nahebrachte.

Die Schweiz und im besondern das alte Gemäuer des Schlößchens Muzot war ihm eine Zuflucht—kein anderer Ausdruck könnte genauer bezeichnen, weshalb Muzot ihm im Februar 1922 zum Ort einer stürmisch wiedergewonnenen dichterischen Produktivität wurde. Zuflucht in einer veränderten Welt, die dem Überschreiten der Landesgrenzen und dem Wohnen in fremden Städten und Landschaften plötzlich früher nicht gekannte Hindernisse in den Weg legte. Zuflucht vor allem in dem gesteigerten Sinn, daß sich hier Fluchtlinien des alten, des nun völlig imaginären Europa Rilkes trafen.

Überblickt man die Biographie Rilkes im ganzen, so scheint der Ausgangspunkt *Prag* eine bedeutende und den Dichter prägende Rolle zu spielen. Er selbst hätte das nicht oder doch nur unter negativem Vorzeichen wahrhaben wollen. Kehrte er später und immer nur für kurze Zeit in seine Geburtsstadt zurück, überfielen ihn gleich die alten Beklemmungen seiner Kindheit. Diese Kindheit nachzuholen, sie nachträglich in künstlerischer Transformation zu "leisten," war für Rilke ein Hauptpunkt seines poetischen Programms. Es ist ein Grundthema des *Malte* und noch der *Duineser Elegien*. Aber es hat nichts zu tun mit sentimentaler Rückerinnerung an Prag. Diese Stadt, von der die Kafka sagte, daß sie ein Mütterchen mit Krallen sei und einen nicht loslasse, hat auch Rilke nicht losgelassen—aber in einer noch komplizierteren Weise als Kafka. Es hat ihn in die Flucht getrieben. Das Bewußtsein, nirgends verwurzelt zu sein, hat sich in dieser Stadt zuerst eingestellt, und es hat verhindert, daß Rilke anderswo sich jemals auf die Dauer häuslich einzurichten und niederzulassen vermocht hätte.

Von Prag aus wurde Rilke zum "homme qui voyage," zum homo viator, der gerade als solcher doch immer wieder bekannte, zum Reisen nicht geschaffen zu sein, und immer auf der Suche nach einer Zuflucht für sein Werk war.

Würde man die Reisewege Rilkes bis zum Jahr 1914 auf einer Karte einzeichnen, es ergäbe sich ein dichtes Netz, ausgespannt zwischen Rußland, Skandinavien, Frankreich und Nordafrika. Gewiß, von 1902 an bildete Paris einen gewissen sicheren Mittelpunkt in diesem Netz. Aber auch das nur, weil Paris ihm mehr war als eine Stadt und ein bestimmter Ort, nämlich eine Landschaft und eine ganze Welt.

Aus dem Prag seiner frühen Kindheit wurde Rilke bald schon, nach dem Scheitern der Ehe seiner Eltern, vertrieben. Er kam zur Ausbildung auf österreichische Militärschulen, erst in der Nähe von Wien, dann in Mähren. Sein Vater hatte ihn zum Offiziersberuf bestimmt. Rilke hat später seine ganze Schulzeit als einen düsteren Irrtum betrachtet—und wer wollte ihm da widersprechen. Als Jüngling kehrte er nach Prag zurück, um sich durch Privatunterricht auf ein verspätetes Abitur vorzubereiten. Zugleich entwickelte er hier eine hektische Betriebsamkeit als junger Literat mit einer Fülle überstürzter und unreifer Publikationen, die er schon bald danach wieder bereute. Es ist nur zu verständlich, wenn er sich später mit Unbehagen an seine Prager Anfänge erinnerte.

Auch seine nie abgeschlossenen Universitätsstudien hat Rilke noch in Prag begonnen. Dann ging er nach München, reiste von hier aus an den Gardasee und nach Venedig, und fand endlich einen ersten menschlichen Halt in der Freundschaft mit der 15 Jahre älteren Lou Andreas-Salomé. Diese Tochter eines russischen Generals französischer Herkunft, Schülerin von Sigmund Freud, die als junges Mädchen die Zuneigung Nietzsches gewonnen hatte, jetzt eine reife und mütterliche Frau, holte den jungen Rilke endgültig aus jeder provinziellen Enge und Wirrnis heraus. Er folgte ihr nach Berlin, und ihr verdankt er vor allem auch die Erfahrung der beiden großen Reisen nach Rußland, in den Jahren unmittelbar vor der Jahrhundertwende. Rußland hat Rilke immer als die entscheidende Station auf dem Weg zu seiner künstlerischen Selbstfindung bezeichnet.

Kurz zuvor hatte er auf einer erweiterten Italienreise sich mit Florenz vertraut gemacht und in der geschlossenen Kunstsphäre dieser Stadt und ihrer Renaissance-Landschaft war das Florenzer Tagebuch konzipiert worden, in dem die bis in die Spätzeit hinein maßgebenden Themen Rilkescher Dichtung schon notiert sind. Rußland dagegen gab ihm den Eindruck seiner unendlichen Ebenen, in die sich das mystisch gesteigerte Gefühl seiner Stundenbuch-Dichtung ausströmen konnte. Hier begegnete er dem Volk in einer dem Westen unbekannten Bedeutung. Er sah seine Armut und Knechtschaft, aber auch die davon unberührte innere Freiheit. Man besuchte Tolstoj auf seinem Landgut und verehrte in ihm die Verkörperung der russischen Dichtung. Pasternak gibt in seinen Erinnerungen eine impressionistische Moment-Aufnahme von Lou und Rilke, denen er als Knabe mit seinem Vater zufällig auf dem Weg nach Jasnaja Poljana begegnet war.

In diesen Jahren sucht Rilke die Gemeinschaft der Maler, die sich in Worpswede in der norddeutschen Ebene zu einer Künstlerkolonie zusammengefunden haben. Sein Buch über Worpswede spricht eindringlicher als von den Kunstwerken seiner Freunde von der Landschaft, in der sie entstehen. Auch hier ist es der tiefliegende Horizont und das Gefühl der Weite, in der jede Einzelheit bedeutsam wird, das Rilkes eigner Stimmung dieser frühen Jahre ein unmittelbares Äquivalent im Sichtbaren schafft.

Aber Worpswede vermag ihn auf die Dauer nicht zu halten, auch nicht die Heirat mit der Bildhauerin Clara Westhoff, die Freundschaft zu Paula Modersohn, der bedeutendsten Malerin des Kreises.

Er geht 1902 nach Paris, sucht und findet den Anschluß an Rodin, dessen Schülerin seine Frau gewesen war. Auch für ihn selbst wird Rodin zum eigentlichen Lehrmeister. Von ihm übernimmt er die Devise des "toujours travailler," an seinen Werken entwickelt er die Theorie des Kunstdings, die dann in seinen eigenen "Dinggedichten" zur poetischen Realisation kommt. Die Pariser Jahre bringen den Durchbruch Rilkes zu seiner Meisterschaft als Lyriker, und hier entstehen auch die *Aufzeichnungen des Malte Laurids Brigge*. Im Salon d'Automne von 1907 lernt er das Werk von Cézanne kennen, an ihm vertieft sich seine Einsicht in das Wesen der Kunst.

Es ist kein Zufall, daß bildende Künstler die eigentlichen Lehrmeister und Vorbilder Rilkes wurden. In ihren Ateliers vollzog sich die

Umsetzung ins Kunstwerk direkter und greifbarer als an den Schreibtischen der Schriftsteller.

Literarische Vorbilder im eigentlichen Sinne hat Rilke nicht gehabt. Als in seinen spätern Jahren die Literarhistoriker ihn mit Fragen nach den literarischen "Einflüssen" bedrängten, unter denen sein eignes Werk in den Anfängen gestanden habe, wich er aus. Oder er nannte immer wieder nur den einen Namen des Dänen Jens Peter Jacobsen, dessen Bedeutung mindestens für den *Malte* nicht zu übersehen ist, aber auch nicht überschätzt werden darf.

Es ist auch kein Zufall, daß Rilke als Dichter deutscher Sprache in einer französischen Umgebung endgültig zu sich selber fand. Sein Dichterkollege Richard Dehmel machte ihm daraus einen Vorwurf und fand es unbegreiflich, wie ein Lyriker ohne ständigen Kontakt mit der eigenen Sprache leben könne. Rilke versuchte vergeblich, ihm deutlich zu machen, daß gerade die Distanz zur im täglichen Gebrauch vernutzten deutschen Sprache ihm notwendig sei, um sie in sich selber zur Sammlung und Klarheit zu bringen.

Man kann Rilkes dichterische Verfahrensweise und damit auch seine Biographie nicht wirklich verstehen, wenn man nicht berücksichtigt, daß er solche Distanzierungen, Umwege und förmliche Verfremdungseffekte unbedingt brauchte, um zu sich selber und seiner eigentümlichen Leistung zu gelangen. Rilke war kein im konventionellen Sinn literarisch "gebildeter" Mensch. Seine Militärschul-Erziehung hatte eine frühe Beschäftigung mit der Literaturgeschichte verhindert. Auf eine Umfrage nach den zehn Büchern, die einem jungen Menschen unentbehrlich sind und sein geistiges Existenzminimum bilden, antwortete er im Jahre 1907:

Eine Reihe von Umständen ließ mich nie zu jener Leichtigkeit im Umgang mit Büchern kommen, die junge Leute sich in einer gewissen Zeit mühelos und fast wider ihren Willen aneignen. Noch jetzt sind meine Beziehungen zu Büchern nicht ohne Befangenheit und es kann geschehen, daß ich mich in großen Bibliotheken geradezu einer feindlichen Übermacht ausgeliefert fühle, gegen welche jede Gegenwehr eines einzelnen sinnlos wäre. (SW. VI, 1020 f.)

Anläßlich eines Wohnungswechsels in Paris gesteht er seinem Verleger Anton Kippenberg, der ja auch ein großer Bibliophile und Büchersammler war, es habe ihn erschreckt, daß seine eigne kleine Bücherei schon sechs bis sieben Kisten fülle. Er möchte am liebsten auf dergleichen Eigentum verzichten und findet mit dem alten Strindberg, "daß der Lebensfluß in keinem Verhältnis steht zu dem, was er fortwährend Schweres, Materielles, Niederschlägiges absetzt und zurückläßt" (Anton Kippenberg, 293). Er möchte Bücher nicht sammeln, sondern wie der Evangelist sie buchstäblich verschlingen.

Rilkes Einstellung zur literarischen Überlieferung ist damit exakt beschrieben. Wir wissen aus seiner Dichtung, wie stark sein Bezug zur Tradition, zum geschichtlich Gewordenen ist. Aber es ist ein lebendiger, aneignender und verwandelnder Bezug. Nur in den Phasen der Unproduktivität empfindet er seinen Mangel an Belesenheit und spielt selbst als Vierzigjähriger mit dem Gedanken, nochmals die Universität zu beziehen. Für seine eigene Hervorbringung zählt aber im Ernste nur das, was er sich in einem Akt der unmittelbaren Aneignung einverleiben, was er wirklich verschlingen kann. So kommen jene für ihn typischen späten Begegnungen etwa mit Goethe oder Hölderlin zustande, die dafür unmittelbar produktiv werden.

Ende 1913 schreibt er an die Fürstin Thurn und Taxis: "Las jetzt den ganzen Kleist, vieles zum ersten Mal. . . . das hat ja sein Gutes, daß die Umstände mich verhindert haben, mir, wie es sonst jungen Leuten passiert, die ganze Dichtung in zu frühen Jahren vorwegzulesen; so steigt mir das Gewaltigste niegesehen herauf vor dem reifern Gemüt" (von Thurn und Taxis, 416).

Diese Selbsteroberung des geistigen Kontinents prägt Rilkes Verhältnis zur Tradition, ein unverbrauchtes und intensives Verhältnis. Es macht ihn offen für Entdeckungen in- und außerhalb der deutschen Literatur, und es bindet den Traditionsbezug an das Zustandekommen einer wirklichen Begegnung.

Rilkes Europäertum ist nicht der Effekt einer Erziehung oder einer sehr frühen, aber zunächst rein literarischen Aneignung, wie bei Hofmannsthal. Gewiß war es nicht unwichtig, daß die Mutter aus Snobismus mit dem Knaben gern französisch sprach. Gewiß hat ihm die Position der deutschen Minorität in Prag, die sich zugleich als die Bildungsschicht dieser Stadt empfand, die spätere Wanderung zwischen den Nationen gleichsam vorgezeichnet. Aber der Gewinn einer geschichtlich verankerten europäischen Substanz ist seine persönliche Leistung, und sie war nur in unermüdlich erneuerten Durchgängen und Konfrontationen zu erbringen.

Wir wollen nicht unterschlagen, was dabei am Rande liegenblieb und nie in Rilkes innern Gesichtskreis getreten ist. Die Berührungen mit der angelsächsischen Kultur blieben flüchtig, trotz der Übersetzung der Sonette der Elizabeth Barrett-Browning im Frühjahr 1907 auf Capri. Rilke hat England nie betreten, und gegen Amerika hegte er das unter den Gebildeten verbreitete Vorurteil. Die Anziehungskraft des mediterranen Bereichs, die größere Vertrautheit mit den romanischen Sprachen verhinderten offenbar den Sprung über den Kanal oder gar über den Atlantik. Rilke reiste viel, aber nie planlos oder nur aus touristischer Neugier. Er suchte stets die ihm angemessene Landschaft, und Landschaft bedeutete ihm sehr viel mehr als Sehenswürdigkeit. Er hatte früh eine besondere Bindung an Italien. Aber es findet sich bei ihm keine Spur der berühmten Italiensehnsucht deutscher Dichter und Denker. Die romantische Verklärung der blauen Ferne war ihm fremd. Aus ähnlichem Grund hat er als Schriftsteller und Lyriker nie "Reisebilder" geschrieben. Er kannte die Lust des Aufbrechens, irgendwohin. Er genoß es, in einer fremden Stadt umherzugehen, in der kein Mensch ihn vermutete. Aber in einem Brief aus den letzten Lebensjahren bekennt er auch, sich vom Reisenden zum Siedler gewandelt zu haben, und hier erst kommt der letzte Antrieb seiner Reisen zum Ausdruck: "Je n'allais plus dans des pays éloignés en visiteur curieux, je m'y installais, je les habitais, et je corrigeais amplement le hasard d'être né quelque part, par une naissance plus vaste et plus amoureuse" (A une amie, II, 813).

Im Rückblick erscheinen schon die frühen russischen Reisen als ein solcher Versuch, den Zufall des Geburtsortes durch eine neue Geburt zu überholen. Wir geraten hier in den Umkreis von Rilkes letztem und wichtigstem poetologischem Prinzip, dem der Transformation, der Verwandlung. Das Reisen, das Besitzergreifen von fernen Landschaften ist die biographische Spiegelung dieses Prinzips und mit ihm aufs Engste verbunden. So erst erklärt es sich, daß der junge Rilke sich in ein hastiges Studium der russischen Sprache stürzte, um die russische Landschaft in seinem Sinne wirklich zu erfahren, in ihr eine Wiedergeburt zu vollziehen. Das hat nichts mit dem bloßen Aufsammeln von Eindrücken zu tun, um sie poetisch zu verwerten. Es geht um eine Neugeburt als Dichter, und nichts könnte diese Absicht stärker verdeutlichen als der Umstand, daß Rilke, noch nicht einmal der russischen Grammatik wirklich mächtig, sogleich beginnt, für Lou eine ganze Reihe von Gedichten in russischer Sprache zu schreiben. Es liegt darin sicher ein voreiliger und überstürzter Versuch des jugendlichen Rilke, eine poetische Neugeburt in ihrer Totalität zu vollziehen. Aber noch in seiner Voreiligkeit und seinem technischen Scheitern ist der Versuch charakteristisch.

Rilke wurde danach vorsichtiger und ließ sich für die folgenden zwei Jahrzehnte höchstens auf gelegentliche Entwürfe in französischer Sprache ein, die erst lange nach seinem Tod aus dem Nachlaß zum Vorschein kamen. Aber die Übersiedlung in die Schweiz und das Fußfassen im Canton du Valais belebten dann von neuem seine Neigung, sich auch außerhalb der Muttersprache poetisch zu manifestieren. Ein wesentlicher Teil seiner Gedichte aus den letzten Lebensjahren ist in französischer Sprache geschrieben. Sie stellten sich nach Rilkes eigner Äußerung fast unbeabsichtigt, wie unter Diktat ein. Selbst in italienischer Sprache liegen ein paar, allerdings rasch wieder aufgegebene Versuche vor.

Schon die ersten Proben seiner *Poèmes français*, noch zu Lebzeiten Rilkes veröffentlicht, erzeugten kuriose Mißverständnisse. Manche Kritiker schienen nicht gewillt, einem inzwischen längst berühmt gewordnen Dichter deutscher Sprache einen solchen Wechsel des Idioms zuzugestehen. Hätten sie etwas von dem Gesetz der Transformation geahnt, unter dem Rilkes Hervorbringung stand, sie würden gelassener reagiert haben.

Der waghalsige Ausbruch ins Russische am Beginn und der entspannte Umgang mit dem Französischen in der Spätphase von Rilkes poetischer Wirksamkeit sind nur die besonders sichtbaren Pole seiner unaufhörlichen Verwandlungen. Dazwischen liegen Metamorphosen, die nicht bis zum Übergang ins fremde Idiom getrieben werden konnten und dennoch für die innere Biographie Rilkes nicht von geringerer Tragweite sind.

Die nächstliegende Form, in der ein Lyriker den Austausch mit fremden Kulturkreisen betreibt, ist die der Übersetzung. Vom Capreser Winter an ist Rilke immer wieder als Übersetzer tätig geworden. Der Gedichtübertragung aus dem Englischen folgten solche vor allem aus dem Italienischen, dem Französischen, aber auch dem Russischen und den skandinavischen Sprachen. Freilich hat Rilke seine Übersetzertätigkeit mehr als Nebenbeschäftigung in jenen Phasen geübt, in denen seine eigne Produktion stockte. Eine Ausnahme machen die Übertragungen von Werken Valérys, den er nach dem Weltkrieg für sich entdeckte und in dem er sogleich, nach der Isolierung durch die Kriegsjahre doppelt willkommen, den tief Geistesverwandten erkannte. Valéry war ihm so etwas wie die Bestätigung seiner eignen inneren Affinität zur mediterranen Welt und zum europäischen Symbolismus.

Der eigentliche Austausch Rilkes mit der europäischen Umwelt vollzog sich aber nicht in erster Linie auf diesem konventionellen Weg der übersetzerischen Vermittlung. Die Übertragungen sind nur Reflexe der Wiedergeburten, die Rilke in der Begegnung mit Menschen, Völkern und Landschaften unmittelbarer erfuhr. Bei der Niederschrift französischer Gedichte machte er die Beobachtung, daß dasselbe Thema bei der Ausarbeitung eine andere Wendung nahm, je nachdem ob er es deutsch oder französisch zu gestalten suchte. Das bestärkte ihn in der Auffassung, daß Lyrik im Grund unübersetzbar ist. Er begrüßte und bewunderte die Übertragung seines Malte ins Französische durch Maurice Betz, aber er war überzeugt, daß sein deutschsprachiges lyrisches Hauptwerk ins Französische nicht adäquat zu übersetzen sei. Das ist nicht, wie es auf einen ersten Blick scheinen könnte, ein Selbstwiderspruch Rilkes. Es entspricht nur der Einsicht, daß zur Aneignung des Fremden noch andere Transformationen nötig sind als die der Übersetzung.

Als wichtigste Konfrontation in seinem Leben hat Rilke nach dem Erlebnis Rußlands und dem Heimischwerden in Paris die Begegnung mit der spanischen Landschaft empfunden. Es war eine Begegnung, die sich ohne literarische Hilfe vollzog. Eine beträchtliche Rolle spielte wieder ein Maler: El Greco. Ihn hatte Rilke schon Jahre zuvor in Paris kennengelernt, besonders sein Toledo-Bild hatte ihn getroffen. Im Spätherbst 1912 kommt Rilke in diese Stadt und findet seine ganze Erwartung bestätigt: es ist, wie es ihm die ekstatische Kunst des Greco angekündigt hatte, eine Stelle, an der die Lebenden, die Toten und die Engel zusammenwohnen. Rilke sucht das Elementare, die Genesis, die vollständige Verwandlung und Neugeburt. Er glaubt sie zu fassen, und dann entgleitet ihm alles wieder. Er steckt mitten in der großen Krise. Die poetische Wiedergabe des Sichtbaren verfängt nicht mehr. Das Prinzip der sogenannten Ding-Gedichte ist gebrochen. Was er früher erfahren und künstlerisch bewältigt hat, rückt in eine neue Beleuchtung. Er erinnert sich in Toledo der flandrischen Städte und glaubt nun zu erkennen, wieviel Spanisches in ihnen noch lebendig war. Er hatte damals schon, in Brügge, das Stadtbild in einer charakteristischen Brechung gesehen: das Spiegelbild in den Grachten war ihm wirklicher gewesen als die Dinge selbst. Rilkes Dichtung wird schwieriger und immer imaginärer.

Als zehn Jahre später die Vollendung der Elegien glückt, weiß er, daß hier "lyrische Summen" gezogen sind. Hier dominiert keine einzelne Landschaft mehr. Alles ist zusammengefaßt. Rom wird beschworen und der Nil. Die fünfte Elegie, "Les Saltimbanques," ist auf eine Reminiszenz aus Paris gegründet und zugleich von den Saltimbanques Picassos inspiriert. Dichte Beziehungen laufen quer durch Raum und Zeit. Die späte Dichtung Rilkes ist mit europäischer Substanz gesättigt. Die Anschauung vieler Länder ist in sie eingegangen und durchdringt sich in ihr. Kühne Umkehrungen werden möglich. Die Verwandlung ins Unsichtbare wird zum Leitsatz.

Auf dieser letzten Stufe der Meisterschaft ist Rilkes Dichtung nicht mehr im früheren Sinne lokalisierbar. Der Abschied wird zum Gesetz der Begegnung. Das Bleibende erschließt sich im Durchgang. Tod und Leben bilden einen großen Zusammenhang, beide zusammen erst ergeben das volle Dasein. Das Vergangene ist gegenwärtig, der Weltinnenraum reicht bis an die Gestirne. Der Tod selbst ist eine letzte Geburt.

In dieser poetischen Welt der unaufhörlichen Transformation, des Austauschs zwischen Hier und Dort, ist alles einmal Erfahrene aufgehoben. Das Bild Europas erstreckt sich von den Tagen der Schöpfung, als zum erstenmal das Licht in die Schluchten des Kontinents brach, bis zu seinen äußersten, gewagtesten, gerade noch möglichen Manifestationen in den großen Kunstwerken der europäischen Geschichte. Rilke harmonisiert nicht, er versucht die Spannungen zu bestehen, die in einer solchen Geschichte und ihrer Erfahrung liegen.

ANMERKUNGEN

[1] Rainer Maria Rilke, *Sämtliche Werke*, herausgegeben vom Rilke-Archiv in Verbindung mit Ruth Sieber-Rilke besorgt durch Ernst Zinn (Frankfurt am Main, 1955 ff.), VI, 863. Zitiert im Text als SW mit Band und Seitenzahl.

[2] Rainer Maria Rilke, *Briefe*, herausgegeben vom Rilke-Archiv in Weimar, in Verbindung mit Ruth Sieber-Rilke besorgt durch Karl Altheim (Wiesbaden, 1950), p. 504. Weitere Zitate durch Namen des Empfängers und Seitenzahl der zweiten Auflage von 1966.

[3] ebda.

[4] ebda.

ESSAYS IN GERMAN LITERATURE

The Odd Guest at the Wedding

John G. Kunstmann

My original plan, with respect to your *Festschrift*, was to offer you a *tertium quid* that would combine some of the features of Cicero's *Cato* and some of the same author's *Laelius*. I had hoped to speak to you *senex ad senem de senectute*—after all, you have almost outgrown your boyishness!—and I had expected to do so in the spirit of the friendship that exists between you and me, *amicus ad amicissimum de amicitia*.

Then tragedy came into my life and I had to devote all my time and all my strength to taking care of my wife. There was no intermission for the writing of an article. But although she was sick unto death, she never forgot my original commitment, and she talked about it and encouraged me to make at least an effort to show our esteem and love for you and your wife.

These lines are, therefore, not only a tribute from me to you, Herman. They are, in addition, an expression of my late wife's and my own love and esteem for Herman and Marion Salinger. Accept them as such, despite their imperfections, some of which are there because *in tormentis scripsi*.

Something of *de senectute* is carried over: I am old enough to admit that I have worked long hours for years, even decades, at certain matters and that I still know not the answer or answers, at least not indisputably. In the following paragraphs I shall report one such case. Nothing of paramount importance is involved. I shall deal with two lines of a folksong that have intrigued me and that I have tried to understand, i.e., I have attempted to find out what these lines meant to the sixteenth-century person when he heard them, or read them, or sang them. The two lines read: "Der Sittig was eyn frembder gast / der kam auff die hochzeyt gladen." In other words, the *psittacus* (popinjay, parrot) was a strange or alien?, exotic?, odd? guest; he came to the wedding, invited or because he had been (especially) invited?

These lines are a part of a German folksong known today as *Die Vogelhochzeit* (abbreviated hereafter as VH) or "Bird Wedding." When the VH was first printed, early in the sixteenth century, the song was then already *zusammengesungen*; i.e., it represents in the earliest version that has come down to us a combination of two songs, one about *fischen* (*coire*) and another song about *vögeln* (*coire*).

I shall not try to impress you with a detailed study of all the sixteenth- and seventeenth-century versions of the VH in which the two lines about the *Sittig* or *Sittich* (modern spelling) are found—among them the 1527, 1603, 1613, 1650, and several undated versions. Either they contain substantially the same VH text with very minor variations in spelling, capitalization, etc., or they become, as time marches on, longer (and filthier) through the addition of birds and their frequently obscene activities not mentioned in the oldest sixteenth-century versions.

Most good university libraries own a copy of *Die älteste deutsche Vogelhochzeit. Jörg Graff, Das Lied vom Heller*. Nürnberg, Kunegund Hergotin, o. J. "Zwickauer Facsimiledrucke," No. 11 (Zwickau S., 1912), containing a charmingly written introduction by A. Goetze. Because of the easy accessibility of this booklet, I prefer to publish a different text of the VH. It is the one I have named the Hiersemann text of the VH.

The Hiersemann text became known through the following description in Karl W. Hiersemann, Leipzig, Königstr. 29. *Kat. 602*, pp. 73–74, where it is offered for sale:

884.– Hübscher lieder zwey// das Erst/ Es wolt eyn Rayger fischen/ etc. Das Ander/ Von dem Haller/ fast kurtzweylig zu singen. 4 Blatt, m. Titelholzschnitt (2 Frauen m. Reiher in Landschaft). Kl.–8 0.0. u. Druckerangabe 1527. Neuer Pgtbd.   430.—

Völlig unbekannter Druck der an sich schon überaus seltenen Flugschrift, meines Wissens ein Unikum.

I have not seen the original. Karl W. Hiersemann, however, kindly granted permission to my late friend, Martin Lippmann, then Technical Director of the Deutsche Bücherei Leipzig, to make a copy for me of the former of the two *Lieder*, *Es wolt eyn Rayger fischen*. I became reasonably certain that this 1527 print of the VH is identical with the VH print in the Zwickauer Ratsschulbibliothek, Sammelband XXX, 5, 20/32. In 1927, I obtained, again through the good services of Martin Lippmann, a description of this *unicum* from the then Director of the Ratsschulbibliothek, Prof. Dr. O. Clemen. According to Dr. Clemen, the woodcut and the type of XXX, 5, 20/32 are the same as those of Zwickauer Ratsschulbibliothek XXX, 5, 22/4, now available in "Zwickauer Facsimiledrucke," No. 11, originally published in Nürnberg by Kunegund Hergotin, the widow of the Nürnberg printer (*Buchführer von Nürnberg*) Johann Herrgott.[1]

I am unable to agree with Dr. Clemen. There are slight differences in spelling and arrangement between the two versions:

Zwickau XXX, 5, 20/32	Zwickau XXX, 5, 22/4
Hübscher lieder zwey/ das Erst/ Es wolt eyn Rayger fischen/etc. Das Ander/Von dem Haller/fast kürtzweylig zů singen.	Hübscher lieder zwey/ Das Erst/ Es wolt ein Rayger fischen/etc. Das ander/ Von dem Håller/ fast kurtzweylig zů singen.
Special title of first song: Das lied vom Storch. First strophe: Es wolt eyn Reyger fischen/ auff eyner grünen hayden/ Da kam der Storch/vnd stal jm seyne kleyder.	No special title for first song. First strophe: ES wolt ein Rayger fischen/auff eyner grünen heyde/do kam der Storch/ vnd stal jm seyne kleyder.

The text and the arrangement of the VH in the Hiersemann print are, as well as I can judge from the copy made for me, exactly the same as those of Zwickau XXX, 5, 20/32, except that the *kurtzweylig* in Hiersemann lacks the "e" over the "u" (Clemen: "das e über dem u kaum zu sehen"), that the "zu" in Hiersemann lacks the "o" over the "u," and that the end of the first strophe in Hiersemann reads "/und stal. . . ." Martin Lippmann, on the other hand, who copied the Hiersemann text for me, has "vnd," exactly as Clemen. I assume that Martin Lippmann made an accurate copy of the *original* Hiersemann-VH (the copy was checked several times against the original). And so I must label the "es" and the "Rayger" (p. 73 of *Kat. 602*) and the "und" (top of p. 74 of *Kat. 602*) typographical errors made by the typesetter or not caught by the proofreader of *Kat. 602*. And I conclude, therefore, that the VH of Zwickau, Ratsschulbibliothek, Sammelband XXX, 5, 20/32 is identical with the VH offered for sale by Hiersemann in *Kat. 602*.[2]

Karl W. Hiersemann has very kindly given permission to me to publish the text of the VH of *Kat. 602*, no. 884, from the copy made for me by Martin Lippmann. I print it below, first, because this 1527 version of the VH has, as far as I know, never before been published and, secondly, in order to give by means of at least one complete version of the VH the context in which the *Sittich*-passage appears. In the original the strophes are not numbered.

Das lied vom Storch.
(1) ES wolt eyn Reyger fischen/ auff eyner grünen hayden/
    Da kam der Storch/ vnd stal jm seyne kleyder.

(2) Da kam der Sperber here/ vnd brache [?] vns newe meere/
wie das die prawt schon aussgegeben were.
(3) Fraw Nachtigal die was die prawt/ der Kolman gab seyn tochter auss/
d'Widhopff/ der selbig tropff/ der hupffet vor der prewt auff.
(4) Die Troschel hat die heyrat gmacht/ vor eynem grünen walde/
die Amschel mit jrem gsang/ die lobt die prawt mit schalle.
(5) Der Gümpel was der preutigam/ der Adler auff die hochzeit kam/
der Fasshan/ die zween die waren fornen dran.
(6) Der schwartze Rab der was der koch/ das sach man an seynen kleydern
wol/ der Grünspecht/ der war des küchenmeysters knecht.
(7) Die Alster die ist schwartz vnd weyss/ die bracht der prewt die hoffspeyss/
der Fincke/ der bracht der prewt zu trincken.
(8) Der Pfaw mit seyne langen schwantz/ der fürt die prawt (?) wol zu dem
tantz/ der Emerling/ der bracht der prewt den mehel ring.
(9) Die Henn wol zu dem tantze gieng/ der Han der fürt den reyen/
der Greyffe must auff der hochzeyt pfeyffen.
(10) Der Gutzgauch was der kemmerling/ der fürt die prawt zu schlaffen/
der Baumheckel/ kam auch hernach gelauffen.
(11) Der Stiglitz mit seyner witz/ der wolt die prawt ansingen/
der Rodtkropff/ mit seynem kopff/ der wer auch gern drinnen.
(12) Der Eyssuogel was wol geziert/ das Behemlin der prewt hoffiert/
der Schnepffe/ der wolt die prawt anzepffen.
(13) Der Sittig was eyn frembder gast/ der kam auff die hochzeyt gladen/
der Stare/ wolt mit der prewt nur baden.
(14) Da kam sich auch die Turteltaub/ vnd bracht der prewt eyn grüne schawb/
die Mayse/ wolt mit der prewt aussraysen.
(15) Die Gans mit jrem langen kragen/ die fürt der prawt den kammerwagen/
Die Ente/ die fürt das Regimente.
(16) Noch weyss ich eynen Vogel gut den darff ich euch nicht nennen/
ja wenn jhrn secht/ jr würdt jn all wol kennen.

The lines "Der Sittig was eyn frembder gast/ der kam auff die
hochzeyt gladen" turn up, then, with minor variations in the three
prints mentioned so far. They are found, additionally, in the following
VH-prints, except for three seventeenth-century VHH:

(a) Four sixteenth-century VHH, each one slightly different from the other
three: two of them have the same woodcut on the front page as the one
described in the Hiersemann *Kat. 602*; two have entirely different frontispieces;
one of the four is "Gedruckt zu Nürnberg durch Valentin Newber."[3] In all four
the *Sittig*-strophe is No. 13.

(b) A fifth sixteenth-century VH. This broadside should really be treated in
detail. Here I shall merely say that it was "Getruckt zů Nürnberg durch Kunegund Hergotin"—*sine anno*. This VH is found in Weimar, Sammelband 14, 6:60^e
st. 59 (50). It is published in M. A. Pfeiffer, ed., *Das Weimarer Liederbuch* (1918–
1920), on pp. 298–300. I have a photostatic copy of this VH. On the first text-

page of my copy, near the bottom, is a stamp with this legend: *Ex Bibl. Regia Berolin*. I am unable to account for this statement of ownership. Its presence makes me doubt whether my photostat is actually a copy of the Weimar broadside. The only "proof" that I ordered and paid for a photostatic copy of Weimar Sammelband 14, 6:60^e is a receipted bill. Further inquiry has not brought any light. The mystery deepens upon comparison of Pfeiffer's "exact reprint" ("wortgetreuer Neudruck") with my copy. There are numerous differences, slight ones, to be sure, but nevertheless differences. The discrepancy in the numbering of this VH in Kopp, "Ein Liederbuch aus dem Jahre 1650," *ZfdP*, XXXIX (1907), 215 [14, 6:60^e st. 59 (50)] and in the Pfeiffer edition [14, 6:60^e, Nr. 49/1] is due, I take it, to the fact that this famous Weimar Sammelband contains only seventy numbers, which are counted as no. 1 to no. 80, no. 55 following immediately after no. 44. In my copy, strophe 13 reads: "Der Sittig was ein frembder gast/ kam auff die Hochzeit gladen," and in Pfeiffer's "exact reprint" the *Sittig*-strophe is also the thirteenth.[4]

(c) Seventeenth-century VHH: 1603. —*Philippi Hainhoferi Lautenbuecher* . . . , in which the second part of strophe 22 reads: "Der sittich gruen, der sittich gruen war bey ihn über de (?) massen schön."[5] 1605. —*Fliegendes Blatt*. The second part of strophe 17 reads: "Der Sittig grün :/ War bey jhn vber dmassen schön."[6] 1613. —*Fliegendes Blatt*. "Ohne Angabe des Druckortes." Strophe 13 reads in part: "Der Sittig was ein frembder Gast, kam auff die Hochzeit geladen."[7] 1650. —*Das Newe vnd grosse Lieder-Buch/ In zwey Theile. Dessen Erster Theil in sich begreift CXIV. Lieder/ Alle auß dem Daphnis auß Cymbrien vnd der Frühlings-Lust zusammengesetzet . . . Gedruckt im Jahr MDCL*. No. LXXIII is a very long VH. The pertinent strophe appears here thus: "Fraw Side war ein frembder Gast: kam auff die Hochzeit geladen."

The *Sittich*, to use the modern spelling, drops out of the later versions of the VH, beginning around 1650. Its place is taken, if it is indeed the *Sittich*'s place that is taken, by the *Papagei* or the *Kakadu*. In the 1603 Hainhofer text cited above, there appears, in addition to the "sittich gruen" (in str. 22), "Der Papagei" (in str. 15): "Der Papigay hat ein groß gschray . . ." In some nineteenth- and twentieth-century texts *Papagei* and *Kakadu* appear together—e.g., in a VH published in the collection called *Macht auf das Tor: Alte deutsche Kinderlieder, Reime*, ed. Maria Kühn (1910), pp. 128 f.: "Der Kakadu, Der bringt der Braut die neuen Schuh . . . , Der Papagei mit krummem Schnabel, der bringt den Gästen Messer und Gabel." I found the same combination in F. Köhler, *Die Mutterschule* (1840), quoted in Hoffmann-Richter, *Schlesische Volkslieder* (1842), pp. 74–75.

With the disappearance of the *Sittich*'s name there also disappear the mention of the fact that the bird was "ein fremder Gast" and the information that the *Sittich* attended the wedding as an invited guest. The reason for this disappearance may be the fading from the memories of the persons singing or reading the VH of the lore of the "original" *Sittich*, i.e., *psittacus torquatus, der grüne Halsbandsittich*, which became known in Western Europe, including Germany, in the Middle Ages. Then, and into the sixteenth and seventeenth centuries, there are frequently statements made about the *green* color of the bird, with mention of its "guildin halszband."[8]

Before trying to determine what the people in Western Europe, including those in Germany, saw in the *psittacus torquatus* in the Middle Ages and in the sixteenth and seventeenth centuries, I should like to call attention to the fact that the expressions "frembder Gast" and "auf die Hochzeit kommen" were in existence for a long time, so that it was not necessary for the author of the *Sittich*-lines in the VH to coin them for use in his folksong.

Concerning "ein frembder Gast," Matthias Lexer in his *MHD Handwörterbuch*, III (1878), s.v., "vremde," cites examples for "den gegens. bezeichnend von gewöhnlich; auffallend, befremdlich, seltsam, wunderlich, sonder-, wunderbar, selten (nicht vorhanden)." More revealing are the references in Grimm, *DWB*, IV, 1, s.v., "gast," esp. coll. 1454, 1455, 1459, 1466:

gast—fremder, so völlig erhalten noch im 16. jh.; wechselt mit "fremdling, fremder"; ellende oder "fremde geste", jenes um die heimatlosigkeit zu verstärken, dieses um den gegensatz zu dem lande, in dem sie auftreten, hervorzuheben. "fremde geste" von fremden im lande ist geläufig geblieben tief in die nhd. zeit hinein [with examples]; auch für "gast" als wol aufgenommener besuch steht schon mhd. und lange "fremder gast", was doch anfangs durch "gast" allein schon bezeichnet war, dann aber besonders von "fremden" galt [with examples]; der fremde ist entweder ein lieber, willkommener, gern gesehener gast u.a., oder das gegenteil."[9]

"Auff d' hochzeit kommen," too, seems to be a set phrase. Here are a few examples: Friedrich Dedekind's *Grobianus* [1551] in Neudrucke deutscher Literaturwerke, ed. G. Milchsack, (1882) 34–35, l. 4297: "Dacht ich will dir auff d' hochzeit komen . . ."; Fischart, *Der new Eulenspiegel Reimenweiß*, "Vorrede," p. 19, l. 29, *DNL*, (1882) 18, 2. Abt.: "Pochhansen, die vns auff die Hochzeit kommen wöllen . . ." and p. 120, ll. 2789–90: "Was? sol ich laden erst die braut? Sie seind doch schon auff d hochzeit kommen?"; Fischart, *Aller Practick Großmutter*, (1623), in *Das Kloster*, ed. T. Scheible, 8 (1847), 636: "Man wird Hund, Fliegen vnd Fercklein nicht dörffen auff die Hochzeit betten, sie werden ohn das darzu tretten."

My question is now: what is the particular significance of "fremder Gast" and "auf die Hochzeit kommen geladen" when employed with reference to the *psittacus torquatus* and that bird's presence at a wedding, specifically a VH?

It should be kept in mind that, from early medieval times, certain "facts" concerning the *psittacus torquatus* or *Sittich* (henceforth abbreviated as S.) were known to the people of Western Europe who had access to such authors as Aelian, Apuleius, Aristotle, Arrianus, Ctesias, Ovid, Pausanias, Philostorgius, Pliny, Solinus, Statius,[10] and who knew the Bible and how to interpret biblical passages to suit their fancy. Thus there existed throughout the Middle Ages and was extant during the sixteenth and seventeenth centuries what might be called the lore of the S.

This lore is not a fixed number of data and, consequently, not every item of this body of lore is necessarily present every time the S. turns up as guest in the VHH of the sixteenth and seventeenth centuries. As a matter of fact, "contradictions" are occasionally observable as, e.g., when Pliny makes the S. out to be a lascivious bird[11] and when Vincent of Beauvais calls the S. "avis . . . luxuriosa nimium, bibitque vinum,"[12] and when, quoting Aristotle, Konrad von Megenberg writes of the S.: "Aristotiles spricht, daz der sitich gern wein trink und ist gar ain unkäuscher vogel, und daz ist niht ain wunder, wan der wein ist ain ursach der unkäusch. es spricht auch Aristotiles, wenn der vogel trunken wirt von wein, so schawet er gern junkfrawen an und ist an dem anplick gar lustig."[13] The "normal" tradition emphasizes the purity and chastity of the S. One must expect such "contradictions" and look upon them as the exceptions that prove the rule. When one disregards them, he does not, thereby, endanger the validity of his conclusions because they are based on what undoubtedly is the overall consensus of the majority of writers concerning the S.

And so, instead of quoting in detail from the authors enumerated a while ago I prefer to cite a few "later" passages that, in turn, refer to these, chiefly classical, sources and that mention certain facts about the S. that, I hope, will shed light on the *Sittich*-passage in the VH.

Let me begin with two very late "riddles," because they represent a sort of summary of all that has been written about, and attributed to, the S. from antiquity to about 1700. They are taken from Jani de Bisschop *Chorus Musarum* (1700), and appear there in the section entitled "Aenigmata" as nos. 216 and 217 on p. 384:

no. 216 —Os et honos avium; cui plumae in corpore vernant,
Blanditur multa dominoque epulisque salute:
Contentus minimo, suspenso amplectitur ungue:
Innocuo adludit rostro, responsaque reddit.
Infantem in cunis, credas vagire jacentem,

Vel derisoris laetos audire cachinnos:
Nunc felem jures simulare, latrare molossum,
Gallinam cantare, animare in bella cohortes,
Tantus amor fandi est, meditata ut saepe retractet.

no. 217. —Gloria sum volucrum; praesto discrimine vocis,
Ingenioque homini; sed amoeni dotibus oris,
In blandos domini mores me vertere novi.
Est mihi rara fides, et rari forma coloris.
Mille sonos modulans docili de gutture fingo:
Quod sono, non brutum est; humanas exprimo voces.
Mulceo jucundis aures, et cantibus auras.
Non volo, quando volo: me carcer claudit honestus,
Qui me, fit quamvis mutus, facit esse loquacem.
Saepe choras duco lepidos, et amabile carmen
Succino; saepe salit dulcis mihi risus ab ore.
Comiter excipio venientem. Sacchare pascor.

One of the earlier passages concerning the S. is found in Isidore of Seville: "Psittacus in Indiae litoribus gignitur, colore viridi, torque puniceo grandi lingua et ceteris avibus latiore. Unde et articulata verba exprimit, ita ut si eam non videris, hominem loqui putes. Ex natura autem salutat dicens 'ave,' vel χαῖρε: cetera nomina institutione discit" (*Etym.*, XII, c. vii, § 24).

This passage is the source of the Merovingian statement about the *septacus* or S., cited in Karl Strecker (ed.), *Poetae Latini Aevi Carolini*, Tom. IV, fasc. II and III (1923), pp. 545–59. It is also the source of Vincent of Beauvais, *Spec. nat.*, lib. XVI, cap. xxxv, coll. 1230–31, as well as the source of *Summa que Catholicon appellatur fratris Johanis . . . emendata per . . . Petrum Egidium* (1520), s.v., "psitacus." The Isidore passage, to give one more example, is also reflected in Hugo de S. Victore, *De bestiis et aliis rebus libri quatuor, quorum primus et secundus Hugonem de Folieto ut videtur auctorem agnoscunt*, Migne, *P.L.*, CLXXVII, coll. 94–95.

Generally speaking, Albert the Great brings the same information about the S. as found in the Isidore passage. But his chapter on the S. contains an important biblical addendum. It reads: "Aquam pluviae non sustinet, sed alias aquas bibit et sustinet et ideo in montibus Gelboe in quibus raro pluit nidificare dicitur."[14] The "montes Gelboe" are the ones mentioned in 2 Sam. 1:21: "Montes Gelboe, nec ros nec pluvia veniant super vos, neque sint agri primitiarum!" "Ye mountains of Gilboa, let there be no dew, neither let there be rain upon you, nor fields of offerings . . ." (King James Version).

From the information contained in these ancient and medieval passages it is apparent that the home of the S. is in the Orient and that the bird, therefore, is a "fremder Vogel" as far as Europe and, especially, Germany are concerned, "fremder Vogel" meaning, first of all, strange, exotic, alien, not domestic bird. Sir David Lyndsay, writing in 1530, is aware of the far-away original home of the "papyngo": "Be thy travell, thou hes experience,/ First, beand bred in to the Orient."

I shall not go into detail concerning the color of the feathers of the S. The bird is referred to often, up to the time of Fischart and later, as having green plumage: "der Sittich grün." Rather should I like to emphasize two traits ascribed to the S. again and again that seem to have impressed writers and artists more than any other thing told or written about this bird—its ability *to speak* and the fact that the S. is a *pure* fowl. These are two traits that ultimately establish a connection between the S. and the Virgin Mary, and that explain the expression "fremder Vogel" to include the meaning: a strange, odd bird, one that really cannot be expected to be present in that sort of company, a pure, virginal bird at the wedding that is attended by dirty, phallic, obscene birds.

The S. is able to speak. It is said to have greeted Caesar or the Emperor with the word "$\chi\alpha\hat{\iota}\rho\epsilon$" or "ave" and to have had the ability, generally, to imitate human speech. Thus the S. joins the long line of talking birds, such as the raven in *Oswald* and *Ruodlieb* and the other "aves hominum sermone fruentes" we meet in *Ruodlieb*, and the talking birds of Celtic literature, etc.[15]

These two words, "$\chi\alpha\hat{\iota}\rho\epsilon$" and its Latin equivalent "ave," especially mentioned as part of the vocabulary of the S., turn up in Luke 1:18, where the angel greets the Virgin Mary with the words "$\chi\alpha\hat{\iota}\rho\epsilon\ \kappa\epsilon\chi\alpha\rho\iota\tau\omega\mu\acute{\epsilon}\nu\eta$," rendered in the Vulgate by "ave, gratia plena." In my opinion, a person in the Middle Ages, looking for connections, could easily establish a connection between the little flying creature speaking these words and the winged angel saying them to Mary. Such a connection, once established, would set the little bird aside from the common flock. The S. would become something "special," a creature worthy to be associated with the Virgin Mary—being as chaste and pure as she. If this is true, the S. would ultimately become one of the "Sinnbilder und Beiworte Mariens," to use a part of Anselm Salzer's title of his outstanding *Programm: Die Sinnbilder und Beiworte Mariens in der deutschen Literatur und lateinischen Hymnenpoesie des Mittelalters* (1886).

This is exactly what has happened![16]

The S. is a chaste, pure, immaculate bird. Sir David Lyndsay, writing in 1530, knew that one of the most outstanding traits of the parrot or S. was purity: "I am content, quod the pure Papyngo" (l. 1074) and "Adew, Brether! quod the pure Papyngo" (l. 1130).

As was the sparrow the bird of Venus, so was the *Sittich* the bird of

Mary or, at least, one of the birds of Mary. Konrad von Würzburg in his *Goldene Schmiede*, l. 1850, explains the role the Mountains of Gilboa play in bringing the S. and the Virgin together:

> swie gar der wilde siticus gruene als ein gras erliuhte,
> er wirt doch selten fiuhte von regen noch von touwe.
> dem tete gelîche, vrouwe, dîn magetlich gemüete,
> daz von unkiuscher vlüete nie wart genetzet hâres grôz,
> swie gar dîn herze wandelbloz in vrischer jugent gruonte,
> dô dîn geburt versuonte mit got uns algemeine.[17]

There is abundant evidence that the S. is considered a clean, pure, chaste bird and, therefore, fit to be associated with the Virgin. Here are merely a few examples. In John Lydgate's poem "Ballade at the Reverence of Our Lady, QWENE of Mercy", Mary is addressed: "O popinjay, plumed in clennesse."[18] Johannes Rothe's *Das Lob der Keuschheit* is a fairly good summary of the lore of the S. and the bird's association with the Virgin:

> l. 5370 disser togend schilt einen sittich had,
>   des federen sint grün alss ein blad,
>   umme den halss einen gelen ring
>   recht als ess si ein gulden ding.
>   ein zungen her had di ist gross;
>   wan di wirt gesneten loss,
>   so lernet her danne sprechen
>   di worte ane gebrechen.
>   sin snabel ist gar harte,
>   gar sedig ist sin geferte.
> l. 5380 her isset unnd trincket nicht vil,
>   unnd wer en etwas leren wil,
>   der muss en mit eime ysern drade twingen,
>   so leret her sprechen unnd singen.
>   unnd sine fusse langet her zu den munde,
>   also ein mensche isset zu aller stunde.
>   den regen kann her nicht geliden,
>   bi deme tode so muss her en miden,
>   sinen zagel her vor allen dingen bewart.
>   alss sal auch sin des kuschen ard,
> l. 5390 der sal sedig sin, zuchtich unnd vol gude
>   unnd sines lichams underteil behude
>   unnd genen in eime togentsamen dinge.
>   umme sinen halss mit eine gulden ringe
>   also saltu dissen vogil beschauwe;
>   den schilt furen di van Buchenauwe.[19]

Normally, when the S. is associated with a biblical or religious person, that person is the Virgin Mary. I know of only one "religious" passage in which the S. is not associated with her, but with Christ. It is found in Goldstaub-Wendriner, eds., *Ein Tosco-Venezianischer Bestiarius* (1892), pp. 61, 208, 420–22. Goldstaub-Wendriner translate the pertinent lines thus: "Der Papagei ist ein Typus für Christus, der an Reinheit seines Gleichen nicht hatte noch haben wird, eine Folge der unbefleckten Empfängnis, der makellosen Geburt wie seines sündenfreien Denkens, Redens und Handelns: So blieb er allein in dieser Welt der Sünde rein und fehlerlos."

The Johannes Rothe passage cited above serves also as an introduction to still another "proof" of the purity of the S.: "den schilt furen di van Buchenauwe" (l. 5395). The S., because of its association with the Virgin, easily becomes an allegorical representation of something good and virtuous, in this case of "zucht."[20] One is, therefore, not astonished to find the S. among the armorial birds of the Middle Ages.[21] Closely connected with the representation of the S. in coats-of-arms, where it is found because it stands for virtue in general and for chastity in particular, is the representation of the S. on clerical and similar vestments (*casula, dalmatica, tunica*, etc.).

A fairly long list of *Sittiche* embroidered on vestments used in connection with cathedrals, etc., can be put together from the following studies: Fr. Bock, *Geschichte der liturgischen Gewänder des Mittelalters . . .* , I (1859), 251, 278 f., cf. II, 282. Joseph Braun, S.J., *Die liturgische Gewandung im Okzident und Orient* (1907), p. 225. Fritz Witte, ed., *Die liturgischen Gewänder und kirchlichen Stickereien des Schnütgenmuseums-Köln* (1926), pl. 80, No. 2. Essewein in *Anzeiger für Kunde der deutschen Vorzeit* (1869), Nr. 1, coll. 4–5. *Dictionnaire Historique de l'ancien langage François*, VIII, 173. Du Cange, *Glossarium*, VI, ss. vv., "papagallus" and "Papagen." There should be added the "Geier" mentioned by Fr. Bock, *Geschichte*, I, 279. Bock writes: "Auf dem untern Blättchen sitzt in grünem Gefieder ein kleiner Geier (vulture?), oder ein Falke, kenntlich an dem roten Halsbande." Bock evidently took this bird (from his own description it is definitely a *Halsbandsittich*—see the *psittacus torquatus* entry in *Brehm's Tierleben*, ed. Pechuel-Loeschke, 'Vögel,' V/2 [1891], 331) for a "Geier" because the name of the donor is Johann von Geyen ("wie der Name und das Wappen anzudeuten scheint").

The belief according to which there exists a close association between the Virgin and the S.—something that, in my opinion, is responsible for the designation of the S. in the VH as "fremder Vogel"—a bird out of place at a wedding otherwise attended by smutty, phallic birds— was most assuredly still a living and common belief in the sixteenth and

seventeenth centuries, shared by persons interested in such "poetry" as
the VH and by artists such as Dürer and Antonis van Dyk (1599–1641).

A museum in Basel owns a *Marienbild* by Dürer (H. Knackfuss,
Dürer [1904], p. 65). It is described in Ludwig Lorenz, *Die Mariendarstel-
lungen Albrecht Dürers aus der Zeit von 1485 bis 1514* (1904), on pp. 41–42
("Die heilige Familie mit dem Hasen"). He mentions the "Papagei" in
the picture.[22] Especially significant is the painting by Antonius van Dyk.
It used to hang in the St. Petersburg Eremitage. I am not sure about the
present whereabouts of the painting. It bears the name "Die heilige
Familie mit den Rebhühnern." More or less easily accessible is the
reproduction in the "Blaues Buch" by Ewald Vetter called *Maria im
Rosenhag* (1956), p. 62: in the tree, above the resting Virgin, is perched a
S.

It seems to me that I may have made, after all these years, a case for
my interpretation of "Der Sittig was ein frembder gast." But I still am
not sure about the exact meaning of the next line in the VH: "der kam
auff die hochzeyt gladen." Is it possible that the need for a word that
rhymes with "baden" in the next line—"der Stare/wolt mit der prewt
nur baden"—is at least in part responsible for the choice of "auff die
hochzeyt gladen"?

Should someone ask me what, precisely, went on in the mind of
Kunegund Hergotin when she looked over her copy of the VH and there
came across the *Sittich*-passage, I should be obliged to confess that I am
still unable to give a satisfactory answer. It may have reminded her of an
acquaintance by the name of Sittich![23]

You may remember that in the *Ecbasis cuiusdam captivi per tropologiam*
the *psittacus* is a prominent performer at the court of the sick lion at
Eastertime. There, together with the stork, "he" sings religious songs in
Hebrew, Greek and Latin. After the singing the *psittacus* asks for wine:
" . . . quod mihi poscenti non dantur pocula vini" (l. 987). I would not
blame you, should you, Herman, having been forced to deal with these
disiecta membra of the S., feel the need of liquid refreshment and the urge
to ask the author of the article the question of Persius: "Quid expedivit
psittaco?"—What hath it profited the parrot?

NOTES

[1] Johann Herrgott had been publicly beheaded in Leipzig on the Monday following
Cantate-Sunday, i.e., 20 May 1527, but was given nevertheless an honorable burial for
which the city treasury paid: "Sabbato post Cantate. Vom Hergot zubegraben dem Toden-

greber 6 gr." Albrecht Kirchhoff, *Johann Herrgott, Buchführer von Nürnberg, und sein tragisches Ende 1527*, (1877) especially pp. 18, 24, 43. See also Joseph Benzing, *Buchdruckerlexikon des 16. Jahrhunderts* (1952), pp. 131–32.

[2] Zwickau XXX, 5, 20/32 is cited by Kopp, "Ein Liederbuch aus dem Jahre 1650," *Zeitschrift für deutsche Philologie*, XXXIX (1970), 215.

[3] Benzing, *Buchdruckerlexikon*, pp. 132 and 135.

[4] Karl Goedeke, *Grundriss zur Geschichte der deutschen Dichtung* (1886), II, 249, E; 87, 3.

[5] Quoted from the copy in the Herzog August Bibliothek in Wolfenbüttel.

[6] This text was published in F. L. Mittler, *Deutsche Volkslieder*, 2d ed. (1865), pp. 440–43. This same text appears in a *Fliegendes Blatt*, s.l., (Basel?, 1613); here the second part of strophe 17 reads: "Sittig grün War bei ihn über d Maß schön." Published in Wilhelm Wackernagel, *Deutsches Lesebuch*, 2d ed. (1841), Part 2, coll. 229–32. Both broadsides, 1605 and 1613, have 32 strophes.

[7] *ZfdA*, III (1843), 38.

[8] Selected general references concerning this problem occur in: Hugo Suolahti, *Die deutschen Vogelnamen: Eine wortgeschichtliche Untersuchung* (1909), pp. 1–2, 455–56, 466–72; Friedrich Seiler, *Die Entwicklung der deutschen Kultur im Spiegel des deutschen Lehnworts*, Part 2: *Von der Einführung des Christentums bis zum Beginn der neueren Zeit* (1921), pp. 156–57; Lexer's and Grimm's dictionaries and Du Cange, *Glossarium mediae et infimae Latinitatis*, VI, s.v., "papagallus," and NED, s.v., "popinjay"; H. Bächtold-Stäubli, ed., *Handwörterbuch des deutschen Aberglaubens*, VI, 1387–88 (an article written by Hoffmann-Krayer).

[9] Cf. Wolfgang Golther, ed., *Das Lied vom Hürnen Seyfrid nach der Druckredaktion des 16. Jahrhunderts* (1889), Neudrucke deutscher Literatur des XVI. und XVII. Jahrhunderts, 81–82 (1911), Str. 84: "Do schwůren sie zůsammen / Zwen ayd, die fremden gest" (i.e., the giant Kuperan and Seyfrid); *Schweizerische Volkslieder. Zwei Sammlungen in einem Band*, ed. Ludwig Tobler (1917), p. 82: 'da komt uns frömbde gest' (from "Schlacht bei Glurns-Schwabenkrieg, 1499"); and from Valentin Boltz, *Der Weltspiegel* (1550, 1551) in Jakob Bächtold, ed., *Schweizerische Schauspiele des sechzehnten Jahrhunderts*, II (1891), 117, line 28: "Bürger vnd frembde Gest." See also Hugo Hayn, *Bibliotheca Germanorum Nuptialis* (1890), p. 69, no. 420: "entdeckt von Einem Frembden Hochzeit-Gast" [dated 1658]; cf. Hayn-Gotendorf, *Bibliotheca Germanorum Erotica & Curiosa*, III (1913), 307.

[10] These authors are mentioned in connection with the S. in Samuelis Bocharti *Hierozoicon sive de Animalibus S. Scripturae*, ed. by E. F. C. Rosenmüller, III (1796), 97 ff.

[11] Cf. Pliny, *nat. hist.*, ed. Mayhoff, X 42 (58).

[12] Vincent of Beauvais in *spec. nat.*, lib. XVI, cap. CXXXV, coll. 1230–31.

[13] Konrad von Megenberg, *Das Buch der Natur*, ed. Franz Pfeiffer, (1861), p. 222.

[14] Alberti Magni, *de animalibus*, ed. Hermann Stadler, lib. XXIII, tract un, cap. XXIV, pp. 1509–10.

[15] Zimmer, "Keltische Beiträge," *ZfdA* XXXIII (1889), 188 f., 204, 211 ff. Talking parrots in French Literature: "Le Papegant," "Le Chevalier du Perroquet," "las Novas del Papagai" (Provençal Poems). The reference in Karl von Kraus, ed., *Mittelhochdeutsches Übungsbuch* (1912), pp. 174 ff. is to the "psitacus" (see 1. 50) and not to the "Papagei." When the bird is a messenger, it is often, not always, able to speak; see Wallner, *ZfdA*, L (1908), 209 f.; the MHD poem *Wigalois*, ll. 2517 f., 2589 ff., 2768 ff. Norman Douglas, *Birds and Beasts of the Greek Anthology* (1927), pp. 89–90: Crinagoras has the S. say "Hail" to the Emperor. Heinrich von Morungen: "Wêr ein sitich ader ein star, die mohten sît/ gelernet han daz si sprechen 'Minne'" (see, e.g., *Minnesangs Frühling*, 4th ed., p. 144 and note on p. 388 or Bartsch-Golther, *Deutsche Liederdichter des zwölften bis vierzehnten Jahrhunderts* [1901], p. 49). - Jean Tixien, i.e., Johannes Ravisius Textor, *Dialogi Aliquot* (1616), pp. 202b–06, 'dialogus avium,' with mention of *psittacus* who *humana voce* says "χαιρε." See also the following two editions of *Mandeville's Travels*, ed. P. Hamelius, p. 182 and ed. Arthur Layard, p. 175, where the words "salven men" are rendered "Salve (God save you!)." Kristân von Hamle: "Ich wolte daz der anger sprechen solte/ als der sitich in dem glas," in Carl von Kraus, *Deutsche Liederdichter des 13. Jahrhunderts*, I (1952), 221 ("in dem glas" or "im Fenster"?). Cf. Wilbert's *Vita Leonis IX*: "Hahn, der die Worte *Papa Leo* krähte/Hund, der *Deus meus* sprach/ Papagei, der die Worte *ad papam vado* wiederholte," in Max Manitius, *Geschichte*

der lateinischen Literatur des Mittelalters, Part 2 (1923), p. 384. Riddle no. 782 in P. Franciscum à S. Barbara e Scholis Piis, *Oedipodiania seu Sphingis aenigmata* . . . (1732): the answer is "Psyttacus." The papyngo, the Scottish form of "popinjay" in Sir David Lyndsay, *The Testament and Complaynt of our Soverane Lordis Papyngo, Kyng James the Eyft*, written in 1530 and printed for the first time in 1538, ed. by David Laing, I (1879), 61–104, can do the following (on pp. 64–65):

> l. 92 Syng lyke the merle, and crawe lyke the cocke,
> Pew lyke the gled, and chant lyke the laverock,
> Bark lyke ane dog, and kekell lyke ane ka,
> Blait lyk ane hog, and buller lyke ane bull,
> l. 96 Gaill lyke ane goik, and greit quhen scho wes wa.

The talking bird tradition, with special reference to the S., goes on into our times: Berta Ragotzi, *Freude am Wellensittich. Aufzucht, Pflege, Sprechunterricht* (1951). Ovid apparently numbers the S. among the *piae volucres* (together with the stork, the phoenix, the ostrich, and the dove); he mentions the bird's *humana vox*. In Fischart's *Ehezuchtbüchlein* the term "Schwetzen" is applied to the "Papigey oder Sickust, i.e., *psittacus*. Similarly, in a poem printed by Hans Knobloch in Strassburg in 1554 the Sitticus is characterized as "schwetzerig überus," BLVS, CV (1870), pp. 278–84; see also Suolahti, *Die deutschen Vogelnamen*, pp. 466–72. "Sprechen" and now "schwatzen"—the mighty have fallen!

[16] Cf. *Das Marienleben des Schweizers Wernher aus der Heidelberger Hs.*, ed. M. Päpke and A. Hübner, Deutsche Texte des Mittelalters, XXVII (1920), pp. 64–65; also Max Päpke, *Das Marienleben des Schweizers Wernher. Mit Nachträgen zu Vögtlins Ausgabe der Vita Marie Rhythmica*, Palaestra, LXXXI (1913), p. 134, and *Vita beatae virginis marie et salvatoris rythmica*, ed. A. Vögtlin, BLVS, CLXX (1888), p. 82. This *vita* originated in the first half of the 13th century.

[17] See also Albertus Magnus quoted above in the text and *Petri Berchorii reductorium morale*, in *Opera omnia* (1631), II, p. 507, 10, l. 7c. 67.

[18] *The Minor Poems of John Lydgate*, ed. H. McCracken, Early English Text Society, Extra Series, CVII (1911), 238.

[19] Deutsche Texte des Mittelalters, ed. Hans Neumann, XXXVIII (1934), 150–51.

[20] *Das Lob der Keuschheit, ein Lehrgedicht von Johannes Rothe*, ed. Hans Neumann, Palaestra, CXCI (1934), pp. 103–4; cf., in the 1650 VH "Fraw Side"—without a doubt, the S. is connected with 'Sitte'; see also 'Sitikus' connected with 'Frau Zucht' and 'Frau Ehr' in Peter Suchenwirt's *Werke*, ed. Alois Primisser (1827), p. 97.

[21] Supporting material is found in Du Cange, *Glossarium*, s.v., "Stelligeri," where is cited, i.a., Albertus Argentinensis, anno 1218: "Alii vero fecerunt viridem psittacum in albo campo." See also Alwin Schultz, *Das höfische Leben zur Zeit der Minnesinger*, 2d ed., I (1889), 349–450; II, 91, note 7 and 93 (green S. in red field). Also, Eberhard Graff, *Althochdeutscher Sprachschatz* (1836), III, 370: "Die Preising von Wolnzach fuhren im Schildt einen Sittich." I have not seen "Die Sterner und Sitticher zu Basel," a novella in *Varnhagens Denkwürdigkeiten und vermischte Schriften* (1840), V, 383–434.

[22] Cf. Max Sandaeus, *Aviarum Marianum* (ca. 1631); Praz, *Studies in 17th Century Imagery* (1939), p. 180; and A. Spamer, *Das Andachtsbild* (1930), p. 170.

[23] For *Sittich* as a family name at the beginning of the 16th century see the reference to Ulrich Sittich, a cousin of Eberlin von Günzburg, in the series *Deutsche Literatur*, "Reihe Reformation," II: "Die Sturmtruppen der Reformation. Ausgewählte Flugschriften der Jahre 1520–25," ed. A. E. Berger (1931), p. 54, bottom; 142, ll. 7–8; 152, ll. 6–7.

Medievalism in Renaissance Germany

Frank L. Borchardt

The literature of Germany in the fifteenth and sixteenth centuries presents extraordinary problems to the literary historian. The problem of medievalism, one of the many, recurs with rhythmic regularity. The exploitation of medieval names, motifs, settings, and conventions characterizes texts that are otherwise alien to the form and sense of the Middle Ages. It may, at times, seem to the unwary reader of a fifteenth-century prose romance that he has stumbled upon some early incarnation of Sir Walter Scott. The same reader, however unwary, would never take his text for a genuinely medieval work. The incidental similarities drown beneath the drastic differences in style and outlook that distinguish the great verse epics from their curious progeny in the fifteenth and sixteenth centuries.[1]

These similarities and differences have, in the development of literary historiography, become imprisoned in the category "late Middle Ages." If the terminology were neutral in value and merely chronological, there would be no quarrel. "Late," however, in almost any context, implies some less than desirable state of affairs: deceased, old, tardy, epigonic. And it implies nothing better in "late Middle Ages." The literary comet of the year 1200 and the decades surrounding it was among the most brilliant in the history of German literature, indeed of world literature. But that brilliance has so dazzled German literary historiography that subsequent events—however significant in themselves or for the future course of literature—have rarely been regarded in any light but that cast from the year 1200. It is as if one were told: if you must enjoy the flamboyant facade of the cathedral at Rouen, you must, at the very least, apologize for its failure to measure up to the Sainte Chapelle—as though they had very much more in common than pointed arches and a blithe disregard of the materiality of stone.

If the category "late Middle Ages" performs any service at all, it is to stress the orderly transition of one style out of the other. But its fundamental disservice spoils even this. In literary history "late" is equivalent to epigonic. When German literary history lumps together everyone from Konrad von Würzburg (ca. 1225–1287) to Hans Sachs

(1494–1576), it extends the notion of epigonism beyond the useful. Even in the case of Konrad von Würzburg, who might in truth be called an epigone, it would be better to face him forward toward the coming tradition (at least as far as Hermann von Sachsenheim, 1365–1458) than to wrench his head around on his shoulders merely to have him look back on the Golden Age as the scholars do.

Epigonism applies to literary history where living consciousness of tradition or absolute continuity prevails. One can hardly feel inferior to the poet of the *Nibelungenlied* if one has never read him or can no longer understand him.[2] Certainly by the year 1400 much had been forgotten and the little remembered was seen through a glass darkly. Allegory and the so-called florid style had, in the hands of the medieval German poets, been occasional devices. In the hands of their successors these devices dominated entire works.[3] The tastes of the fourteenth century sifted through the available literature and passed on fragments of the great tradition. The fifteenth century finished reshaping the remnants to its own taste: prose in preference to verse, civic virtue in preference to chivalry, marital fidelity in preference to courtly love.

To be sure, conservative forces returned to the works of the high Middle Ages, even early into the sixteenth century, but they were no longer truly conserving a living tradition; rather, they were trying to revive a forgotten one. When the antiquaries come on the scene, like Jakob Püterich von Reichertshausen (1400–1469), one can hardly speak of a revival.[4] It is more like a disinterment. The lyric traditions of the high Middle Ages give the illusion of longer life, chiefly because of the appearance of a fine poet in the fourteenth century, Oswald von Wolkenstein (1377–1445). But these too had the *signum mortis* on their brow: anthologies, like antiquaries, being a sure indication of imminent demise. Reinmar and Walther—and they alone from the period before the Great Interregnum—found their way into the *Hausbuch* of Michael de Leone (ca. 1350) amidst numerous inferior poets.[5] Frauenlob was dead only fifty years when he was anthologized by Johannes von Neumarkt (ca. 1369).[6] A similar fate awaited Peter Suchenwirt, Oswald, Muskatplüt, and Hermann von Sachsenheim in the songbook of Clara Hätzlerin (1471).[7] This is not to say that all traditions were disrupted totally, but only that the traditions of vernacular literature were so sufficiently disrupted as to make nonsense of the concept of epigonism for the German literature of the "late Middle Ages."

Certainly, parts of the "Medieval Model," as C. S. Lewis called it, survived the Middle Ages and even the seventeenth and eighteenth centuries.[8] No one, however, would call either Grimmelshausen or Goethe "late medieval." One of these survivals was the cosmology. The

new sciences may have been simpler and more accurate, but they lacked
the elegance and, especially, the conformity with human experience of
the Aristotelian and Ptolemaic explanations and so were impotent to
dislodge them from the poetic imagination. Another survival was the
encyclopedia, by which I mean the conventions of organizing large
bodies of knowledge. The display of learning in chapter 26 of the *Acker-*
mann aus Böhmen latches on to the encyclopedic tradition.[9] It appears
there without apology, as it does throughout "Meistersang," whenever
the Seven Liberal Arts are praised.[10]

When Thomas Prischuh von Augsburg, within twenty years of the
Ackermann, produces a similar catalog and similarly displays his learning, he does so self-consciously, reflectively, explaining to his audience
that such displays are demanded by tradition:

> ich tets doch nun in der figur
> mim ticht zů ainer floritur.[11]

> [This have I done only for the figure of speech,
> to give my poem a flourish.]

This would be a shocking anomaly if the tradition had been unquestionably intact. In a sense, the tradition was intact, in that it still represented an ideal. But a new audience had arisen, unaware or only dimly
aware of it, an audience for whom the tradition was not essential to
communication as it was to the learned, an audience that had to be
educated into it. This audience was the new bourgeoisie. The good
burghers, who spent their energies in manufacture and trade, were
generally innocent of the clerical and chivalric experience of the past,
however much they admired their idea of it.

Such admiration goes a long way toward explaining the apparent
atavism of "late medieval" letters. A rash of chivalric literature broke out
in the fifteenth century. As with the preceding literature, remote time or
exotic place provided the setting. This does not, however, imply a
particularly intimate insight into the preceding literature. Chivalry is
regularly transported into alien time or space. The here and now has
almost always been unsuited to grand gestures and noble deeds. The
superficial similarity collapses under the fundamental differences in
presuppositions and outlook. The trappings of romance—festivities,
adventures, parted lovers—envelop the immensely popular little novels
of the fifteenth and sixteenth centuries. But *Die schöne Magelone* could
not have less in common with an epic of the high Middle Ages, even if
Count Peter's jousts were multiplied a hundred-fold.[12] An entirely foreign, not to say hostile, ethic permeates the later work. The tenderness

of parental concern, the models of civic virtue (Magelone founds a hospital), the proprieties of courtship, the rewards of fidelity, all are more likely to suggest Hauff and the Biedermeier than the stark nemesis of *Tristan* or the *Nibelungenlied* or the relentless pursuit of virtue in Hartmann von Aue or Wolfram von Eschenbach. The panoramas of the high medieval epic, peopled with towering figures, yield to a narrower focus that follows familiar and rather ordinary human beings through their fairytale-like adventures. The poets, translators, adapters of the fifteenth and sixteenth centuries venerated what they knew of the tradition, but not to the extent that they would betray their own values. No force on earth could have moved the compilers of the *Tristan* chapbook to admire adultery. Something has undoubtedly happened to that art of courtly love if the *Tragedia . . . von der strengen Lieb Herr Tristrant mit der schönen Königen Isalden* can end:

> Das stäte Lieb und Treu aufwachs
> im ehling Stant, das wünscht Hans Sachs.[13]

> [That love and troth forever wax
> in the state of marriage: thus Hans Sachs.]

Allegory has fallen on strange days indeed, if Lady Poverty is obliged to come upon the scene with the words:

> Ich pin die ehrlich frau armuͤet
> Ob ich gleich nit pin reich an guͤet
> So pin ich aber reich an duͤegent.[14]

> [I am honorable Lady Poverty,
> although I am not rich in wealth,
> I am rich in virtue.]

The appearance of medieval motifs and conventions is so extensive in the fifteenth and sixteenth centuries—but so different from what preceded—that it should be considered characteristic of a distinct style, one not to be judged by malicious comparison to the tradition no matter how much it was admired by the poets.

In the examples just cited, admiration of past traditions is coupled with the blindest possible lack of comprehension, the thinnest veneer concealing none too opaquely a new system of values. Other examples could demonstrate profounder comprehension, such as Luther betrays in his hymn, "Kom heyliger geist herre Gott." He prays the Holy Spirit to grant the strength:

> das wyr hye ritterlich ringen,
> durch tod und leben zu dyr dringen.[15]

[that we may fight chivalrously,
to press through death and life to Thee.]

Luther's use of "ritterlich'" was surely not a reference to the sorry knighthood of his own day. It was an appeal to the admiration of past traditions. Despite the appalling state of the knightly class and its bitter hostility to the bourgeoisie, there was probably no higher compliment a good burgher could receive than that his behavior was "knightly." An analogue in modern American usage would be "courteous," referring to good manners and suggesting the standards of a past and better age as it is imagined in the present. Luther's metaphoric use of "ritterlich" is similar but also implies a point of comparison little changed from the ideals of the courtly poets of the high Middle Ages. Even then real chivalry was never at home in the present, but always at home in the heroic past. In addition to valor and devotion, nostalgia was intrinsic to this field of ideas from the very start. Nor is Luther's application of the term to the spiritual life any daring departure from tradition, considering Wolfram's Parzival, Meister Eckhart's doctrine of nobility or Cola di Rienzo's Knighthood of the Holy Spirit.

Luther's exquisite poem, "Sie ist mir lieb die werde Magd," is likewise bound to the past.[16] It betrays nothing of the new theology. It is finely tuned to the conventions of erotic mysticism; and that ancient tradition was to survive well into modern times. The mystical tradition consistently lends inspiration, authority, and vocabulary to movements of spiritual renewal in Western Christianity, to Luther's, to those of his rivals, to those that preceded and succeeded the Reformation.[17] Luther's comprehension of that tradition was anything but superficial. But by the time he was writing even the earliest of these hymns (1524), Luther had taken his movement on an irreversible course far beyond any medieval antecedent. In one sense unaltered continuity of tradition and real survival of medievalism apply to Luther. In a more important sense tradition was here wholly subjected to a revolutionary force.

It may seem, at the very least, impertinent to mention the vulgar literature of the fifteenth and sixteenth centuries in the same breath with Luther's hymns. They have, however, one important feature in common: they are both revolutionary. They accompany and ratify two of the great innovations of the period: the Reformation and the reshaping of the social structure. This is not to say that the social and religious revolutions were identical. Not all burghers became Protestants; not all Protestants became burghers. But these innovations generally coincide with other changes—in art, music, architecture, statecraft, warfare, and public affairs—and their literatures are evidence of the character of the period.

Another feature common to both these literatures is medievalism, more specifically, the survival of courtly and clerical conventions in a new setting, where they could be perfectly at home. One has only to regard the burgher churches of Nürnberg, Ulm, and Prague to see how suitable the Gothic style could be to burgher piety and pride, and how different from the Gothic of a brilliant monarchy like Charles IV's in the soaring space of the Cathedral of St. Vitus. Yes, the Gothic style survived, but it served new purposes.

Survival was, however, not the only form of medievalism in the Renaissance. The Gothic style, for example, was revived to serve even newer purposes—and well before the medieval fever of the nineteenth century. Even into the seventeenth century Gothic churches were still being built. The Bishop of Würzburg and Duke of Franconia, Julius Echter (reigned 1573–1617), had his secular buildings constructed in Renaissance style—the University, the hospital, his residence on the Marienburg—as befitted a great Renaissance prince. As a Counter-Reformation zealot he built parish churches for his flock, furnishing the somber little structures with Gothic windows.[18] He deemed Gothic good for the piety of the people. All that glistens is not gold; all that is Gothic is not medieval.[19] The Gothic revival of Julius Echter—which I have heard called, perversely, "Spätstgotik"[20]—provides a precise analogue to the second, the more important and characteristic form of medievalism in the Renaissance: the discovery of the medieval past or the Middle Ages revived.

In the argument that follows, I lay no claim to originality in the broad characterization of the medieval sense of the past,[21] nor do I maintain that the generalizations prevail without exception. It is only in the transition to newer forms of thought about time that I believe my interpretation of the evidence to depart from previous interpretation.

The process of discovery or revival presupposes the existence of a separate entity to be discovered or a lost past to be revived. This in turn presupposes a consciousness of the present as somehow discrete from the past, a view of history that departs from the timeless eye of God. The Middle Ages seemed to preserve some sense of the pastness of human events, most strikingly in periods of rapid change. Indications of this appear in forgery of legal documents. Most of them were set in prior time. The forgers summoned up the past either to justify a present state of affairs or to condemn it, to maintain or restore on the basis of ancient authority the just conditions that, supposedly, once prevailed.[22] The usual response to an odious forgery was not a critical reading and subsequent exposure of the falsity of the document. It was another forgery. The forgers and their audience failed to understand the principle of anachronism, and this failure made them express the past in the language of the present. Forgery in any era is a rich source of information about that era. Medieval forgery reveals a conception of time that fused the past and present into one familiar entity. The past was rather like the present: ancient Rome had consuls, as did medieval Strassburg; ancient Rome had a Caesar, as did medieval Germany.

Insofar as antiquity was past and not present it held little charm for the Middle Ages. By all calculations, the present era began sometime around the birth of Christ: the sixth *aetas* according to Isidore;[23] the fourth *imperium*, according to Orosius;[24] the second *status*, according to Joachim.[25] No one was certain how much longer the present would last, but there was little disagreement as to when it began. The past was more or less equivalent to pre-Christian times. One can hardly speak of antiquity as a past so desirable to the Middle Ages that it should be revived. That would mean restoring an era without grace. Classical antiquity nonetheless enjoyed great authority; otherwise Alexander the Great would not have had God at his side,[26] nor Dante Virgil, nor would poor Ovid have been moralized beyond recognition. The very attempt to christianize the admired ancients betrays, however, the grave handicap that accompanied their authority. And more importantly, it demonstrates the refusal of the Middle Ages to regard them as truly past. The admired ancients were made to behave as though they were good medieval Christians. The apparent dislocation of time makes perfect sense in a view of history that looked to the timeless eye of God, "in a perspective which stretched from Creation to the Last Judgment."[27] It is a logical corollary of the history of salvation: although the Fall of Adam and the act of redemption were unique moments in time, their consequences apply equally to all human time since the Fall. The history of salvation in its entirety is constantly present to man.

The one reserve of prior time not truly present to the Middle Ages was the heroic past, which I use broadly to mean all better times, separated from the present by some abyss. It may have been the setting of the epics and romances or the Golden Age or just the "good old days." Sacred history provides the authoritative model: the sojourn of man in the Garden of Eden, the one period of time not present to the history of salvation. The heroic past is a reproach to the present and an example for the future. This particular sense of the pastness of human events differs, I believe, little from the longing for better times in all eras and does nothing to distinguish the Middle Ages from any other period.

The slow shifts in the sense of the heroic past do, however, give a clue concerning other changes in the overall sense of time. As long as the heroic past remained sufficiently remote, either nebulous or relatively ancient, it could not disturb the broad present of the medieval mind. Early in the fourteenth century, one Jacques de Longuyon inserted into a romance several strophes on the "Nine Worthies," three from among the pagans: Hector, Alexander, and Julius Caesar; three from among the Jews: Joshua, David, and Judas Maccabee; and three from among the Christians: Arthur, Charlemagne, and Geoffrey of Bouillon.[28] He wrote this for the episcopal court at Liège and included Geoffrey for reasons of local patriotism. The Nine Worthies have a colorful history thereafter, well into the seventeenth century, in both literature and art. They took different directions in various countries. In England and Scotland they became the subject of heavy moralizing. In France and Flanders they glorified chivalry in the courts. In Germany they decorated the burghers' homes and city halls in the shape of woodcuts and statues.[29] They entered Germany in the second half of the fourteenth century and were by far the most popular secular motif of graphics there in the fifteenth century.[30] The constellation of these heroes, particularly the presence of Geoffrey in the company of Arthur and Charlemagne, suggests that the good burghers who paid hard cash for these figures endowed at least the earlier Middle Ages with heroic stature and sought to borrow some of it for themselves. A relatively recent period that was a mere two centuries past, the early twelfth century had begun to slip from the broad sense of the present.

One can picture the town fathers of Cologne assembled under the impressive statues of the Nine Worthies to discuss taxes, tolls, and market conditions. It must surely have struck some of them in the course of a dreary meeting that these discussions were not quite the same as blowing down the walls of Jericho or Jerusalem. Others, no doubt, took occasional inspiration from the virtue of the Worthies to exact the toughest possible terms in a trade treaty. In either case, the crowns and armor of the Worthies could not have provided a stronger contrast to the fur-lined robes of the patricians. The former invested the business of military conquest; the latter invested the business of business. The one was basically alien, the other familiar. The one past, the other present.

Some early indications of this citizenship-in-the-present arise in the vernacular historiography of the fourteenth century. It is the unlatined burghers who require history to be written in their language. Those who do the writing are still learned clerics, but they write for the "intelligent laymen . . . who take greater pleasure in the reading of new things than of old."[31] This is an extremely significant statement, and astonishing for a man about to write a universal history from Adam to his own time. He wishes to serve up the past to an audience basically ignorant of it be-

cause it is so involved in the present. The burgher chroniclers soon dis-
cover that the traditional history on which they depend has little room
for them. So they must make room. And local history gets tacked on to
imperial and papal history with the unavoidable inference that it is
somehow different.[32] By the end of the first decades of the fifteenth
century, several historians have the temerity to present mere eyewitness
reports as though they were as authoritative as written tradition.[33] Of
these the most famous are Tilemann Elhen von Wolfhagen with his
Limburger Chronik (1402) and Ulrich von Richenthal with his best-selling
report on the Council of Constance (1420). Yet a third historian, Gobelinus Persona (ca. 1420), even does field-work.[34] Attention is called to
contemporary language and literature, sporadically to be sure, but nonetheless precedent-setting.[35] The historical folksongs of the period supply ample evidence for burgeoning interests in current events.[36]

People care about what is happening in the great world. They know
it affects them, and they want to be informed. The present acquires
identity and character; it turns into a mental entity. The span of the
present is drastically reduced to exclude much of what it once included.
With intensifying awareness of the presentness of certain events, regularly and perhaps necessarily comes intensifying awareness of the pastness of other events. Add to this the crisis atmosphere of the later
fourteenth and fifteenth centuries—plague, schism, heresy, insurrection
—and one finds the growing conviction that things were not now as
they had once been. And the "once" was not very long ago. This is in
total defiance of the most authoritative of medieval historians, Orosius,
who wrote his *Seven Books of History Against the Pagans* precisely in order
to prove that the past was just as wretched as the present.[37]

A new view arises in competition with the old, seeing history less as
the unfolding of an ultimately inscrutable divine plan than as an expla-
nation of the present. In the new view, the present ceases to be an
ordinary time span, generally similar to other time spans, and like them,
basically negligible in the court of eternity. The present becomes extraordinary, and the past is called upon to serve it. This, and not the sense
of anachronism, seems to me to be the key factor in the decay of the
medieval sense of time. It may be the humanists who most perfectly
express this sense of the extraordinary present: "Happy is our age
which witnesses the revival of good letters" is their single most wide-
spread cliché.[38] But the humanists were neither the first nor the only
ones to believe that their own time announced the arrival of something
new. They were anticipated in this by the apocalyptic thinkers of the
thirteenth century who, like the humanists, saw the new as the restora-
tion of the old.[39] The same belief accompanies every revolutionary

movement of the period, culminating in the Reformation, which no less than the others reduced the past to servile dependence on the present.

The past served the present as an authorizing antiquity, now drawn from available traditions, now invented on the spot, in both cases a form of propaganda. The interests thus served included every aggressive political, social, and religious force of the period: imperial, dynastic, national, provincial, bourgeois, peasant, papal, conciliar, or reforming. And it was not only the remotest past that served those who needed or wanted reinforcement or legitimation of their present. Dietrich von Nieheim repeatedly dips into medieval history to strengthen the imperial position at the Council of Constance, comparing the present situation to the papal "pornocracy" of the tenth century and calling upon Sigismund to act like Otto the Great.[40] The pretensions of the Wittelsbachers received massive learned support at the hands of Andreas von Regensburg (ca. 1428), who invented connections for them with Charlemagne and all the great medieval emperors.[41] Perhaps the most famous example is the foundation myth of the Swiss, Wilhelm Tell, created in the mid-fifteenth century to coincide with the struggle for a form of national independence from the Hapsburgs.[42] The setting is, as everyone knows, a glorified and rather recent past. The greater glory of Thuringia is served by the mythical and medieval "Sängerkrieg auf der Wartburg" in Johannes Rothe's chronicle.[43] The good burghers of Ulm traced their genealogies to notable figures of the medieval past as well as to those of dimmest antiquity.[44] All evidence points to a new attention to the Middle Ages, perhaps not quite so authoritative as biblical and classical antiquity, but authoritative nonetheless, and like classical antiquity at least, distinctly past.

Only when the Middle Ages had become properly past could they become the subject of a revival. In the reign of Maximilian I the medieval revival is in full bloom. Maximilian's commissions alone would suffice to prove it. His genealogical investigators may have traced the Hapsburgs back to Noah or Troy, but even the fantastic Max was a bit skeptical about that. He seems, however, to have believed that Arthur, Theodoric, Clovis, and Geoffrey of Bouillon genuinely belonged among his ancestors—witness his monument at Innsbruck.[45] His autobiographical epics sing his praises in tunes of allegory and chivalry no Gottfried or Wolfram could have recognized. He rescued the *Gudrun* and Hartmann von Aue's *Erec* in Hans Ried's *Heldenbuch*. One can hardly speak of the continuity of tradition, if the survival of important medieval works rests on the antiquarian whim of an imperial dilettante.

Among the humanists there is a great flurry of antiquarian activity earnestly directed toward the German Middle Ages. Conrad Celtis's discoveries of Hrotswitha and the *Ligurinus* of Günther of Pairis are the most renowned instances, but they are on the merest tip of the iceberg. The catalog of German authors of the magic abbot, Johannes Trithemius, perforce centers upon the Middle Ages. Here the learned world hears for the first time of Otfrid von Weissenburg after centuries of oblivion.[46] The important medieval histories of Jordanes, Einhard, and Otto von Freising were published by such humanists as Hermann von Neuenar, Conrad Peutinger, and Johannes Cuspinianus. The great collectors, Emperor Maximilian himself, Trithemius, Hartmann Schedel, stuffed their libraries with German medievalia.

The single feature that distinguishes this form of medievalism from all others is its insistence on the German. This discovery of the medieval past was, in part, a discovery of the German past. The Middle Ages being revived were, in part, the German Middle Ages—one of those regrettable fictions associated with the Romantics but in truth created by the patriots of the reign of Maximilian. They began to rewrite political and intellectual history, replacing the Roman *Imperium* with a German *Regnum* and their cosmopolitan heritage with an explicitly German life of the mind.[47] The notions of a German national monarchy and a nationally distinct cultural tradition were utterly alien to the Middle Ages, even or especially in Germany. The thrust of the imperial constitution was centrifugal, encouraging diversity and guaranteeing local autonomy. The geography of Germany, its fragmentation, its supranational emperor made it a natural crossroads, invited the invasion of ideas, and assured them sanctuary somewhere amidst the countless competing jurisdictions. The Renaissance patriots were blind to these virtues, much like their nineteenth-century successors to whom they point directly. All appearances to the contrary, they do not point back to the Middle Ages. Their invention of a lost national grandeur for the Middle Ages is a *nova*, unknown to the medieval firmament.

It is difficult to say what brought them to this unholy extreme. To all appearances, the humanists seem to have been reacting to Italian cultural supremacy. Yet this fails to explain the similar sentiments arising among vernacular writers ostentatiously ignorant of the new learning. It fails to explain the eruption of similar patriotism all over Europe from Petrarch's "Italia mia" to Ronsard's *Franciade*. Perhaps this patriotism, this discovery of the "national past," this revival of a lost antiquity, this medievalism ought not to be explained at all, only observed as one sign of a general phenomenon: the rise of a new order on the ruins of the old, a phenomenon generally called the Renaissance.

84 *Frank L. Borchardt*

NOTES

1 Alois Brandstetter, *Prosaauflösung: Studien zur Rezeption der höfischen Epik im frühneu-hochdeutschen Prosaroman* (Frankfurt, 1971), pp. 23 and 136–37.

2 Indeed, some maintain that he was not understood even in his own time: cf. Hugo Bekker, *The Nibelungenlied: A Literary Analysis* (Toronto, 1971), p. 4, n. 3.

3 Hans Rupprich, *Vom späten Mittelalter bis zum Barock: Erster Teil*, Geschichte der deutschen Literatur, IV 1 (Munich, 1970), 168.

4 Ibid., pp. 53–55.

5 Peter Keyser, *Michael de Leone und seine literarische Sammlung* (Würzburg, 1966), pp. 47–52.

6 Joseph Klapper, *Johann von Neumarkt, Bischof und Hofkanzler: Religiöse Frührenaissance in Böhmen zur Zeit Kaiser Karls IV.* (Leipzig, 1964), pp. 11, 35, and 166.

7 Carl Halthaus, ed., *Liederbuch der Clara Hätzlerin* (1840; rpt. Berlin, 1966), pp. 24–25, 63–66, 99–112, 203–5, 252, and 279–83.

8 C. S. Lewis, *The Discarded Image* (London and New York, 1967), p. 13.

9 Willy Krogmann, ed., *Johannes von Tepl: Der Ackermann* (Wiesbaden, 1954), pp. 128–29 and 204–9.

10 Bert Nagel, *Meistersang* (Stuttgart, 1962), pp. 73–74.

11 "Des conzilis grundveste," in Rochus von Liliencron, ed., *Die historischen Volkslieder der Deutschen vom 13. bis 16. Jahrhundert* (1865–69; rpt. Hildesheim, 1966), I, 240.

12 Karl Simrock, ed., *Deutsche Volksbücher* (Frankfurt, 1845–65), I, 39–122.

13 Adalbert von Keller, ed., *Hans Sachs*, XII (Tübingen, 1879), 185.

14 Ibid., p. 265.

15 Gerhard Hahn, ed., *Martin Luther: Die deutschen geistlichen Lieder* (Tübingen, 1967), p. 3.

16 Ibid., pp. 43–44.

17 Steven E. Ozment, *Mysticism and Dissent: Religious Ideology and Social Protest in the Sixteenth Century* (New Haven and London, 1973), p. 1: "These writings [of the medieval mystics] would furnish refuge and weaponry to nonconformists in any age." Cf. also p. 14.

18 The church of St. Gertrude at the Pleich in Würzburg is paradigmatic. Other examples can be found at Aub and Dettelbach, both in Franconia. The pilgrimage church at Dettelbach is decorated with portal and pulpit in Renaissance style, the latter in its explicitly "Gothic" version.

19 The art historians are in this matter, as in most, well ahead of the literary historians: cf. "Der Kirchenbau," Gustav von Bezold, *Die Baukunst der Renaissance in Deutschland, Holland, Belgien und Dänemark*, 2d ed. (Leipzig, 1908), pp. 127–46.

20 The guidebooks call it "Nachgotik," "Echtergotik," or "Juliusstil": Alexander von Reitzenstein and Herbert Brunner, *Bayern: Baudenkmäler*, 7th ed. (Stuttgart, 1970), p. 222; and Max H. von Freeden, *Würzburg*, 10th ed. (Würzburg, 1969), p. 52.

21 Peter Burke, *The Renaissance Sense of the Past* (London, 1969), pp. 1–20.

22 Horst Fuhrmann, et al., "Die Fälschungen im Mittelalter: Überlegungen zum mit-telalterlichen Wahrheitsbegriff," *Historische Zeitschrift*, CXCVII (1963), 539–40.

23 *Etymologiarum sive Originum Libri XX*, W. M. Lindsay, ed. (1911; Oxford, 1957), V, 28–29.

24 Roy J. Deferrari, trans., *The Seven Books of History against the Pagans* (Washington, 1964), pp. 285–86.

25 I oversimplify Joachim's exceedingly complex view of history: Marjorie Reeves, *The Influence of Prophecy in the Later Middle Ages* (Oxford, 1969), pp. 131–32.

26 Victor Junk, ed., *Rudolf von Ems: Alexander* (1928–29; rpt. Darmstadt, 1970), pp. 445–46.

27 Burke, *The Renaissance Sense of the Past*, p. 150.

28 Karl Josef Höltgen, "Die 'Nine Worthies,'" *Anglia*, LXXVII (1959), 281.

[29] R. L. Wyss, "Die Neun Helden: Eine ikonigraphische Studie," *Zeitschrift für schweizerische Archeologie und Kunstgeschichte*, XVII (1957), 85 and 104.

[30] Cf. Paul Heitz, *Einblattdrucke des Fünfzehnten Jahrhunderts*, XXV (Strassburg, 1911), plates No. 1–9; and cf. D. J. A. Ross, *Alexander Historiatus: A Guide to Medieval Alexander Literature* (London, 1963), p. 108: "from the first half of the fourteenth century to the middle of the seventeenth, no theme is more frequently encountered in the art and literature of Western Europe."

[31] "Die klûgen legen" . . . "ouch hant die menschen me lustes zû lesende von nuwen dingen denne von alten," in Jakob Twinger von Königshoven's chronicle (1382–1420): Carl Hegel, ed., *Die Chroniken der Oberrheinischen Städte: Straßburg*, Die Chroniken der deutschen Städte vom 14. bis ins 16. Jahrhundert, VIII (1870; rpt. Göttingen, 1961), 230.

[32] On Twinger's predecessor, Fritsche Closener (1362) see Hegel's general introduction, ibid., pp. 50 and 62–63.

[33] This is not without precedent in the Middle Ages, considering ambassadorial reports, memoirs, and travel literature. But no medieval chronicler would have pretended that these wore authority until they were hoary members of the written tradition.

[34] See Frank L. Borchardt, *German Antiquity in Renaissance Myth* (Baltimore, 1971), pp. 28–39 for an appreciation of this neglected historian.

[35] On songs sung popularly: Arthur Wyss, ed., *Die Limburger Chronik des Tilemann Elhen von Wolfhagen*, MGH, Deutsche Chroniken, V 1 (Hannover, 1883), p. 15, nn. 16 and 17; on the songs of the Theodoric cycle see Jakob Twinger, ed. cit., p. 376 f. and n. 1, p. 377; on language see Gobelinus Persona in Henricus Meibom, Jr., ed., *Rerum Germanicarum Tomi III* (Helmstedt, 1688), I, 159, 235–36.

[36] See n. 9 above.

[37] Ed. cit. (n. 24 above), p. xviii f.

[38] Cf. Margaret Aston, *The Fifteenth Century: The Prospect of Europe* (London, 1968), pp. 47, 175 ff., and 193, for a start, and similar utterances by Trithemius, Hutten, Erasmus, and most of their friends.

[39] Here I throw my lot in with one side of the controversy of another generation: Konrad Burdach, *Rienzo und die geistige Entwicklung seiner Zeit*, Vom Mittelalter zur Reformation, II 1 (Berlin, 1913–28), 396 and 565.

[40] Heinrich Finke, ed., *Acta Concilii Constanciensis*, 4 vols. (Münster, 1896–1928), IV, 615.

[41] Georg Leidinger, ed., *Andreas von Regensburg: Sämtliche Werke* (Munich, 1903), pp. 517 and 598. Cf. p. ix for the editor's analogous myth-making.

[42] Richard Feller and Edgar Bonjour, *Geschichtsschreibung der Schweiz vom Spätmittelalter zur Neuzeit*, 2 vols. (Basel and Stuttgart, 1962), I, 100–1.

[43] Rochus von Liliencron, ed., *Düringische Chronik des Johann Rothe* (Jena, 1859), pp. 330–36.

[44] Gustav Veesenmeyer, ed., *Fratris Felcis Fabri Tractatus de civitate Ulmensi* (Tübingen, 1889), pp. 117–18.

[45] E. Heyck, *Kaiser Maximilian I* (Bielefeld and Leipzig, 1898), pp. 1–9.

[46] *Catalogus illustrium virorum* (ed. princ., 1495), in M. Freher, ed., *Opera historica*, 2 vols. (1601; facsimile rpt. Frankfurt, 1966), I, 127 f.

[47] Trithemius pleads for a drastic revision of the concepts of medieval history. For Roman Emperor he would read German King; for imperial free cities, royal free cities: *Joannis Trithemij . . . Tomus I [Tomus II] Annalium Hirsaugiensium* (St. Gall, 1690), II, 3–4. He also attaches himself to the young tradition (14th century) of praises of German virtue when he compiles the catalog: cf. Freher, ed. cit., I, 122.

Language and Reason in the Thought of Hamann

James C. O'Flaherty

One of the indispensable clues to an understanding of Hamann's thought is his concept of reason. In fact there is no subject with which he is more concerned throughout his entire career subsequent to the London conversion than the question of the powers and limitations of human reason. A glance at the concordance of the Roth-Wiener edition of his works reveals, for instance, that there are more references to the terms "Vernunft" and "Verstand" than to any other subject, including the next most frequently occurring terms such as "Gott" and "Natur."[1] (Despite the fact that this particular edition is incomplete, there is no reason to suppose that a concordance to his complete works and letters would yield a different result.) It is ironical that a thinker whose primary concern was to underscore the importance of faith should have in actuality addressed himself more frequently to the question of the nature of reason, and in so doing became the counterpart of his compatriot and friendly adversary, Immanuel Kant, a thinker who had deliberately ruled out faith in order to deal with the problem of reason. Further, it is interesting to note that, long before Kant turned his attention to the question of cognition, Hamann had been wrestling in his own way with the problem of the nature and limits of reason. That these two great thinkers came to radically different conclusions should not obscure the fact that they were concerned to a great extent with the same problem.

Unlike Kant, however, Hamann offers no systematic analysis of the function of reason. Indeed, his highly impassioned indictments of reason as "ein *Ens rationis,* ein Ölgötze, dem ein *schreyender* Aberglaube der Unvernunft *göttliche Attribute* andichet"[2] and statements to the effect that "alle *Abstractionen willkührlich* sind und seyn müßen" (3,190) might easily mislead the reader into the belief that Hamann's contribution to the subject amounts to no more than a virtuoso performance resulting only in highly colored and supercharged invective. The fact is, however, that underlying all his remarks on the subject is a remarkably self-consistent and clearly definable concept of reason.

In order to comprehend Hamann's understanding of reason it is necessary to distinguish between two modes of cognition, namely, the intuitive and the abstract. Although he does not employ the term *intuitive* (*anschauend*) in programmatic fashion to designate a basic mode of reasoning, we may confidently adopt it as descriptive of his thought. For it was none other than Immanuel Kant who, writing to Hamann in 1774 to ask the latter's help in the interpretation of an obscure passage of Herder's *Älteste Urkunde des Menschengeschlechts*, requested that Hamann reply "wo möglich in der Sprache der Menschen," adding "denn ich armer Erdensohn bin zu der Göttersprache der *Anschauenden Vernunft* garnicht *organisirt*."[3] Though Kant is here using the phrase "intuitive reason" as a bit of raillery, it is a very accurate and felicitous one to describe Hamann's procedure. The term abstract, on the other hand, is frequently used by Hamann to denote the rationalism of the Enlightenment and kindred movements.

The characteristics of Hamann's use of reason emerge most clearly when we investigate the effects of his thinking upon language. Since in his view there is no thought apart from language, it seems quite appropriate that we should look to language for the earmarks of reason. It will be seen that there are six salient features that characterize the language of *anschauende Vernunft* or intuitive reason, i.e., reason functioning within its appropriate limits. To be specific, we may say that intuitive reason manifests itself in language by the following: (1) the abundance of concrete images ("Bilder"); (2) the employment of analogical reasoning; (3) the frequent recourse to paradoxes; (4) the presence of multiple levels of meaning; (5) paratactic sentence structure; (6) the presence of affective terminology. Of these six characteristics Hamann lays down at one point or another the principles which govern all except the fifth, which is, however, clearly manifested in his use of language. As we shall see in the sequel, abstract reason affects language in precisely the opposite ways from intuitive reason. It is true that Hamann does not subsume the six characteristics listed above under one head as defining a mode of reasoning. Nevertheless, it is clearly advantageous to see these characteristics in their essential relationship to one another and to the problem of reason in Hamann's thought. Adopting this procedure will help us to understand his otherwise contradictory statements regarding reason. Let us now consider briefly each of the characteristic earmarks of intuitive reason as they manifest themselves in language.

1. Imagery ("Bilder")

Hamann maintains that natural language is, to adopt Bergson's phrase, "molded on reality." Ordinary language or "the language of nature" ("die Sprache der Natur," 2,211) is for him the historically developed vernacular of a people, which has been "unimproved" by grammarians or the creators of technical jargon. It is this kind of language that can be raised to the level of poetic expression. Opposed to it is the "unnatürlicher Gebrauch der Abstractionen" (2,207) on the part of the philosophers. Such abstract terms are "wächserne Nasen, Gemächte der Sophisterey und der Schulvernunft," again "Hirngespinnste"[4] and "Luftschlösser" (G,16). Abstract terminology can never be transformed into poetry, inasmuch as it has forsaken the wellsprings of all inspiration, "the language of nature." To say that the abstract word can never become the poetic word is to say that it can never speak meaningfully of spiritual matters. It is a striking fact that Nietzsche, whose religious views are diametrically opposed to those of Hamann, should have composed lines that accord so perfectly with Hamann's sentiments regarding the relation of poetry to truth: "Die Sphäre der Poesie liegt nicht außerhalb der Welt, als eine phantastische Unmöglichkeit des Dichterhirns: sie will das gerade Gegenteil sein, der ungeschminkte Ausdruck der Wahrheit, und muß eben deshalb den lügenhaften Aufputz jener vermeinten Wirklichkeit des Kulturmenschen von sich werfen."[5]

Hamann's conviction, unlike Nietzsche's, is grounded on the essential nature of both God and man. Hence, God "der Poet am Anfang der Tage" (2,206) always speaks to man in poetic language: "Die Schrift kann mit uns Menschen nicht anders reden, als in Gleichnissen, weil alle unsere Erkenntnis sinnlich, figürlich und der Verstand und die Vernunft die Bilder der äußerlichen Dinge allenthalben zu Allegorien und Zeichen abstracter, geistiger und höherer Begriffe macht" (1,157–58). It is clear from this passage that Hamann conceived of the abstracting process as one that, among other things, removes the "external images of things" and replaces them with empty terminology. This process is fatal to language as a vehicle for the expression of veridical knowledge. Thus he says in the *Aesthetica in nuce*: "Sinne und Leidenschaften reden und verstehen nichts als Bilder. In Bildern besteht der ganze Schatz menschlicher Erkenntniß und Glückseeligkeit" (2,197).

Rationalistic theologians like the Göttingen Orientalist Johann David Michaelis (1717–1791), had objected that the earthy, picturesque language of the Scriptures, particularly the Old Testament, could not possibly be regarded as the Word of God in any literal sense, since it would be unworthy of Deity to speak in the unpolished and imprecise vernacular. If God were to speak directly to man, He would choose more intellectual, more abstract language, that is, the language of the philosophers. Such a view of revelation fails, according to Hamann, to take into account the fact that God's infinite love for man is revealed precisely in His willingness to condescend to man's estate. God has humbled himself to the extent of speaking in the everyday idiom of the people by means of "kleine, verächtliche Begebenheiten" (2,43) and "menschlich thörichter, ja sündlicher Handlungen" (1,99). God has not seen fit to couch His revelation in a form "die ein Voltaire, ein Bolingbroke, ein Schaftesbury annehmungswerth finden würden, die ihren Vorurtheilen, ihrem Witz, ihren moralischen, politischen und magischen Grillen am meisten ein Genüge thun würde" (1,10). To speak in the rarified language of these philosophers would be to ignore the needs of the "ganzen menschlichen Geschlecht" including, ironically, the rationalistic philosophers themselves, who fail to recognize their own deepest spiritual needs. For Hamann does not subscribe to any form of the double-truth theory: spiritual truth does not require two forms, one for the philosopher, another for the masses. "Daß Moses für den Pöbel allein geschrieben, ist entweder ohne allen Sinn oder eine lächerliche Art zu urtheilen" he wrote in the *Biblische Betrachtungen* (1, 12).

Philosophically speaking, the "images" ("Bilder") of natural language represent for Hamann "objects" ("Gegenstände"), which may be defined as uncritically perceived entities of ordinary experience, principally visual in nature. Abstract or discursive reason has the power, however, to eliminate such objects and to replace them with terms that actually stand for relations.[6] Therefore, he may say that "academic reason" ("die Schulvernunft") deals in "lauter Verhältnisse, die sich nicht absolut behandeln lassen; . . . keine Dinge, sondern reine Schulbegriffe, Zeichen zum Verstehen nicht Bewundern, Hülfsmittel, unsere Aufmerksamkeit zu erwecken und zu fesseln" (G,513). "Dasein [i.e., concrete existence in a world of real objects] ist Realismus," he wrote to Jacobi in 1787, "muß geglaubt werden; Verhältnisse sind Idealismus, beruhn auf Verknüpfungs- und Unterscheidungsart" (G,507). In his indictment of the Kantian critical philosophy he writes that metaphysics misuses "alle Wortzeichen und Redefiguren unserer empirischen Erkenntnis" by transforming them into "lauter Hieroglyphen und Typen idealischer Verhältnisse . . ." (3,285). In other words, the language of nature deals in the relations of objects, whereas abstract language deals in the relations of relations, a procedure that can only result in "eine gewaltthätige Entkleidung wirklicher Gegenstände zu nackten Begriffen

und bloß denkbaren Merkmalen, zu reinen Erscheinungen und Phäno-
menen" (3,385).

Another fundamental aspect of imagery is, of course, its strong
appeal to the emotions, a quality that is lacking in the case of abstract
terminology. Our concern in this section has been to consider briefly the
epistemological implications of Hamann's insistence that language
robbed of its imagery is inauthentic. We shall return below to the subject
of the affective aspect of natural language.

2. Analogy ("Analogie"; "Analogon")

The second characteristic of Hamann's use of reason is his preference for *analogical* as opposed to purely *logical* thinking. Whereas the
rationalist establishes a principle, whether deductively or inductively,
and thereupon proceeds to draw inferences from it, the intuitive thinker
establishes a model on nonrational grounds, as, for example, instinct or
faith, and thereupon proceeds to draw parallels to the model. This latter
procedure accords, in Hamann's view, with the proper use of reason,
despite the fact that reasoning from analogy does not yield the certainty
one might desire. Thus, he writes "daß die Vernunft nichts als Analo-
gien auffassen kann, um ein sehr undeutlich Licht zu erhalten" (1,302).
Following the lead of Francis Bacon, Hamann maintains that man in his
original state thought analogically rather than logically. This idea is
clearly stated in the famous passage at the beginning of the *Aesthetica in
nuce*: "Poesie ist die Muttersprache des Menschengeschlechts; wie der
Gartenbau, älter als der Acker: Malerey,—als Schrift: Gesang,—als De-
klamation: Gleichnisse,—als Schlüsse: Tausch,—als Handel" (2,197).
Thus, Hamann places analogical thinking, as opposed to the later development of discursive thinking, within the framework of his general
anthropology with its emphasis on man's retrograde development away
from his primordial state. It is more natural for man to think in similes or
parables ("Gleichnisse"), which involve analogical thinking, than to
arrive at deductions ("Schlüsse") based on rational principles. Early in
his career Hamann wrote in *Biblical Reflections*: "Alle endliche Geschöpfe
sind nur im Stande, die Wahrheit und das Wesen der Dinge in Gleichnissen zu sehen" (1,112). By this token, rationalism emerges only as
man's life becomes more estranged from nature and therefore more
artificial.

For Hamann, as for most of his contemporaries, Socrates was the
most revered of all philosophers. But instead of seeing the Greek phi-

losopher as the arch-rationalist, dedicated to purely logical thought after the manner of the Enlighteners, Hamann saw him as an anti-rationalist, guided by his "sensibility" ("Empfindung," 2,73) and his "tutelary spirit" ("Dämon," 2,75). Further, he saw in Socrates the prime exemplar of the analogical method. Thus, at the beginning of his *Socratic Memorabilia* he asserts: "Ich habe über den Sokrates auf eine sokratische Art geschrieben. Die *Analogie* war die Seele seiner Schlüsse, und er gab ihnen *Ironie* zu ihrem Leibe" (2,61). He then footnotes the term "analogy" with a quotation in English from Edward Young's *Night Thoughts*: "*Analogy*, man's surest guide below," as if to underscore the importance of this mode of reasoning (cf. 3,39).

The fundamental importance of analogical thinking in Hamann's philosophy is underscored by the fact that it furnishes us with one of the few instances in which he felt it necessary to label his procedure with an abstract term, namely, "metaschematism." The word derives from a term used by the Apostle Paul in writing to the members of the church at Corinth exhorting them to cease from quarreling among themselves. But instead of addressing himself directly to their situation Paul draws an analogy between his relationship to his followers, on the one hand, and the relationship of Apollos to his followers, on the other hand (I Cor. 4:6). The Apostle uses a Greek word that is translated in the Revised Version as "transfer in a figure." From the Greek original Hamann created both the abstract noun "Metaschematismus" (2,150) and the verb "metaschematisiren" (3,144). For Hamann, to metaschematize means, then, to substitute one set of objective relationships for another, analogous set of subjective, personal or existential relationships, or the reverse, in order to throw some light on their meaning. One of the best examples of his use of metaschematism is the *Socratic Memorabilia*.[7] For in this treatise he adopts the role of Socrates, while assigning the role of Socrates' adversaries, the Sophists, to his own philosophical adversaries. Metaschematism is, of course, a form of indirect communication, a method that, with certain differences, was later on to be made famous by Kierkegaard. It is quite characteristic of Hamann that he appeals to the authority of a Scriptural model in establishing this concept, as if to announce to his hyperrationalistic adversaries that theirs is not the only intellectually respectable way of thinking but that the operation of the divine Logos in history provides us with a different and a better way.

Still another way in which Hamann exploits the possibilities of analogical thinking is his use of typology. This ancient hermeneutical device is to be carefully distinguished from allegory. Whereas the latter clothes an abstract idea in concrete form, the former involves the establishment of a parallel or analogy between a given concrete historical event and another that succeeds it in time. In biblical hermeneutics this means the foreshadowing in the Old Testament of important events in the New: thus, the Paschal Lamb foreshadows the Sacrifice of Christ on the cross, or again Adam foreshadows the Christ. In his interpretation of Scripture Hamann uses this method consistently. However, he also sees in the events of his own life (as that of a typical believer) a sort of recapitulation of the history of the Jews, both collectively and individually (cf. 2,41). So enamored of this method is Hamann that he transfers it from sacred to profane history. Interesting instances of this procedure may be found in his *Sokratische Denkwürdigkeiten* where Socrates is seen as foreshadowing the Christ, or the general public in the Athens of Socrates' day as foreshadowing the general public in eighteenth-century Germany. In fact, scattered throughout the essay are at least twelve typological themes.[8] Typology differs from metaschematism in always involving the historicity of the events that it connects. Further, meta-schematism always involves the existential moment, whereas typological relationships may or may not do so.

Apart from typology and metaschematism, however, Hamann also recognizes the uses of analogical thinking in connection with *ideas* or *ideals* that may also anticipate the historical event. Thus he writes in *Golgotha und Scheblimini*:

Nicht nur die ganze Geschichte des Judentums war Weissagung; sondern der *Geist* derselben bechäftigte sich vor allen übrigen Nationen, denen man das *Analogon* einer ähnlichen dunkeln Ahndung und Vorempfindung vielleicht nicht absprechen kann, mit dem *Ideal* eines Retters und Ritters, eines Kraft- und Wundermanns, eines Goel's, dessen Abkunft nach dem Fleisch aus dem Stamme *Juda*, sein Ausgang aus der Höhe aber des *Vaters Schooß* seyn sollte. (3,311)

In this important christological passage Hamann has doubly emphasized the term "Analogon" by utilizing the Greek form and then italicizing it.

But it is not only these devices that characterize Hamann's variations of the analogical method; there are others that would merit closer attention if space did not forbid. We may note in passing, however, that an interesting and illuminating book has been written by Wilhelm Koepp on the subject of the Magus and his masks.[9] Hamann's tendency to adopt numerous suggestive and often provocative masks as well as his habit of veiling his references to others is the subject of Koepp's book. Since in each case the mask, while concealing an identity, reveals at the same time a particular quality of the person or thing masked, a likeness or analogy is therefore established between the mask and that which it conceals.

Although the abstract thinker is ready to admit that the appeal to analogy may yield genuine knowledge, he is quick to point out that "arguments from analogy are . . . precarious unless supported by considerations which can be established independently."[10] Such considerations are, of course, those that may be established on purely logical or empirical grounds, hence acceptable to the thoroughgoing rationalist. For Hamann, however, "the considerations which can be established independently" are those that are grounded in faith. Bolstered by Hume's insistence on faith or belief as the basis on which our propositions are ultimately grounded, Hamann maintains that the most certain kind of knowledge is that which derives from the revelation in nature, history, and Scripture, and he thereupon proceeds to draw analogies to the truths there revealed. It must be conceded that Hamann utilizes the analogical method to an excessive degree, and that his philosophy would undoubtedly have profited by considerably more concession to discursive thinking and by a somewhat higher regard for academic reason or "Schulvernunft." On the other hand, it is interesting to note that recent philosophical thought is moving toward a higher evaluation of the analogical method even in the realm of pure science. In a recent work Wilfrid Sellars argues, somewhat against Kant, that analogy is even more fruitful for modern science than it has been traditionally for theology, holding that it is "a powerful tool for resolving perennial problems in epistemology and metaphysics."[11] This would seem to constitute one more impelling reason why it is misleading to label Hamann an "irrationalist."

3. Paradox ("Widerspruch")

An important aspect of Hamann's conception of reason as it emerges from his use of language is his acceptance of the paradox as a vehicle for the expression of spiritual truth. The reason for such a positive view of the paradox is in the last resort theological. Since God has condescended to reveal Himself in lowly, even contemptible form—as the Scriptures everywhere attest—the paradox possesses the highest possible legitimation. "Man muß mit Bewunderung sehen," he writes in the *Biblische Betrachtungen*, "wie Gott sich in alle kleine Umstände einläßt und die Offenbarung seiner Regierung in gemeinen Begebenheiten des menschlichen Lebens den seltenen und außerordentlichen vorzieht" (1,36). Or again:

Welcher Mensch würde sich unterstehen wie Paulus von der Thorheit Gottes, von der Schwäche Gottes zu reden. 1 Cor. I.25. Niemand als der Geist, der die Tiefen der Gottheit erforschet, würde uns diese Prophezeyung haben entdecken können, deren Erfüllung in unseren Zeiten mehr als jemals eintrifft, daß nicht viele Weisen nach dem Fleisch, viele Mächtige, viele edle zum Himmelreich beruffen wären, und daß der große Gott seine Weisheit und Macht eben dadurch hat offenbaren wollen, daß er die thörichten Dinge der Welt erwählt, um die Weisen zu schanden zu machen; daß Gott die schwachen Dinge der Welt erwählt, um die Mächtigen zu schanden zu machen, die niedrigen und verächtlichen Dinge *erwählt*, ja Dinge welche nichts sind um Dinge, die sind, die sich ihres Daseyns rühmen können, zu Nichts zu bringen. (1,6)

The supreme paradox of Christianity is, to be sure, the incarnation in Christ, the appearance of the Creator of heaven and earth in *Knechtsgestalt*, in the form of a servant. Although the main source of Hamann's emphasis on the paradox is certainly the biblical revelation, he is also conscious of carrying on the tradition of Luther in this regard (cf. 2,247,249). Later, Kierkegaard will draw strong inspiration from Hamann's emphasis on the paradox of faith.

It is not only in the revelation to the Jews and in Christ, however, that the paradoxical nature of spiritual truth is manifested. In the *Sokratische Denkwürdigkeiten* Hamann stresses the principle that the religiously inclined among the Greeks accepted the paradox as a matter of course in statements concerning the gods, and that it was only the rationalists among them who refused to accept it:

Die Heyden waren durch die *klugen Fabeln* ihrer Dichter an dergleichen Widersprüche gewohnt; bis ihre Sophisten, wie unsere, solche als einen Vatermord verdammten, den man an den ersten Grundsätzen der menschlichen Erkenntnis begeht. Von solchem Widerspruch finden wir ein Beyspiel an dem Delphischen Orakel, das denjenigen [Socrates] für den weisesten erkannte, der gleichwol von sich gestand, daß er nichts wisse. (2,68)

Since Hamann believed in the essential continuity of classical culture and Christianity,[12] it is not surprising that he found in its religion, at what he considered to be its healthiest stage, an anticipation of the Christian dialectical view of reality.

Hamann's insight into the paradoxical nature of ultimate reality was reinforced by his keen awareness of the contradictions within his own nature. Thus, at the beginning of his career he spoke of "den unzähligen Widersprüchen, die wir in unserer Natur finden und derer Auflösung uns unmöglich ist" (1,224); and years later, just a few weeks before his death, he wrote to Jacobi: "Es ist ein wahres Kreuz, zu thun, was man haßt, und hassen zu müssen, was man selbst thut, und diese Widersprüche mit sich herum zu schleppen" (G,657). At the same time, however, he realized that his was not a unique case: "Dergleichen Widersprüche [i.e., the cross-currents of his own impulses] erfährt jeder mehr oder weniger in seiner Natur oder in seinem Schicksal . . ."(G,1). Hamann's dialectical view of reality derives then not from a theoretical proposition, as for instance in the case of a Hegel, but from experience, both subjective and objective. As Erwin Metzke has said: "Man spürt, wie fern hier der 'Widerspruch' aller Spekulation und logischen Spitz-findigkeit ist, und das gilt für all die Widersprüche, auf die Hamann hinweist."[13]

There is one important exception to Hamann's general refusal to appeal to a metaphysical principle, namely, the idea of *coincidentia oppositorum*. Stressing as he did the contradictory nature of experience and its reflection in the conceptual opposites with which the honest thinker is constantly confronted, it was but natural that he would require a principle by means of which the opposites might be reconciled. In 1782 he wrote to Herder: "*Jordani Bruni Principium coincidentiae oppositorum* ist in meinen Augen mehr werth als alle Kantsche Kritik" (IV,462). A year earlier he had requested Herder's assistance in finding a copy of a work by Bruno in which he (erroneously) believed that the principle was treated, stating that the idea had been in his mind for some years (IV,287). Nicholas of Cusa rather than Giordano Bruno was the real formulator of the principle of the coincidence of opposites, but this fact was unknown to Hamann as well as to most of his contemporaries. Unlike Hegel, who sought to specify in what manner the contradictory elements of experience are reconciled, Hamann never departed from the conviction that such antitheses can only be reconciled in God, and hence the need for faith is not eliminated by his appeal to the principle.

4. Multiple Levels of Language ("Einheit mit der Mannigfaltigkeit")

The fourth characteristic of intuitive reason is that it may produce multiple levels of language, whereas abstract reason may not. Again the biblical revelation is central, for the Hamannian conception of the au-thentic use of language was determined almost entirely by it. Just as Christ had assumed lowly human form, so had the Holy Spirit assumed in the Scriptures the lowly form of ordinary human language. "Gott ein Schriftsteller!" he wrote in the *Biblische Betrachtungen*, "Die Eingebung dieses Buchs ist eine eben so große Erniedrigung und Herunterlassung

Gottes als die Schöpfung des Vaters und Menschwerdung des Sohnes" (1,5). From this standpoint it was natural that Hamann repudiated the strictly rationalistic exegesis of scholars like Michaelis. In fact the *Aesthetica in nuce* is principally an attack on Michaelis's method of biblical interpretation, which requires that all levels of meaning except the literal be rigidly excluded from biblical exegesis. Such an approach to the Scriptures leaves one, however, merely with "the dead body of the letter" (2,203).

The British biblical critic George Benson (1699–1762), whose exegetical views were shared and disseminated in Germany by Michaelis, also comes under Hamann's fire. In an essay on the unity of sense in the Scriptures Benson had written:

It appears to me that a critical interpreter of Holy Scripture should set out with this as a first principle; viz. that no text of Scripture has more than one meaning. *That one true sense* he should endeavor to find out as he would find out the sense of Homer or any other ancient writer. When he has found out that sense he ought to acquiesce in it. And so ought his readers too; unless, by just rules of interpretation, they can show that he has mistaken the passage; and that another is the one, just, true and critical sense of the place.[14]

Such a method of interpretation was in Hamann's eyes simply "exegetical materialism" (2,239). As the passage cited from Benson clearly shows, the rationalistic exegetes allowed no room for a genuinely religious dimension of Scripture, since it must be interpreted like any other piece of ancient literature, as, for example, the *Iliad* and the *Odyssey*. Further, the hermeneutics of Benson and Michaelis sets up an abstract norm in place of the rule of faith as the last court of appeal in biblical interpretation. Hamann was by no means ready to concede that even Homer could be properly interpreted by means of Benson's "just rules of interpretation," let alone the Bible (2,203).

As we have already seen, Hamann's method of biblical interpretation is, generally speaking, typological, although it is on occasion allegorical. To what extent he accepted the traditional hermeneutical principle of the fourfold sense of Scripture, the literal, allegorical, moral, and anagogical, is debatable. Nevertheless, it is clear that both the literal and figurative or spiritual meanings are equally important for him. Therefore his objections to Michaelis's "materialistic exegesis" by no means imply an underrating of the literal sense of Scripture, only dismay and indignation that Michaelis should deny the figurative, and therefore the spiritual sense. The two meanings cannot be separated. Thus he says of the Bible in a letter to his brother in 1760: "Je mehr der Christ erkennt, daß in diesem Buch von ihm geschrieben stehet; desto mehr wächst der

Eyfer zum Buchstaben des Wortes" (II,9). By itself, however, the literal meaning is nothing. In a typically Hamannian thrust at the rationalistic exegetes, he writes that "das äußerliche Ansehen des Buchstabens ist dem unberittenen Füllen einer lastbaren Eselin ähnlicher, als jenen stolzen Hengsten, die dem Phaethon die Hälse brachen" (2,171).

The rationalistic critics had repudiated the principle of the multiple sense of Scripture in the interest of preserving its unity. In the *Aesthetica in nuce*, however, Hamann poses the question "ob die Einheit mit der Mannigfaltigkeit nicht bestehen könne?" (2,203). He had, as a matter of fact, already answered this question to his own satisfaction a few years earlier, in the weeks just prior to writing the *Sokratische Denkwürdigkeiten*. In a letter to his friend J. G. Lindner, 1 June 1759 he reports that a remarkable passage in Augustine's *Confessions* has come to his attention where the great theologian speculates on why the scriptural revelation manifests different levels of meaning. The Magus does not quote the passage from the *Confessions*, but it is illuminating to examine Augustine's own words. Imagining himself in the place of Moses, with a commission to transmit God's message to man, he writes:

I should then, had I been at that time what he [Moses] was, and enjoined by Thee to write the book of Genesis, have wished that such a power of expression and such a method of arrangement should be given me, that they who cannot as yet understand how God creates might not reject the words as surpassing their powers; and they who are already able to do this, would find, in what true opinion soever they had by thought arrived at, that it was not passed over in the few words of Thy servant; and should another man by the light of truth have discovered another, neither should that fail to be found in these same words.[15]

So impressed with this doctrine was the young Hamann that he undertook in the essay on Socrates, as indeed in most of his later writings, to follow its example. It suffices for our present purposes, however, simply to note that his idea of the multiple sense of "the language of nature" is quite basic to his thought, since it stems ultimately from his idea of deity.

5. Parataxis

A fifth effect of Hamann's use of reason manifests itself in a technical but highly important aspect of language, namely, the tendency to produce parataxis as opposed to hypotaxis. Paratactic sentences are characterized by brevity and the absence of long, involved dependent clauses; the word order tends to be natural or to follow an elementary logic in that the subject and predicate are expressed at or near the beginning of the sentence with the other elements following generally in the order of their importance. Aphorisms, epigrams, etc., because of their laconic nature, are necessarily paratactic in structure. Hypotactic sentences, on the other hand, are characterized by greater length, involving as they do longer dependent clauses (or, their equivalent in German, the so-called long attribute); the word order tends toward a certain artificiality in that the full disclosure of the meaning of the sentence may be suspended until the end. Because of its frequent use of dependent clauses, hypotaxis involves the *subordination* of certain elements within a sentence, whereas parataxis involves their *coordination*. Historically speaking, parataxis is associated with Senecan or "Silver Age" Latin prose, hypotaxis with Ciceronian or "Golden Age" Latin prose.

Growing to maturity in the mid-eighteenth century, Hamann was heir to the so-called *Kanzleistil* or Chancery Style, a wooden—and peculiarly German—imitation of the style of Cicero. The fact is that he never completely abandoned the Chancery Style. Since it has been customary to describe him as an "aphoristic" writer, and to cite him along with Lichtenberg, Nietzsche, and others, as a prime example of that literary species, a clarification is in order. For the question arises as to how he could be both a practitioner of the Chancery Style and a master of aphoristic prose.

In order to answer this question one must recognize that both styles do occur in Hamann's writings, and, while the Chancery Style precedes the looser Senecan-type prose, he never really abandons it but returns to it on a number of occasions even in his later writings. A study of the works in which the two styles occur reveals that in his most characteristic and influential writings such as the *Sokratische Denkwürdigkeiten* and especially the *Aesthetica in nuce* the aphoristic mode dominates, more consistently, however, in the latter. It is precisely in these works that we find him employing intuitive as opposed to abstract reason since all the other criteria for determining its use are present. When he does enter the lists against the abstract thinkers, however, he is quite capable of arguing to a great extent on their own terms, as for example, against Moses Mendelssohn in *Golgotha und Scheblimini* (1784) and against Kant in the *Metakritik über den Purismum der Vernunft* (1784). Despite the fact that Hegel considered the former Hamann's most important writing, and despite the growing appreciation of the cogent argument he employs against Kant in the latter, one scarcely considers the prose of these works as examples of Hamann's best or most characteristic style. It is in writings such as these, however, that his recourse to abstract reason most clearly manifests itself. Here is also evidence that, while he was primarily an intuitive thinker, he shows considerable power when he does turn to the abstract mode. One must conclude with Eric Blackall, however, that Hamann "tended towards the aphorism as his natural means of expression."[16] His use of the Chancery Style was, therefore, not natural, but an acquired manner, into which he fell when he had recourse—as he did on occasion—to an abstract mode of thought.

6. Affective Terminology
("Donner der Beredsamkeit, der einsylbichte Blitz")

Perhaps the most obvious of all the earmarks of intuitive reason is its affinity with the affective or emotional elements that characterize ordinary language, and that are present to a heightened degree in poetic language. As we have already noted, discursive reasoning effectively eliminates this aspect of language and therefore robs it of its natural richness. Thus against the philosophers who adopted the point of view of Newtonian physics, he wrote:

O eine Muse wie das Feuer eines Goldschmieds, und wie die Seife der Wäscher!—Sie wird es wagen, den natürlichen Gebrauch der Sinne von dem unnatürlichen Gebrauch der Abstractionen zu läutern, wodurch unse˜e Begriffe von den Dingen eben so sehr verstümmelt werden, als der Name des Schöpfers unterdrückt und gelästert wird . . . Seht! die große und kleine Masore der Weltweisheit hat den Text der Natur, gleich einer Sündfluth, überschwemmt. Musten nicht alle ihre Schönheiten und Reichthümer zu Wasser werden? (2,207)

Natural language, whether the everyday vernacular or its transmutation into genuine poetry, addresses itself to the whole man, to feeling as well as to intellect, for "die Natur würkt durch Sinne und Leidenschaften. Wer ihre Werkzeuge verstümmelt, wie mag der empfinden?" (2,206). Language divested of its affective appeal cannot stir the heart or the imagination: "Leidenschaft allein giebt Abstractionen sowohl als Hypothesen Hände, Füße, Flügel;—Bildern und Zeichen Geist, Leben und Zunge—Wo sind schnellere Schlüsse? Wo wird der rollende Donner der Beredsamkeit erzeugt, und sein Geselle—der einsylbichte Blitz" (2,208). The basic reason that language must not be robbed of its capacity to appeal to the affective and poetic side of man's nature is that God Himself, "the Poet at the beginning of days," has chosen to speak to man in the vernacular and in poetry, as the Scriptures abundantly testify. Here, as we saw in the case of the imagistic nature of ordinary language, the reason for Hamann's view is fundamentally theological.

The emasculation of language is not only a by-product of the abstract world view of the physicists and philosophers who would adopt their method, but is also a result of the deliberate effort of the prescriptive grammarians and indeed of all rationalistic arbiters of language. The most spectacular example of such interference with the natural development of language is to be found in the activities of the French Academy, which Hamann scores in these words: "Die Reinigkeit einer Sprache entzieht ihrem Reichthum; eine gar zu gefesselte Richtigkeit, ihrer Stärke und Mannheit.—In einer so grossen Stadt, als Paris ist, liessen sich jährlich, ohne Aufwand, vierzig gelehrte Männer aufbringen, die unfehlbar verstehen, was in ihrer Muttersprache lauter und artig, und zum Monopol dieses Trödelkrams nöthig ist" (2,136). In this passage Hamann does not deny that the members of the Academy seek to preserve the poetic aspects of the French language. What he questions is their method. As Otto Jespersen says of the dictionaries of the French and Italian academies, they were "less descriptions of actual usage than prescriptions for the best usage of words."[17] Such prescriptions are necessarily derived from norms that are rationally determined, hence they are abstract in nature. As we have seen earlier, abstraction is, in Hamann's eyes, the castration of thought. Therefore he can quite consistently say that the rationalists' attempt to improve language "diminishes its strength and manhood." The language that reason and good taste approve may have originally been possessed of imaginative and affective qualities, but constant usage robs the most vivid expressions of their pristine power. Thus, it does not matter whether language is emasculated indirectly by natural scientists and their philosophical devotees or by humanists who attempt to reform language in the light of reason. The result is inevitably the same: language becomes sterile and colorless, lacking the capacity to speak to the whole man, however precise or "pure" it may be.

Conclusion

Although Hamann does not subsume all the characteristics of his use of reason under the head of *anschauende Vernunft* or indeed of any other definitive term, it is clear that in the case of each of the characteristics save one he has provided us with both a general principle and an abundance of examples illustrating the principle. Since perceptive thinkers from Kant to Georg Lukács[18] have recognized that Hamann was not an irrationalist, but that on the contrary, reason plays an important role in his philosophy, however different it may be from the one it customarily plays in the case of more abstract thinkers. A superficial analysis of Hamann's prose may result in the conclusion that its all-too-frequent obscurity is rooted in sheer irrationalism. This is, however, by no means the case. Its obscurity derives for the most part from an excessive use of intuitive reason rather than from true irrationalism—a quite different matter.

Having seen to what extent Hamann is committed to intuitive or analogical reasoning, while at the same time rejecting the abstractions of the *Aufklärer*, we can more readily understand why he alternates between praise and vilification in his references to *Vernunft*. Thus, when he makes such statements as: "Glaube hat Vernunft eben so nöthig, als diese jenen hat" (G,504); "Ohne *Sprache* hätten wir keine Vernunft, ohne Vernunft keine *Religion* . . ." (3,231); "Weiß man erst, was Vernunft ist, so hört aller Zwiespalt mit der Offenbarung auf" (G, 406), he is obviously referring to what he considers the legitimate use of reason. Or again when he speaks of "den natürlichsten Gebrauch der Vernunft" (3,190), which the rationalists have transformed into "Schulvernunft" with disastrous results, he patently has in mind his own use of reason. On the other hand, the long series of pejorative epithets that he scornfully applies to "die hochgelobte Vernunft" are aimed not only at the philosophical pretensions of the *Aufklärer* but also at their official, therefore privileged, position in the Prussia of Frederick II, indeed at the king himself. Having now examined the principal evidence for the ambivalence in his concept of reason, we are in a better position to understand how he could write the following lines to his friend Jacobi in 1787: "Vernunft ist die Quelle aller Wahrheit und aller Irrthümer. Sie ist der Baum des Erkenntnisses Gutes und Böses. Also haben beide Theile Recht und beide Unrecht, die sie vergöttern, und die sie lästern. Glaube ebenso die Quelle des Unglaubens als des Aberglaubens. Aus einem Munde geht Loben und Fluchen" (G,513). Three decades earlier Hamann had written to another friend, J. G. Lindner, lines that summarize effectively the conception of reason to which he adhered throughout his career: "Wir machen Schlüße als Dichter als Redner und Philosophen. Jene sind öfterer der Vernunft näher als die in der logischen Form, wenn sich das Herz erklärt, so ist unser Verstand nichts als klügeln . . ." (I,201). These lines are by no means the typical romantic assertion of the priority of blind emotion over intellect, but are to be taken quite literally as the most concentrated summation possible of the Hamannian conception of reason.

After recognizing that Hamann's use of reason is quite different from that of more orthodox thinkers, one must still come to terms with the fact that there are general tendencies of his thought that bespeak underlying, hidden assumptions, which, if spelled out, are revealed to be quite abstract.[19] A striking illustration of this fact is his idea of language, which, if full justice were done to it, would require a whole new metalanguage for its precise exposition.[20] Perhaps the most important of all the underlying principles of his philosophy, and one that he is quite willing to acknowledge is, as we have seen, the metaphysical principle of the coincidence of opposites. But Hamann's general aversion to giving abstract formulation to his ideas cannot be considered simply perverse. For his purpose was to avoid what he held to be the arbitrariness, the mendacity, the arrogance, and the dehumanization that he believed invariably accompany the tendency to abstraction in philosophy, with its resulting unfortunate effects radiating out into all areas of human existence. In a remarkably compact statement of the significance of "intuitive knowledge" for human life he wrote in *Die Magi aus Morgenlande* (1760): "Das menschliche Leben scheinet in einer Reihe symbolischer Handlungen zu bestehen, durch welche unsere Seele ihre unsichtbare Natur zu offenbaren fähig ist, und eine anschauende Erkäntniß ihres würksamen Daseyns ausser sich hervor bringt und mittheilet" (2,139).

It is clear from the foregoing that there is a close parallel between the operation of the Hamannian "intuitive" reason and the operation of what today would be called "unconscious mind." It would, however, be quite misleading to psychologize his thought at this point. For not only is he keenly aware of the existence of the unconscious aspect of mind—which he describes as "jenes ungeheure Loch, jener finstere, ungeheuere Abgrunde"—but explicitly warns against dealing *directly* with it: "Nicht daß ich an den Tiefen der menschlichen Natur den geringsten Zweifel hätte," he wrote to Jacobi, "aber diese Schlünde zu erforschen, oder den Sinn zu solchen Gesichten auch andern mitzutheilen, ist mißlich" (G,6). It is the central characteristic of his approach that he equates the "depths" of the human psyche with the depths to be found in the poetic view of the universe as crystallized in genuine poetry, definitively, of course, in the Scriptures. In other words, instead of gazing *directly* into the "subterranean" recesses of his own psyche, he views them *indirectly* as reflected in the mirror of the Scriptures (cf. esp. 1,75–76). This shift from pure introspection to a consideration of the given facts of the "mirror" that sacred poetry constitutes means a shift from subjectivity to objectivity, and is a fact of primary importance for an understanding of his philosophy. It is obvious that Hamann's thought, despite definite parallels with depth-*psychology*, is principally concerned with depth-*epistemology*. Perhaps nowhere is his thinking in this regard more succinctly summarized than in a letter to Jacobi about a year before his death:

Die Wahrheit muß aus der Erde herausgegraben werden und nicht aus der Luft geschöpft, aus Kunstwörtern—sondern aus irdischen und unterirdischen Gegenständen erst ans Licht gebracht werden durch Gleichnisse und Parabeln der höchsten Ideen und transcendenten Ahndungen, die keine *directi* sondern *reflexi radii* sein können, wie Du aus Baco anführst.[21] Außer dem *principio cognoscendi* giebt es kein besonderes *principium essendi* für uns. *Cogito ergo sum* ist in diesem Verstande wahr. (G, 497)

Thus Hamann indicates how genuine access to the unconscious, or in his terminology "subterranean," mind may be gained, namely, by the proper use of language. The implications of this idea are far-reaching, not only for his own thought but also for the philosophy of the *Sturm und Drang* in general as well as for the later development of Romanticism.

NOTES

[1] See *Hamanns Schriften*, ed. Friedrich Roth and Gustav Adolph Wiener, VIII (Berlin, 1842), s.v.

[2] J. G. Hamann, *Sämtliche Werke*, ed. Josef Nadler, III (Vienna, 1951), 225. Hereafter the following volumes of this edition, I (1949), II (1950), as well as the one cited above will be referred to parenthetically in the text by *arabic* numerals only, the first referring to the volume, the second to the page number. All italics in quotations from Hamann occur in the original.

[3] J. G. Hamann. *Briefwechsel*, ed. Walther Ziesemer and Arthur Henkel, III (Wiesbaden, 1951), 82. Hereafter this and the other volumes of the edition—I (1955), II (1956), IV (1959)—will be referred to parenthetically in the text by a *roman* numeral, followed by an *arabic* numeral, the first referring to the volume, the second to the page.

[4] C. H. Gildemeister, *J. G. Hamanns, Des Magus im Norden, Leben und Schriften*, V (Gotha, 1868), 516. Hereafter this volume will be referred to parenthetically in the text simply with the letter "G," followed by the page number.

[5] Friedrich Nietzsche, *Werke*, ed. Karl Schlechta (Munich, 1966), I, 50.

[6] See my *Unity and Language: A Study in the Philosophy of Hamann* (1952; rpt. New York, 1966), pp. 47 ff.

[7] See my *Hamann's Socratic Memorabilia: A Translation and Commentary* (Baltimore, 1967), pp. 51–52, 88–91, 187–88.

[8] Ibid., pp. 207–8.

[9] Wilhelm Koepp, *Der Magier unter Masken* (Göttingen, 1965).

[10] Dorothy M. Emmet, "Analogy," *Encyclopaedia Britannica*, (1969), I, 843.

[11] Wilfred Sellars, *Science and Metaphysics: Variations on Kantian Themes* (London, 1968), p. 18.

[12] *Hamann's Socratic Memorabilia: A Translation and Commentary*, pp. 3–5, *et passim*.

¹³ Erwin Metzke, *J. G. Hamanns Stellung in der Philosophie des 18. Jahrhunderts* (Halle/ Saale, 1934), p. 51.

¹⁴ Quoted by Rudolf Unger in *Hamann und die Aufklärung* (Jena, 1911), I, 243.

¹⁵ *Confessions*, trans. and annotated by J. C. Pilkington (New York, 1943), p. 332.

¹⁶ Eric Blackall, *The Emergence of German as a Literary Language* (Cambridge, Eng., 1959), p. 447.

¹⁷ See my *Unity and Language*, p. 104, n. 26.

¹⁸ Georg Lukács, *Die Zerstörung der Vernunft* in *Werke*, IX (Neuwied, 1962), 100, 111, 114.

¹⁹ Hegel paid Hamann the great compliment of devoting an unusually long review to the Roth edition of his works. In it he states that for Hamann "das Bedürfnis der denkenden Vernunft fremd und unverstanden gelieben ist." Certainly abstract reason or "denkende Vernunft" was alien to him, but that he misunderstood its importance is wide of the mark. A main difference between Hamann and Hegel is precisely their antithetical evaluations of "denkende Vernunft." G. W. F. Hegel, *Berliner Schriften 1818–1831* in *Sämtliche Werke*, XI, Neue Kritische Ausgabe, ed. J. Hoffmeister (Hamburg, 1956), p. 226.

²⁰ But many Hamann scholars argue that such an undertaking would be a betrayal of his intentions, and therefore they would question its legitimacy. Such a position certainly has much validity, but remains nevertheless debatable.

²¹ The terminology of this passage derives from Francis Bacon, who speaks in *De augmentis scientiarum*, Bk. 53, Ch. 1 of three kinds of light rays: direct, refracted, and reflected, corresponding to man's knowledge of God, nature, and man.

"Wandrers Sturmlied":
Once More with Obiter Dicta

Hermann J. Weigand

When and under whatever circumstances young Goethe may have sat down to dash off the unpunctuated lines of "Wandrers Sturmlied" on paper, sometime in 1772, whatever long period of incubation may have preceded the decisive act, the poem that emerged breathes a sense of immediacy that takes us to the heart of the creative process.[1] We see the poet wandering through the countryside in a gusty spring downpour of rain and sleet interspersed with an occasional glint of sunlight, singing and shouting, athrob with a sense of life that makes him feel kin to the elemental powers that buffet him about. He begins with a proclamation of his sense of intimacy with the powers of nature, and this strain, continuing through the first six strophes, culminates in the twice-repeated proclamation of himself as "göttergleich." His mood is jubilant. It ascends to staggering heights of euphoria and hybris.

The first line, an invocation of "Genius," "Wen du nicht verlässest, Genius," is repeated again and again with minor modifications like a refrain, as his spirit surges. The verb that steers the keynote into an assertion, "wird," "wirst," dominates the grammatical structure four times and, despite the grammatical future, pervades the song with an abiding presence. The poem abounds in keywords that call for a perceptive ear: "entgegen," "decken," "um," "innen," "glühen," "Glut." They all recur. The first of these, "entgegen," an ambiguous word of relation, divides in English into two counterparts, toward and against. Here, in the first strophe, where it occurs as "entgegen singen," both meanings combine. There is movement toward and movement against. But the opposition, encompassed in song, is not hostile. It is the antiphonal rivalry of voices in a part-song, each striving to compete and assert itself as a cooperative element in a larger achievement. The poet is not alone in this striving. In the same sentence that invokes "Genius," he hails the lark above as a partner in this strenuous, jubilant exercise. The sense of immediacy in this gesture is complete. When we meet the word "ent-

105

gegen" again, in strophe nine, as a challenge, it has the same antiphonal ring. Let us not forget this.

The second strophe, concerned with the mud and mire underfoot, begins with an image barely glimpsed. Genius will lift him over the slime with fiery wings. Is he not here thinking of the mythical winged steed, Pegasus, offspring of Poseidon and the Gorgon, hero of many adventures, associated with Parnassus, Helicon, the sacred springs and the Muses, since the Renaissance so prevalent a symbol of poetic inspiration down to Goethe's own age as to become a mere emblematic shortcut supplanting live imagery?

The second image here encountered is quite another affair. Within the sweep of one sustained rhythmic curve the poet sketches essentials of the aftermath of the Greek story of the Flood: we see Phoebus Apollo's vast figure bestriding the earth and discharging his arrows at the monster bred out of the steaming slime, and we see the poet emulating him in stance and power. But there is an element of obscurity about the utterance. The reader feels himself stumbling over detached verbal blocks, rather than skimming along the crest of a continuous wave. The poet must take the blame for this. He chopped up the one great line into six short phrases to be followed down the printed page. He followed the same practice in strophes nine and thirteen. In the present instance this leads to gross misunderstanding. Everyone falls into the trap of reading: "Wandeln wird er / Wie mit Blumenfüßen / Über Deukalions Flutschlamm." To my knowledge every commentator explains "Mit Blumenfüßen" as walking over flowers or light-footed. That is the touchstone for the universal misreading. But let us read the passage with an emphatic pause after "Wie," then more or less nonstop, and it will reveal hidden depths: "Wandeln wird er Wie: mit Blumenfüssen Über Deukalions Flutschlamm Python tötend, leicht, gross Pythius Apollo [wandelte]." "Wie" introduces a comparison, but not a literary simile comparing the poet's feet to flower-feet (whatever that may mean), but rather a comparison of the poet with the figure of Phoebus Apollo in all his aspects. This sheds an entirely new light upon "Mit Blumenfüßen." Can we forget in the context of the universal Flood that Phoebus Apollo is not only the heavenly archer, but the sun god as well, the universal source of light, heat, and organic life? Wherever he bestrides the earth vegetation springs forth anew. Flowers spring up under his footsteps and caress his feet. Let me prove this by demonstration. (1) In this poem Phoebus Apollo is visualized as the sun god, source of life. (2) He is personified; we see him striding lightly over the mire. (3) In "Mahomets Gesang," another hymn of the same period, the movement of Islam, pictured as a mountain spring that grows to a mighty river, is also personified as a walker striding down the land to the ocean: "Städte / Werden unter seinem Fuß" (strophe 11). If it is questionable to speak of cities arising under his footstep, how natural, on the other hand, is it to speak of flowers sprouting under the sun god's footstep! (4) The condensation of the sentence into the compound "Blumenfüße" is effected without effort to form a conceit. (5) An automatic corollary of this condensation is the resulting image of the newly sprung flowers as caressing Apollo's feet. Such emotional response on the part of the flowers is not an embellishment; it is a substantial feature of the image. Summing up the present findings, we shall read: "Wandeln wird er wie . . . Apollo" and "Apollo wandelte mit Blumenfüßen."

Although I thought I knew this poem well, having been familiar with it for many years, I came upon the discovery here presented only very recently. Now, after the fact, I am aware that pressure tending toward this reading had long been building up in me by virtue of two passages in the final strophe: "Hoch flog / Siegdurchglühter / Jünglinge Peitschenknall" is a single six-beat phrase without room for the breath to pause, but is nevertheless chopped up into three lines. And the concluding part of the sentence, "Und sich Staub wälzt' / Wie vom Gebürg herab / Kieselwetter ins Tal," involves a comparison that as in the case of Apollo does not repeat the reflexive verb "sich wälzte," but implies it as clearly understood.[2] Persistent misapprehension of literary passages, such as we encounter here, is not altogether uncommon. Somewhere Nietzsche twits the Germans as being so addicted to song that they can only think of God as also singing: "So weit die deutsche Zunge klingt / Und Gott im Himmel Lieder singt." We may surely assume that Nietzsche read "Gott," or had the Germans read "Gott," as a nominative rather than a dative, tongue in cheek.

The slight alteration of the thematic line in strophe three to "Dem du nicht verlässest, Genius" (for *dem, den*) commits an atrocious lapse of grammar in favor of salvaging the rhythm. In this strophe the immediacy of the situation is suspended by predictive analogous reminiscences of divine tutelage. The rigors of camping out at night on a bed of rock are mitigated by the woolen pad of the wings of Genius. No one will think of these wings as detachable blankets; rather, Genius is envisioned as an angelic presence embracing the poet, sheltering him from the cold bare rock with wings tucked underneath, and protecting him against whatever dangers may lurk in the midnight grove, with guardian pinions spread out above. Seraphs, we remember, are equipped with three pairs of wings. "Decken" occurs as a term of protection against unspecified dangers. We shall meet this key word again in a most improbable context in strophe ten.

After this slight digression strophe four again alerts us to the spring tempest. It has now turned into a snow flurry. But the poet endows this with encompassing warmth. Note the *um-* of "umhüllen" which is soon to recur several times. There is an aura of warmth about him that attracts the Muses and the Graces and makes us think of the dance of summer insects around a moving object. Sensing their presence, the poet apostrophizes them in strophe five to reassure them. Pointing to the elements, water and earth, and the slime as their son, he endows them with positive value as elements of a creation in which everything is good and pure. That everything is affirmed as good and pure does not, of course, imply that everything is of equal value. We shall presently see that the poet is very conscious of a hierarchy of values. Here and in the following strophe the poet's pantheistic sense of at-oneness with the totality of nature reaches its climax.[3]

There is a pause. What follows before the mood of the poem has run its course, falls into three divisions: strophes 7 to 9, strophes 10 to 12, and strophe 13. Each of these intones its specific theme with a rhetorical question. Strophe 7 introduces a specific moving object as part of the outer landscape, "Der kleine schwarze feurige Bauer." Except for the skylark he is the first living organism to impinge upon the visionary transformation of the landscape as the poet battles the elements, and even the reality of the skylark has been questioned. Be that as it may, the singing skylark and the little swarthy peasant, brimful of energy, represent a plane of reality quite distinct from Apollo, the sungod-archer bestriding the earth, and the Muses that dance about him enlivened by his inner warmth. The figure of the peasant is used to draw a contrast between his simple, rugged, close-to-the-soil life and the poet's not-so-secure, but lavishly endowed, infinitely enriched form of existence. There is a tremor of danger, of apprehension betrayed by the question. Its emphatic repetition and all that follows is designed to strengthen his reassurance on the rebound. There is a contrast not only between the limited gifts awaiting the peasant, wine and the warmth of his hearth, and the limitless gifts awaiting the poet, but also a subtle play of words involved in the phrasing of their expectation. The peasant expects, awaits his gifts; in the case of the poet, all the bounties of life are ranged about, awaiting him. They are personified. They look forward to meeting *him* in a joyous throng. The repeated use of *um* relative to the throng encircling the poet is particularly notable.

This strophe has invoked the wine god, Father Bromius, in association with the peasant. The name is Greek, and in the Roman tradition, which identified him with an old Italic divinity, he was commonly addressed as *Pater*, Father. Bromius, like Pater Liber, is only one of his many names. In the age of Goethe almost everything Greek was filtered through Roman tradition. Addressing him as Father suggests a relation of affectionate intimacy. To replace the name Bromius, which Goethe certainly encountered in Ovid's *Metamorphoses*, as pointed out by Arthur Henkel,[4] with Dionysus, as some commentators of our poem have done, including Trunz,[5] only leads to confusion. Thanks to Nietzsche, for a century it has been impossible to think of Dionysus without evoking the image of Apollo as his dialectical counterpart, both of them members of a schematic ideology, in which Apollo stands for reason, consciousness, clarity, dialectics, individuation, whereas Dionysus is the god of the dark, subconscious, irrational, terribly eruptive creative powers, the god of divine frenzy and mass madness. There is absolutely nothing to warrant Goethe as having conceived of the god in these terms. In our poem the wine god is seen as a deity of subordinate rank. "Nur deine Gaben" stresses his limits and disqualifies him from the outset from participating in the highest values.

The eighth strophe invokes Father Bromius a second time in an atmosphere of strictures. Addressing him as the Genius of this age, "Jahrhundertsgenius," the poet disparages the age for contenting itself with the wine god as the symbol of its highest aspirations.[6] Now the time has come for our poet to reveal the source of his own inspired singing. It is Pindar, the most celebrated of the singers who immortalized the festival games of the Greeks in honor of their gods. Two letters to Herder of the year 1772 attest Goethe's boundless admiration for Pindar, and our poem, in both its free form and its rhapsodic content, obviously attempts to emulate the glow of inspiration, compared with which everything modern strikes him as tepid. What our modern poets try to achieve by an infusion of wine from without—that, and immeasurably more—Pindar achieved by virtue of his inner glow. The status of the wine god is further reduced by contrasting his gifts limited in quality and time with the limitless gifts of Phoebus Apollo, timelessly bestowed on all the world.

The poet's grief and vexation over the slackness of an age that cannot rise to heights of soul without the artificial stimulation of the wine god finds utterance in his cry, "Weh, weh!" In these words I do not hear the sound of an Old Testament curse, let alone a wail of self-pity; there is rather a tone of intense commiseration. A triple outcry of anguish is followed by a self-exhortation. At this moment the poet must have become aware of a meteorological change. A rift must have appeared in the clouds, showing sharp glints of sunlight. Phoebus Apollo, face him aglow! As in the first strophe, where along with the skylark the poet raised his antiphonal song against the bluster of the rain clouds, he now exhorts himself to make the antiphonal response to the sun god. The dread of failure looms in the background. To default at this test would be disastrous. He conjures up this contingency with apotropaeic intent. Here a new element, the cedar, is projected upon the scene, adding a third participant to the tense situation. The cedar is an element of the inner landscape, located in its stately grandeur at a distance behind the poet. He sees it with his inner eye. Biblical associations make it an object of high nobility. Within the triadic field of tension here depicted, the cedar assumes the role of honor in case the poet defaults. If the poet fails to face the god aglow, the lordly eye of Phoebus Apollo will disdainfully ("kalt") glide over and above the poet to come to rest ("verweilen") upon the cedar, which measures up to the test. Being evergreen, it is alive with an inner glow. It is in perpetual readiness to respond to Phoebus Apollo's encountering glance.

The cedar has given rise to much confused comment. I hold it as axiomatic that the cedar is introduced as a positive replacement for the poet in case he should default. It is contrary to all logic to think of the poet as failing because of weakness and the cedar failing because of self-sufficient pride. If both of them are to be dismissed as failures, what point is there in introducing the cedar at all? To say that the cedar can afford to do without Phoebus Apollo is to ignore the basic condition of all organic life. Some commentators think the poet might default, not because of weakness, but because of self-sufficient pride. These, stressing the attribute of pride as also pertaining to the cedar, would regard the cedar as no more than an emblematic metaphor for the poet, nailed by the disdainful glance of the sun god.

There is a catch, of course. We have the word "neidgetroffen" in the middle of the strophe. General consensus designates it as ambiguous. I discussed this in a paper many years ago.[7] Let me go over the ground again, sorting out the strands of possible interpretation. In our printed text, the apotropaeic passage, "Kalt wird *sonst* . . ." consists of seven lines. This picture is deceptive. The spoken reality reduces these seven lines to five.

> Kalt wird sonst sein Fürstenblick
> Über dich vorübergleiten
> Neidgetroffen
> Auf der Zeder Kraft verweilen
> Die zu grünen sein nicht harrt.

It is the rhythm that counts. In terms of rhythm, we have two pairs of four-beat, quick-march, trochaic lines, asyndetic, i.e., not connected, the first pair separated from the second by the two-beat line, "neidgetroffen." This line shores up the movement. It is ambiguous, pointing both backward and forward. As the reader observed, we left "neidgetroffen" altogether out of account in studying the emotional interrelation of the three principals.

What does "neidgetroffen" mean? What can it mean? It is a participial compound. The nominal element *Neid*, envy, can mean anything from covetousness to disdain to active enmity. That it need not mean covetousness in Goethe's language of this period is shown by the last lines of strophe one of his dramatic monologue "Prometheus," bidding defiance to Zeus: "Mußt mir meine Erde / Doch lassen stehn, / Und meine Hütte, / Die du nicht gebaut, / Und meinen Herd, / Um dessen Glut / Du mich beneidest." How can the lord of the thunderbolts be thought of as coveting the feeble flame of Prometheus' hearth! Yet, in presenting this example of *Neid* in the most general sense of ill-will and hostility, I find myself checked by the fact that the whole first strophe is uttered by Prometheus as a taunt. It would suit his mood of mockery to needle Zeus with the imputation of petty jealousy. As for "getroffen," it is usually a word of action suggesting two participants, one shooting and one shot at, a subject and an object of the action (although both activities can be thought of as combined in one person).

Perhaps the best way to focus the problem is simply to ask: Who is envious? Envious of whom? Remembering that *Neid* can stand for any kind of ill-will, and that, compounded with *getroffen*, it may represent either a static emotion, a grudge lodged in some person, or a dynamic current discharged from one person against another, we are confronted with a confusing variety of choices. To take the simplest case first: the readiest referent for "neidgetroffen" is Apollo's "Fürstenblick." In that case the epithet would seem little more than an expanded elaboration of "kalt," and this would certainly support my contention that reasons of rhythm are primarily, if not exclusively, responsible for the insertion of the two-beat compound. If, however, we take the referent of "Neidgetroffen" to be "dich," which stands closest to it, then Apollo's effect directed against the poet would be highly dynamic. If this is what Goethe meant, why did he write "neidgetroffen," we ask, and not "neidgetroffnen"? This is just the kind of accusative that Goethe uses with signal effectiveness in "An Schwager Kronos," another of the Storm and Stress hymns. Having made elaborate rhetorical preparations in the third strophe from the end, he charges the next run-on strophe with a whole battery of accusatives: "Trunknen vom letzten Strahl / Reiß mich, ein Feuermeer / Mir im schäumenden Aug', / Mich Geblendeten, Taumelnden / In der Hölle nächtliches Tor!" Since this device was demonstrably at Goethe's command, why did he not use it? We must therefore discard this interpretation.

A third theoretical possibility lies open with regard to Apollo as the envier. Many commentators have assumed that Apollo's *Neid* is directed against the cedar. According to this view, the poet and the cedar would be standing at opposite ends of the spectrum as it were, the poet defaulting at the moment of the showdown from weakness, whereas the cedar in brash, self-sufficient pride of stateliness and beauty anticipates Apollo's springtime summons by virtue of its ever-greening life force. This could be brought into line with the Greek conception of "the envy of the gods," which asserts itself when man's good fortune becomes too much of a good thing. However, ignoring some strange variations of this general scheme, I find no reason whatever for the introduction of the cedar if it is not to stand as a positive foil against the hypothetically defaulting poet. To introduce the cedar by way of a warning that even the antiphonal zeal of a living creature may misfire vis-à-vis the gods, seems to me a switch of thought tantamount to a derailment.

There is one more possibility that we must explore. Must the personality harboring *Neid* be Apollo? May it not be the poet directing the shaft of his ill will against Apollo? As we follow this up there unfolds a highly complex dramatic situation. There is a multiple exchange of signals all taking place in a moment. Apollo's lordly glance sweeps over and beyond the poet, who sees himself "mutlos," dispirited, beaten. Seeing himself rejected, he glares with resentment at the god and observes that the contours of the god's eye have softened as it comes to rest approvingly upon the cedar. Accordingly, the poet's own expression of rage is modified to include a blend of jealousy against the preferred object of Apollo's favor. Since this whole exchange of signals takes place in the poet's imagination, and the cedar, unlike the skylark and the swarthy peasant, is only a part of the interior landscape, any naturalistic objection to the effect that the poet would have to have eyes in the back of his head to see the object upon which the god's benevolent glance alights, is pointless. This version, resolving the compressed compound, "neidgetroffen," into "von deinem Neid getroffen," does justice to the hypothetical confrontation of the Sun-god and the defaulting poet.

Here at the end of strophe nine it may be time to pause and recapitulate the points that have led to great divergence in the interpretation of the poem. It is apparent that many interpreters did not take "entgegen singen" in strophe one and "glüh' entgegen" in strophe nine as a friendly antiphonal response. Without this there would have been no grounds for charging the poet with pride and self-sufficiency. He may well be charged with hybris, but never with pride. All the way through he is under the protection of "Genius," whatever divine form this may take. The misinterpretation of Vater Bromius I find more difficult to explain. The reservation in strophe seven, "nur deine Gaben," makes it clear to me that Vater Bromius is conceived as a deity of subordinate rank, not to be compared in dignity or power with Phoebus Apollo, fit only to inspire an age that is destitute of inner glow. In strophe nine our analysis showed that while the ambiguity of "neidgetroffen" cannot be resolved, the logical sense of the strophe does not require it at all. It is, however, a rhythmical necessity of the first order.

To return to strophe seven and the peasant. More than twenty years ago, I transcribed and inserted in my copy of Max Morris, *Der junge Goethe* (1911), the following passage: "If the poor wretch, who is trudging on to his miserable cottage, can laugh at the storms and tempests, the rain and whirlwinds, which surround him, while his richest hope is only that of rest; how much more cheerfully must a man pass through such transient evils, whose spirits are buoyed up with the certain expectation of finding a noble palace and the most sumptuous entertainment ready to receive him!" The passage is from a letter communicated in book 3, chapter 10 of Henry Fielding's novel *Amelia* (1752). The pious sentiments here so eloquently expressed preface the information that the recipient, who has been expecting a legacy of 100,000 pounds, has been ignored in the will of his aunt just deceased, in favor of his avaricious sister. In connection with the passage quoted, in airing his pious sentiments tongue in cheek, the writer remarks that Cicero's *Tusculan Questions*, book 3, present a similar nobility of outlook despite the fact that Cicero was a benighted heathen.

The similarity of pattern between Fielding's sentence and strophe seven is so striking as to make one ask whether this is a mere coincidence. However, in view of the fact that sentences of such conditional correlative pattern might well be encountered in forensic argument or in treatises of eudaemonistic ethics, I scanned book 3 of the *Tusculan Questions* but without finding anything that bore a formal resemblance to Fielding's sentence. I assume it as probable therefore, almost to the point of certainty, that Goethe, who had become an avid reader of English novels during his sojourn in Strasbourg in 1771, had got his hands on *Amelia* and that, regardless of its tongue-in-cheek presentation, or even more probably because of it, the passage stuck in his mind, and its pattern found itself incorporated in "Wandrers Sturmlied." Such transpositions of key, including on occasion not only the borrowing of a formal pattern, but also the verbatim lifting of an alien content, are not unknown in literature.

Like strophes seven to nine, ten to twelve form a tightly knit group. Here, for the first time, the storm itself is apostrophized as a divine personality, Jupiter Pluvius. We must think of Jupiter here only in his specific capacity of rain god, not as supreme ruler of the Olympian twelve, for where would that leave Apollo, the source of all organic life? Similarly, the reference to the Castalian spring in this strophe as a mere tributary, in comparison to the rain god's torrent, should not specifically evoke the image of Apollo as god of the Muses, in addition to his other functions. To be sure, there is a monotheistic (albeit Trinitarian!) overtone in the poet's hailing of the rain god as: "Dich, von dem es begann, / Dich, in dem es endet, / Dich, aus dem es quillt," reminiscent of the biblical triad: "In ihm leben, weben, und sind wir" (Acts 17:28). Thoughts cascade pell-mell in this strophe and the typological correspondence of the torrential downpour and the Castalian spring on the one hand, with the characteristic and the beautiful (strength vs. charm) as two distinct forms of aesthetic expression, as developed in "Von deutscher Baukunst" (1771), cannot be overlooked but should not be pressed too closely.

Like the preceding group that took off from the sight of the peasant, this group too begins with a rhetorical question: why does my song name you last? My song has been pouring you forth all the time. "Dich, Dich strömt mein Lied" is another antiphonal response to the divine power. He feels the deity's grasp as a fluid protection. He feels the downpour as a shielding cover, no different from the guardian pinions of strophe three.

In the next two strophes the confused ad hoc blend of ideological currents subsides into lyricism. These strophes with their weaving rhythms single out two of the most distinguished representatives of the idyllic and pastoral genre, Anacreon and Theocritus, as not having been vouchsafed the grasp of the torrential god. These two parallel strophes, keyed to an initial "nicht," weave the melodic pattern of a descending spiral rationing the breath as it is being released. But the first of these two, having completed its artful circumlocution and arrived at the name of the poet Anacreon as its goal, and calling for a full stop, suddenly jerks the voice upward to apostrophize the storm-breathing deity. Let the reader attempt to repeat this extraordinary feat of the voice and feel the crack in his throat! Was this intended as a danger signal? It is not repeated in the Theocritus strophe.

The last strophe brings another *tour de force* and a final crack-up. Despite the punctuation of the revised version (period and dashes), I can read this strophe, like strophe seven, sighting the peasant, and strophe ten, apostrophizing the storm god, Jupiter Pluvius, only as a deliriously ecstatic question in confident expectation of Pindar's antiphonal response across the ages. Abruptly follows a seizure, a threat of total collapse. Antiphonal song has turned into a plaintive cry for help from whatever divine quarter, to supply that minimum of glow that will sustain his reeling step to reach the hilltop and its sheltering abode. We could let our imagination wander to exploit the comedown in "meine Hütte," to picture a shanty so rude and primitive as to make the peasant's cottage with its wine and its hearthglow resemble a palace.

The British authors Wilkinson and Willoughby have made a case for reading a large dose of humor into "Wandrers Sturmlied."[8] I do not read the poem in those terms. There is hybris reaching its climax in strophes five and six; there is a desperate straining to sustain the mood of antiphonal song vis-à-vis the gods all the way into the final strophe, this followed by a threat of total collapse. There is self-irony in this, to my way of thinking, not humor. We know that Goethe had a great sense of poetic economy. He was loath in collecting his poetic works to lose anything salvageable. Yet he resisted including this great hymn in his first authorized edition of his poems in 1789, and again in the second authorized edition of 1806, dismissing it in the third part of *Dichtung und Wahrheit* in 1812 as "Halbunsinn." Only after an unauthorized printing in 1810 had made its existence known beyond the tiny circle of intimates favored with manuscript copies in the 1770s did Goethe include it with minimal alterations in the third authorized edition of his poems in 1815. Would the poet have been disposed for so long a time to consign this remarkable poem to oblivion if he had conceived it as a *tour de force* of extravagant humor? Two years after writing the poem Goethe sent a copy to Fritz Jacobi (31 August 1774) with the comment: "Hier eine Ode, zu der Melodie und Kommentar nur der Wandrer in der Not erfindet." Quoted by Arthur Henkel[9] among others, and appearing as the well-chosen title of a recently published essay by Heinrich Henel,[10] "Der Wandrer in der Not" characterizes a frame of mind that rules out humorous intent.

NOTES

[1] For the text of "Wandrers Sturmlied," appropriately grouped with other poems of Goethe's *Sturm und Drang*, I refer the reader to *Goethes Werke*, Hamburger Ausgabe, ed. Erich Trunz, I, 7th ed. (Hamburg, 1964), 33–36. Notes, some extended commentary, and a selected bibliography are found on pages 463–67. Recent notable additions to the bibliography would include Gerhard Kaiser, "Das Genie und seine Götter. Ein Beitrag zu Wandrers Sturmlied von Goethe," *Euphorion*, LVIII (1964), 41–58; and Heinrich Henel, "Der Wandrer in der Not: Goethes 'Wandrers Sturmlied' und 'Harzreise im Winter,'" in *Deutsche Vierteljahrsschrift*, LVII (1973), 69–94.

[2] I cannot help mentioning something totally irrelevant that haunted me while writing this paper. In his history of World War II (1971), the British historian, Liddell Hart, repeatedly refers to much valuable information on German plans and strategy supplied to the British after the war by General von Blumentritt. How would a general come by such a name? We can surely not think of him as Apollo's twin.

[3] Casual reading has turned up interesting evidence to show how one of America's distinguished men of letters, James Russell Lowell, exploited his familiarity with "Wandrers Sturmlied" to advantage. There is a covert allusion to our poem in his *Biglow Papers*, part II, 1867. Ever since the publication of the Norsemen's voyages of discovery in three languages, in 1837, American scholars and amateur archeologists had been alerted to the search for evidence, particularly in the form of runes, of traces of pre-Columbian settlements. Lowell has one of his spokesmen, Parson Wilbur, send a communication to the *Atlantic Monthly* on the subject of runes, outlining that there are three kinds; first, those understood by the Royal Society of Copenhagen; second, those understood only by its distinguished secretary; and third, those not clearly understood by any of the authorities and therefore providing a great incentive "to enucleating sagacity." Of the third class, he reports, he is in possession of a specimen found in his own pasture. This he has deciphered to read as follows: "Here Bjarna Grimolfsson first drank Cloud-brother through Child-of-Land-and-Water." This inscription Parson Wilbur interprets to mean: In this pasture the Viking Bjarna inhaled his first tobacco smoke through a reed stem. We cheer Lowell for having fashioned two fine Icelandic kennings by virtue of "Sohn des Wassers und der Erde." The story, of which I have here given a condensed version, is to be found in Samuel Eliot Morison's *The European Discovery of America: The Northern Voyages A.D. 500–1600* (New York, 1971), p. 37.

[4] See Arthur Henkel, "Versuch über 'Wandrers Sturmlied,'" in *Die Gegenwart der Griechen im neueren Denken. Festschrift für Hans-Georg Gadamer zum 60. Geburtstag* (Tübingen, 1960), pp. 59–76.

[5] Erich Trunz, "Anmerkungen" to *Goethes Werke*, I, 464–65.

[6] "Vater Bromius/ Du bist Genius/ Jahrhunderts Genius . . . ." More likely than not, this second, ill-tempered invocation of Vater Bromius was induced by a literary reminiscence lying very close at hand. In 1771, one year before the writing of "Wandrers Sturmlied," Wieland had published *Der Neue Amadis*, that mini-pornographic, mock-heroic, infinitely tedious epic, an exercise of lavish wit and ingenuity upon a wholly unworthy subject. In canto 13, strophe 26, Wieland had hailed Vater Bromius as the provider of some choice Burgundy, or, that being unavailable, a good Assmannshäuser. Knowing how Goethe lampooned Wieland's *Alcestis* in *Götter, Helden und Wieland* a few years later, we can imagine his feeling of disgust in leafing his way through *Der Neue Amadis*. As far back as 1883, Gustav von Loeper had pointed to canto 13 as a source for Vater Bromius. Readers of the second revised edition of *Der Neue Amadis*, posthumously published, will look in vain for any reference to Vater Bromius. Wieland deleted it in favor of a totally altered text. However, in the edition of 1839 (Leipzig: G. J. Göschen) of Wieland's *Sämtliche Werke*, the text of the poem is followed not only by Wieland's appendix of learned notes, but also by a complete list of variant readings showing Wieland's revision of the original text. The "Vater Bromius" variant can be found in vol. 15, p. 332.

[7] Hermann J. Weigand, "Wandrers Sturmlied—'Neidgetroffen,'" *Germanic Review*, XXI (1946), 165–72.

[8] Elizabeth M. Wilkinson and L. A. Willoughby, "Wandrers Sturmlied, A Study in Poetic Vagrancy," *German Life and Letters*, n.s. 1 (1947–48), 102–16.

[9] Henkel, "Versuch," p. 61.

[10] See n. 1.

Escape and Transformation: An Inquiry into the Nature of Storm's Realism

A. Tilo Alt

Non semper ea sunt quae videntur.
(Phaedrus, *Fables*)

Although we consider Storm a writer of some significance, there remains a nagging doubt about his ultimate place in the annals of German literature. Thomas Mann may have sensed some of this when he rose to defend Storm's work in his well-known essay of 1930: "Ich betone die sensitive Vergeistigung, den Extremismus seiner Gemütshaftigkeit so sehr und spreche sogar von leichter Krankhaftigkeit, um nichts auf ihn kommen zu lassen, was auf Bürgernormalität oder -sentimentalität, auf seelisches Philistertum hinausliefe, weil nämlich Fontane von Provinzialsimpelei gesprochen hat. Es ist nichts Rechtes damit, es stimmt nicht."[1] Indeed, we might add, "es stimmt nicht," because however annoying Fontane may have felt Storm's "Husumerei" to be, he merely intended to describe Storm's provincialism as the preservation of subjectivity limited by its own level of experience without intending to canonize or to mythologize the homeland.[2]

This view of Storm's work, based largely on aesthetic and biographical criteria and stressing the "decadent" aspects of his oeuvre for reasons we can well imagine where Thomas Mann is concerned, contrasts sharply with a historical point of view advanced by such diverse critics as Erich Auerbach, Georg Lukács, and, more recently, Robert Minder.[3] All three critics emphasize the backwardness of nineteenth-century German literature in comparison to the literatures of France, Russia, and England in the same period. The most acid comment and, therefore, also the most one-sided comes from Georg Lukács. Lukács, it might be remembered, quotes from an essay by the young Karl Marx in the "Deutsch-Französische Jahrbücher" of 1843:

Wollte man an den deutschen status quo selbst anknüpfen, wenn auch in einzig angemessener Weise, d.h., negativ, immer bliebe das Resultat ein Anachronismus. Selbst die Verneinung unserer politischen Gegenwart findet sich schon als verstaubte Tatsache in der historischen Rumpelkammer der modernen Völker.

. . . Wenn ich die Zustände von 1843 verneine, stehe ich nach französischer Zeitrechnung, kaum im Jahre 1843, noch weniger im Brennpunkt der Gegenwart. . . . Wie die alten Völker ihre Vorgeschichte in der Imagination erlebten, in der Mythologie, so haben wir Deutsche unsere Nachgeschichte in Gedanken erlebt, in der Philosophie. Wir sind philosophische Zeitgenossen der Gegenwart ohne ihre historischen Zeitgenossen zu sein. Die deutsche Philosophie ist die ideale Verlängerung der deutschen Geschichte. . . . Was bei den fortgeschrittenen Völkern praktischer Zerfall mit den modernen Staatszuständen ist, das ist in Deutschland, wo diese Zustände selbst noch nicht einmal existieren, zunächst kritischer Zerfall mit der philosophischen Spiegelung dieser Zustände.

From this Lukács concludes:

Diese Charakteristik des ideologischen Zustandes in Deutschland bezieht sich vollinhaltlich auf die deutsche Literatur dieser Jahre. . . . Was sie [Raabe and Storm] und ihresgleichen erreichten—und das ist nicht wenig—haben sie in Opposition gegen die deutsche Entwicklung nach 1848 errungen. Und wenn dieses Lebenswerk in der Geschichte des europäischen Realismus nicht mehr darstellt, wenn es mit provinziellen, engen und skurrilen Zügen behaftet ist, so deshalb, weil die Opposition Raabes und Storms nicht entschieden, nicht prinzipiell genug war.[4]

Finally, Lukács quotes from Storm's statement concerning his concept of classicism, a statement that has proved irresistible to Marxist critics ever since. Storm's self-imposed limitation to a "Novellistik der Erinnerungen," Lukács thinks, was the natural consequence of a choice between humiliating submission to Bismarck's regime or lonely artistic oddity. It was, presumably, for that reason that Storm said: "Zur Klassizität gehört doch wohl, daß in den Werken eines Dichters der wesentliche Gehalt seiner Zeit in künstlerisch vollendeter Form abgespiegelt ist . . . und ich werde mich jedenfalls mit einer Seitenloge begnügen müssen."[5] Obviously, what has appealed to the Marxist critics such as Lukács, Goldammer, Böttger, and Teitge[6] is the term "abgespiegelt," a term denoting the Marxist concept of the superstructure of culture. According to these critics, Storm cannot mirror any progressive tendencies because there are none to reflect. It would seem, incidentally, that Storm's statement reveals more about his inability to comprehend classicism than anything else.

Both critiques, Thomas Mann's aestheticism and Georg Lukác's social realism, shed light on the "realist" Theodor Storm, yet they are difficult to reconcile in their disparate perspectives. Could it be that the contradictory nature of their assessments has its origin in the contradictory nature of Storm's work itself? What precisely is it that makes Storm a "realist" of some significance and wherein lies his so-called realism? The historical and biographical criteria of our critics require elaboration as well as corroboration by structural criteria.

It is time, therefore, to turn our attention to the terminology employed in the title of this study, "escape and transformation." The two terms characterize the basis of Storm's attitude toward reality, which, in essence, is one of insecurity. Hence, the terms go far toward yielding a typology of his realism. Upon close examination of his work, it is possible to isolate the ways in which this attitude of fundamental insecurity toward reality asserts itself: first, in a conventional imagery and style that accompanies the escapist phase of his work, and second, in the themes of the supernatural and myth that parallel the period of Storm's attempt to transform reality in his quest for a firm basis from which to view reality. These characteristics of theme and style reflect a lifelong struggle with a moral and metaphysical problem (the meaning of life) and the effort to find a solution for it in the myth of tragic man or tragic existence.[7] Generally, the phase of escapism characterizes the sentimental, pathetic, and residually Romantic aspects of Storm's poetry and prose from the beginnings in the late 1840s to the novellas of tragic fate in the late seventies and eighties. The phase of transformation of reality describes his quest for a genuinely tragic view of life, i.e., the implication of a transcendental potential in the supernatural and of an answer to the question of the meaning of life in the theme of myth.

Storm's attitude of insecurity toward reality had historical as well as personal reasons. As a young man Storm already had become utterly disillusioned with the rationalism of his time, and he experienced knowledge as a process of metaphysical disillusionment. Therefore, reality was to him acceptable only in aesthetic terms; otherwise, it appeared to him as a heartless, soulless mechanism. He wrote to Therese Rowohl in 1838: "Die Welt, die wir uns in unserem Geiste bauen, ist alles; wir streben nach Wahrheit und die beglückende Täuschung fällt. . . . Darum liebe ich die Kinder, weil sie die Welt und sich noch im schönen Zauberspiegel ihrer Phantasie sehen."[8] Storm's escapist reaction to his historical situation is evident here.

Richard Brinkmann has shown that the literary realism of the nineteenth century is by no means a question of the objective reflection of the political, social, and cultural conditions of the period but very much a matter of subjectivity, of narrative perspective ("Erzählhaltung") as a means of coming to terms with reality ("Weltbewältigung").[9]

As a formal and statistical matter, it can be said that Storm's novellas reveal a fixed number of recurring structural elements. Of a total of fifty-six novellas, fairy tales, and prose sketches, forty-three can properly be called novellas. Twenty-six of these, or more than half, are frame tales. If we count the other prose pieces as well, approximately one-half of his prose works are told by a narrator who is represented by either the main or a minor character. This narrator tells his story most frequently in the first person and occasionally in the third. The other half of the novellas are related by both the author and narrator, again, either in the first or in the third person. Throughout his works Storm never appears undisguised as an authorial narrator freely addressing his readers with irony, humor, or wit. In fact, it can be said that Storm was intent upon concealing his involvement as the author of his prose. The question that follows from this typology is why Storm preferred the concealment of his "persona" (Wayne Booth's term) or, by Franz Stanzel's definition (in whose sense we propose to use the terms "author" and "narrator"), why the figural and neutral forms of narration (as opposed to authorial narration) predominate in the prose works of Storm.[10] Further, we must seek an answer to the question of Storm's preference for the framed novella and the manuscript fiction of his later works.

The novella and the frame tale are, of course, conventions of the nineteenth century in which Storm simply shared. Yet the ironic attitude of an author toward his fiction, was not solely the prerogative of the novelist (such as Dostoevsky or Trollope, for instance) but is reflected in Keller's novellas as well. That would preclude the argument that the novella does not admit of an ironic perspective. In the foregoing, we have already suggested an answer to the question of Storm's subjectivity. It provided the perspective for his novellas, despite the fact that in his fiction he sought to separate objective reality from subjective experience through an elaborate system of devices. As we have observed already, Fontane's assessment of Storm's subjectivity is essentially correct. Storm could only function in a context with which he was intimately connected, such as his family and his native region.

There are, in the main, three elements which account for the intended impact of Storm's prose and, in part, his lyrics: the concealment of his involvement as the author, i.e., the narrative "Ich" of his stories, the lyrical element, and the conventionality of his language and imagery. All three culminate in a typically Stormian concept of the dramatic that might best be defined as the intent to convey to the reader the same profound emotional impact the writer himself experienced. It is for that reason that he was moved to defend the novella as the genre capable of the highest artistic expression, a genre that deserved to be called the "sister of the drama." By the same token, Storm emphasized in his correspondence with other writers that he meant to move the reader profoundly: "Eins sollte mir leid tun, wenn meine Dichtung nur rührend wäre; sie sollte erschütternd sein."[11] Unfortunately, and by definition, a tragic emotion could not result from most of Storm's production. The three elements which by their common denominator of understatement, served to amplify the atmospheric impact of his themes and motifs (mostly of transiency and death), resulted in a pathetic rather than tragic gesture. This was particularly true of his early novellas, as demonstrated by the near unmitigated sentimentality of *Immensee*, and most certainly for his fairy tales, which are, with the possible exception of *Die Regentrude*, mere allegories of the human mind and condition. Thus we find in his works a tendency toward sentimentality and escapism that evades the confrontation with the strictures of an intellectually and morally weak age, namely that of post-revolutionary and post-Versailles Germany. Further contributing to Storm's pathos was his concept of tragedy, which reflects the relativism of a nihilistic age and which is, in its deterministic aspects, perhaps reminiscent of Georg Büchner. Storm wrote: "Der Kampf, der vergebliche Kampf gegen das, was durch die Schuld oder auch nur Begrenzung, die Unzulänglichkeit des Ganzen, der Menschheit, von der . . . der Held ein Teil ist, der sich nicht abzulösen vermag, und sein und seines eigentlichen Lebens herbeigeführter Untergang, scheint mir das Allertragischste"; and he added parenthetically, "*Carsten Curator, Renate, Aquis submersus*, bei welch letzterem ich an keine Schuld des Paares gedacht habe."[12] The absence of personal guilt and, above all, of a universal order (such as the mythology of the ancients or the *ordo mundi* of the Middle Ages) prevents Storm from creating genuine tragedy. Perhaps *Hans und Heinz Kirch* and most certainly *Der Schimmelreiter* come closest to a convincing portrayal of man's tragic existence as Storm's basic concept of man.

As an illustration of the escapist tendencies in Storm's work, a few striking examples may suffice that exhibit a surprising degree of political and social indifference. In 1864, after his return from exile and after the defeat of the Danes by Prussia, Storm wrote with some degree of satisfaction:

> Wir können auch die Trompete blasen
> Und schmettern weithin durch das Land.
> Doch schreiten wir lieber in Maientagen,
> Wenn die Primeln blühen und die Drosseln schlagen,
> Still sinnend an des Baches Rand.[13]

Or similarly, in 1850, the fairy tale, or what could more accurately be called allegory, *Stein und Rose* (which later became *Hinzelmeier*) was prefaced by these lines:

Ein wenig Scherz in die ernste Zeit
Ein Lautenklang in den verwirrten Streit
In das politische Versegebell
Ein rundes Märchenritornell.[14]

And in 1848, while Germany was in the throes of its first revolution, Storm wrote *Immensee*, a story of unrequited love and resignation. The preface, finally, to the first edition of his fairy tales (*Hinzelmeier, Bulemanns Haus, Die Regentrude*, and *Der Spiegel des Cyprianus*) of 1865 demonstrates that Storm was well aware of the dual, perhaps even ambivalent role of his fairy tales. He wishes to show the impossibility of a Romantic and naive flight from reality on the one hand, and, on the other hand, to search for a new and more profound answer to the meaning of life— however tentative—by means of the supernatural. He tries to coax his readers into accepting a less prosaic view of life: "Und so lade ich denn diesmal außer den Alten auch die Jungen ein, den 'Ritt ins romantische Land' mit mir zu wagen. Es wird zwar sachte aufwärts gehen, zuletzt aber doch hübsch über die Alltagswelt hinweg, und der Schulstaub wird prächtig aus den flatternden Gewändern fliegen."[15] The allusions to Eichendorff notwithstanding, there is no denying the fact that Storm wished to draw his readers' attention to the tragic side of human existence. The contours of the characters and their actions tend to be blurred for the sake of a heavy stress on their inner lives. In order to focus attention on these qualities, Storm thus does not develop his images and symbols beyond a certain conventionality (or blandness), lest they distract from what he wishes the reader to see.

Some of the recurring imagery that suggests this facet concerns a character's physical language (or body language) to express an emotional state. The hands, eyes, the face, and certain typical gestures provide the chief manifestations that, in some form or other, attach to Storm's characters in all his works. Elisabeth's hands in *Immensee*, revealing her sorrow, come to mind: "Und diese blasse Hand verriet ihm, was ihr Antlitz ihm verschwiegen hatte. Er sah auf ihr jenen feinen Zug geheimen Schmerzes, der sich so gern schöner Frauenhände bemächtigt, die nachts auf krankem Herzen liegen."[16] In *Aquis submersus*, the eyes in Katharina's portrait painted by Johannes tell the old aunt (Bas Ursel) that the young lady is in love, and Hauke Haien's flashing eyes describe his anger or his fierce pride. Likewise, white and red roses denote sorrow and passion. Musical elements, chiefly the leitmotif, but also purely lyrical passages in otherwise objectively conceived narrative situations (or simply in contrast with the realism of the novella) are typical for this musical quality of Storm's language. The figure of old Matten in *Zur Chronik von Grieshuus* punctuates her speeches with the words, "Bei

Gott ist Rath und That!"[17] (when the actual situation suggests otherwise). Magister Bokenfeld, the narrator of the second part of the same novella, refers to the wolves by the phrase, "Der Wolf, der griese Hund," giving the role the beasts play in the story a kind of foreboding quality to emphasize the state of decline for the house of Grieshuus and echoing the motif of violence struck early in the novella when Squire Hinrich kills his brother in a duel. It was Walter Silz who pointed to the "mood value" of the musical elements in *Der Schimmelreiter*.[18] One such example makes clear the lyrical quality of Storm's prose whenever he wishes to impress upon us an especially deeply felt occasion (usually a feeling of horror or loneliness in the face of transitoriness): we are made to feel the horror that still broods over the desolate beach (after a storm) where the hideous corpses were lying and the loneliness into which Hauke Haien, still a boy, ventures: "Er lief weiter und weiter, bis er einsam in der Öde stand, wo nur die Winde über den Deichen wehten, wo nichts war als die klagenden Stimmen der grossen Vögel, die rasch vorüberschossen; zu seiner Linken die leere weite Marsch, zur anderen Seite der unabsehbare Strand mit seiner jetzt vom Eise schimmernden Fläche der Watten: es war als liege die ganze Welt in weißem Tod."[19]

A brief look at one of Storm's best-known poems, "Über die Heide," will show clearly the importance of the cliché and its monotonous effect as an atmospheric device:

> Über die Heide hallet mein Schritt;
> Dumpf aus der Erde wandert es mit.
>
> Herbst ist gekommen, Frühling ist weit—
> Gab es denn einmal seelige Zeit?
>
> Brauende Nebel geisten umher;
> Schwarz ist das Kraut und der Himmel so leer.
>
> Wär ich hier nur nicht gegangen im Mai!
> Leben und Liebe—wie flog es vorbei![20]

The poem was written in 1875, recalling a time with Constanze, ten years after her death, in the course of a visit to Segeberg, her birthplace. It fuses the memory of shared happiness with the muffled echo from the steps on the ground, alluding to death as the anonymous companion ("wandert es mit") during the walk. The dark quality of the vowels in "dumpf" and "wandert" further suggests the meaning for the neutral pronoun "es." In the last couplet the unrounded and front vowels in "wär," "hier," "im Mai," and the alliteration of the two nouns in the last verse ("Leben und Liebe") dissolve the act of recalling into almost pure sound, a soft lilt that signals the overpowering feeling of nostalgia for that moment of happiness long ago. The heavy stress on the opening and closing syllables in every verse (the dactylic-trochaic meter and masculine rhymes) provides the weighty beat for the somber atmosphere of death. It is not difficult to see that "Über die Heide" is not at all a moorland poem, but one of leave-taking, a final farewell to the memory of his wife. The poem is almost pure sound and rhythm, evoking a mood. The commonplace of the heath and the entirely evocative character of the poem contrast with its complex structure. The two-part lines ("Langzeilen") in verses 3, 6, and 8 lend additional weight to the second half of each verse ("Kurzzeilen"). Thus every half-line ("Kurzzeile") emphasizes one thought, the feeling of transiency: "Frühling ist weit," . . . "Der Himmel so leer," . . . "wie flog es vorbei." The reminiscent mood of the poem culminates in sheer fright: "Wär ich hier nur nicht gegangen im Mai!" The conventional imagery further amplifies the morbid atmosphere, since the profound and essential rhythm is more important than the poem's thought content. The sentimental "so" in "der Himmel so leer," which renders the image of the empty sky in purely emotional terms (the only flaw in the poem, by the way), shows the problematical side of Storm's precept of the pure lyric. In this way, the immediate experience and cliché blend completely (according to Storm's lyrical canon the poem must be the immediate expression of an experience). The alliteration "Leben und Liebe" and the month of May are as commonplace as love and spring. The pronoun "es" of the second verse would be another instance of conventional poetic association, namely that of the heath as the habitat of demons and ghosts. Hence the heath as a landscape plays no role at all; rather, it is a very personal point of departure, something very necessary for Storm as a link with his own inner world—or as a point of reference in an otherwise chaotic universe.

In most of his novellas, Storm used a similar technique. Here, as well as in his poetry, the unique, the private experience, had to stand for the whole. We said earlier that by far the greater number of his novellas involve a narrator represented by a figure in the story as one of the guises the author assumes ("authorial medium," according to Stanzel). Frequently, in the frame tales of his later period (mostly his chronicles), the narrator (as chronicler) introduces the story as the chance discovery of certain facts, data, faded manuscripts, an old ruin and the like, to create the illusion of authenticity for what follows.

Turning to certain structural features for a moment, let us examine some of its aspects in *Ein Doppelgänger* and *Hans und Heinz Kirch*. *Ein Doppelgänger* belongs to the type where the author functions as a temporary first-person narrator in the frame as well as in the story proper.

Only, this once, Storm appears practically undisguised as a "lawyer and poet" in the opening and closing frames. This appearance of the writer goes beyond the ambiguities of an authorial narrator, because it occurs on the same level with Storm's authorial mask and private identity. Moreover, the "familiar sounds of home" ("der Heimatklang") in the narrator's native Low German accent support the thesis that narrator and author are identical. The tale of John Hansen alias John Glückstadt, devoted father and husband as well as ex-convict, would clearly make this a story whose meaning and reason for being lie in the distorted image his surviving only daughter has of her father. Its meaning would also rest with the personal plight of a former criminal who is willing and anxious to be reintegrated into society. It also rests with the issue of social conditions in Storm's time. As has been pointed out elsewhere, however, there is one structural element that contradicts this interpretation and reinforces the subjective link that the narrator establishes at the beginning of his story by making it clear that he has a personal interest in it. In the concluding segment of the frame the narrator remarks unexpectedly that he had been in a dreamlike state while recounting the story of the two lives and sides of John Hansen:

Mir kam allmählich das Bewußtsein, daß ich weit von meiner Vaterstadt im Oberförsterhause an dem offenen Fenster stehe; der Mond schien von drüben über dem Walde auf das Haus, und aus den Wiesen hörte ich wieder das Schnarren des Wachtelkönigs. Ich zog meine Uhr: es war nach eins! Das Licht auf dem Tische war tief herabgebrannt. In halb-visionärem Zustande—seit meiner Jugend haftete dergleichen an mir—hatte ich ein Menschenleben an mir vorübergehen sehen, dessen Ende als es derzeit eintrat, auch mir ein Rätsel geblieben war. Jetzt kannte ich es plötzich.[21]

This surprising admission lends a different emphasis to the story itself and to its conclusion in the frame. Since the humanitarian impulse of fusing the two disparate sides of her father's life for Christine was the narrator's justification for the entire narrative in the first place, the narrator's trancelike state conflicts with his reason for the story's being. If it is mere fiction, then the temporary first-person narrator might have admitted to its subjective nature from the outset. Indeed, one might infer that the real role of the narrator was to make the dreamlike vision the object of interest and not its discovery and denouement. It is a narrative perspective, therefore, which borders closely on the interior monologue technique, and once more shows Storm to be a precursor to the impressionist writers and their subjective style. The vision itself is one of tragic fate, that is, the story represents the tragedy of an individual within Storm's purview. Therefore, *Ein Doppelgänger* is not concerned primarily with the plight of a social class or the author's intent to moralize or even to issue a call for social change.

Hans und Heinz Kirch, written entirely in third-person style, concerns a "culpa patris" theme of sin and expiation. There are structural incongruities, however, that tend to obscure the issue of crime and punishment and hence of genuine tragedy. There are lyrical scenes in the novella which exist chiefly to protect its tragic core but also to betray (unintentionally) the narrator's involvement. The tragic core (or more accurately, pathetic core) consists of two elements, namely the transitoriness of youth, love, and innocence, and of the conflict between father and son that is ordained by fate and circumstances. The final scene between the old man, Wieb (Heinz Kirch's fiancée), and the social democrat, a carpenter, serves to cast some light upon the author's intention: Hans Kirch says to the carpenter, "Er ist tot, aber in der Ewigkeit, da will ich meinen Heinz schon wieder kennen." To the disreputable carpenter, whom the townspeople called the "social democrat" and who interrupted Hans Kirch with the question, "Was haben wir Menschen mit der Ewigkeit zu schaffen?," he now replies, "Du kennst mich wohl nicht, Jürgen Hans? Ich bin Hans Kirch, der seinen Sohn verstoßen hat, zweimal! Hörst du es, Jürgen Hans? Zweimal hab ich meinen Heinz verstoßen, und darum hab ich mit der Ewigkeit zu schaffen!" The carpenter's answer is, " . . . 'Das tut mir leid, Herr Kirch,' . . . und wog ihm trocken jedes seiner Worte zu, 'die Ewigkeit ist in den Köpfen der alten Weiber!' "[22] It is characteristic of Storm that he leaves the final answer open. Neither the rationalistic skepticism of the carpenter (which largely corresponds to Storm's personal opinion in religious matters) nor Hans Kirch's predilection for the visionary (the reader has no knowledge of his son's fate, except the father's vision of his son's death at sea) is held to be absolute truth. The ironic description of the carpenter (he is described as a small mind, tending toward smugness in his anticlericalism) implies a critical distance to his point of view as well, and Hans Kirch's visionary (or supernatural) experience points to no more than a potential answer to the question. But the narrator knows that if a reconciliation is possible at all, it will be so in eternity or never. The tragedy is that life could not resolve the conflict—only death could. He says of Hans Kirch after Heinz's disappearance, "Heinz hatte sich gemeldet [as an apparition], Heinz war tot, und der Tote hatte alle Rechte, die er noch eben dem Lebenden nicht mehr hatte zugestehen wollen."[23] At the end of the story we see Hans Kirch old, broken, and feeble and Wieb utterly distraught and helpless: the one filled with remorse and grief over personal guilt, and the other with the pathos of fate that seems utterly arbitrary, with death the ultimate victor.

Theodor Storm's lifelong flirtation with the motif of the supernatural and his artistic struggle with the integration of private experience projected upon an objective frame of reference found its resolution in *Der Schimmelreiter,* which was completed in 1888, the year of his death. As he wrote to Paul Heyse in 1886, "weiterhin in Arbeit: Der Schimmelreiter, eine Deichgeschichte; schwierig, denn es gilt eine Deichgespenstersage auf die vier Beine einer Novelle zu stellen, ohne den Charakter des Unheimlichen zu verwischen."[24] Storm achieves this intended blending of legend and reality by employing a triple frame involving three narrators. The story (the term "character novel" would not be out of place)[25] represents an optimum of objectivity in his works, because it succeeds in integrating the author, i.e., the first-person narrator, into the narrative without sacrificing the objective attitude of the two narrators of the second and third frames. The opening frame introduces the author-narrator who cannot recall the exact title of a magazine, where he had once come upon the tale of the rider on the white horse in his youth. What he does recall, however, he now has the author of the magazine story tell us. He, in turn, proceeds to tell how he had come upon the tale of Hauke Haien on a stormy day at an inn near the Hauke-Haien Dike. There, an aging schoolmaster relates—in the third person—the story proper.

It is perhaps fair to say that the novella's basic technique rests on deliberate ambiguity. Without committing himself, the author presents reason and irrationality, intelligence and ignorance, enlightenment and superstition in constant juxtaposition. This principle determines the structure of the whole. The triple frame is not only, as Silz points out, a proper setting for such a rich painting inside,[26] but also an integral part of its structure. The narrator of the opening frame thus emphasizes the fact that he cannot recall the exact source for his story nor vouch for its accuracy. By this means he contrives to give its contents a greater degree of probability than if he had insisted upon the truth of it. A similar effect is achieved by the other two narrators. The magazine narrator relates only the "actual" story just as he heard it from the schoolmaster. He is for this reason reporting fact rather than fiction:

Da der Zeitschrift-Erzähler nur eine Mittlerfunktion hat, wirkt seine Erzählung von dem gespenstischen Reiter als die Wiedergabe eines Tatsächlichen. Die unheimliche Erscheinung ist damit als etwas Wahrscheinliches in die Erzählung eingeführt. Die Gültigkeit dieses Phänomens wird sehr bald unterstrichen durch die Reaktion der in der Gaststube Versammelten auf den Bericht des Ankommenden: Eine "Bewegung des Erschreckens" geht durch sie. Für sie alle hat der Schimmelreiter offenbar eine ganz konkrete Bedeutung.[27]

The balance achieved in the narrative is one of giving equal space to the superstitious fears and ignorance of the villagers and to Hauke Haien's intelligence and high level of awareness. Moreover, the rationalistic schoolmaster with his modern skepticism contrasts with the uncanny subject of his tale. Again, as has been shown before, the schoolmaster's attitude toward his story must be taken with a grain of salt. He is described as a sickly and deformed man who is critical of society and his mental inferiors and who loves to champion in Hauke the representative of the enlightenment. This puts the proper perspective upon the schoolmaster's words in the closing frame "when he aligns Hauke Haien with Socrates and Christ as one of those spiritual leaders whom humanity has 'ever crucified and burned'."[28] Both enlightened figures, Hauke and the schoolmaster, are not only set off from the supernatural aspects of the story, but they are also linked with them. The phantom rider appears three times. Each time he is acknowledged as a real occurrence by his observers. Immediately preceding his second sighting, even the schoolmaster is moved to remark, "Weiß Gott Herr! Es gibt auf Erden allerlei Dinge, die ein ehrlich Christenherz verwirren können."[29] This transformation of the hero into a supernatural phenomenon has been criticized as being in direct conflict with the neutral narrative perspective toward the rational and irrational in the story. We would suggest, however, that the novella's real aim was to create the myth of a modern tragic hero whose legend, as exemplified by his creation, his monument, the dike, survives, and whose tragedy stands as a meaningful sign in a quasi-Faustian sense. It is, of course, not the Goethean promise of a metaphysical redemption but points to the possibility of a transcendental meaning to reality.

To return to some structural considerations: just as there is a bipolar structure to the story as a whole, so there is a notable dialectic of the death motif as a collective and an individual tragedy, that is, as a deterministic and an ethical problem.

First, deterministically, nature is seen as a deadly and vicious force (the storm, the sea) and so is the central motif of death, which occurs about midway in the novella in the form of an inscription on the headstone of the last dikegrave: "Dat is de Dot, de allens frit,/ Nimmt Kunst un Weetenschop di mit,/ De kloke Mann is nu vergahn,/ Gott gäw em selig Uperstahn."[30] Its central location in the novella makes this motif one of prefiguring not only Hauke's death, but the death of all men. At the center of the tale stands the dike, symbolically providing the battle line between darkness and enlightenment (between the hostility of the villagers, and specifically their leader Ole Peters, and Hauke's superior intelligence) and between man and natural disaster. It is also the line between the natural and the supernatural, the sea constantly gnawing at its foundations and man's defenses being eroded.

The individual side of the tragedy, on the other hand, is of equal importance. The personal, ethical guilt of the hero is stated in classic Aeschylean terms. Hauke is guilty of hubris, the overweening pride that is in violation of the natural order of things—to be sure, only in an ethical and moral sense, because of the absence, here, of any concept of universal myth or *ordo mundi*. His pride in the new polder, his life's work, prompts him to think: "Hauke-Haien-Koog! Hauke-Haien-Koog! In seinen Gedanken wuchs fast der neue Deich zu einem achten Welt-wunder; in ganz Friesland war nicht seinesgleichen! . . . er überragte sie [the Frisians] um Kopfeslänge, und seine Blicke flogen mitleidig und scharf über sie hin."[31] A fatal flaw causes his undoing when he permits himself to be persuaded, against his better judgment, to have only superficial repairs in the dike carried out. Again, in classical terms, the hero is conscious of his tragic guilt: "Herr Gott, ja, ich bekenne es, ich habe meines Amtes schlecht gewaltet!"[32] Hauke's death, finally, is an act of self-sacrifice for the sake of his work, the dike, and as an ac-knowledgment of the myth-giving power of the people who, earlier, during the construction of the new dike, wanted to immure a dog, because only a living being could secure the dike. Hauke, then, had prevented the sacrificial rite. Accordingly, he not only atones for his guilt but also secures his legend, and thus his death is more than just an act of despair or his material extinction, an ending otherwise so preva-lent in Storm's work.

As Jost Hermand has pointed out, there is also a monumental side to Hauke's character[33] who, in some ways, like Nietzsche's superman, represents the ideal of a *Gründerzeit* hero in the imperialistic age of Bismarck. The tragic hero, then, is Storm's tentative answer to the vicis-situdes of the materialistic nihilism of his age. To be sure, ethics as a substitute for a universal order, monumentality, but also genuine tragedy make Storm's myth of a modern tragic hero an eclectic concept.[34] Yet, measured against the almost exclusively deterministic view of tragedy in his other works, his frequent sentimentality and, at times, escapist atti-tudes, *Der Schimmelreiter* with its fully contoured hero, who is held accountable for his actions and who is at once real and mythical, repre-sents Storm's crowning achievement.

As we have seen, the typology of Storm's realism is constituted by the pathetic and tragic aspects of his work. The pathetic aspect is repre-sented by the phenomena of escapism and conventionality and the tragic aspect by his will to transform reality whenever he employs the motifs of the supernatural and myth. The quintessential problem of Storm's poetry and prose lies in the intended portrayal of genuine tragedy. Yet the frequently resulting sentimentality proves that there exists a discrepancy between a world devoid of meaning and the constant struggle of the poet to infuse it with sense through the nexus of ethos of middle-class life and the nexus of continuity provided by history. His realism fundamentally was a matter of subjectivity, that is, of representing private experience as the reality that is the most profoundly moving of all. Storm's problem was that he could never quite overcome the difficulty posed by a technique of writing that insisted on separating objective reality from experienced or subjective reality. Only in *Der Schimmelreiter*, by balancing the real and the mythical, did he succeed in creating a genuinely tragic effect without leaving the question of personal experience and outward order unresolved.

Storm's realism is closely linked with the problem of nineteenth-century realism in general. In the absence of any unifying concept that can assign a total meaning to reality and that is the precondition for any classical literature, the artists of the time could only deal with its fragments and bestow a meaning upon the pieces that they did not actually possess. One sign for this fragmenting of reality was the overwhelming preference for short forms of literary expression such as the novella and the short story. This tendency toward an open-ended approach to reality wherein only subjective or private experience played a role (*Der Schimmelreiter* notwithstanding) culminates in the near total subjectivity of Impressionism whose outward manifestation was the increasing absence of plot resulting, for example, in purely atmospheric prose and a preference for one-act plays. In this sense the representatives of "Poetic Realism"—Theodor Storm among them—can be regarded as the forerunners of the symbolists and impressionists whose aestheticism signified the ultimate capitulation in the struggle against a meaningless reality.

NOTES

[1] Thomas Mann, *Adel des Geistes: Sechzehn Versuche zum Problem der Humanität* (Stockholm, 1955), pp. 460 ff.

[2] Paul Böckmann, "Theodor Storm und Fontane," *Schriften der Theodor-Storm-Gesellschaft*, XVII (1968), 88, 92.

[3] Erich Auerbach, *Mimesis. Dargestellte Wirklichkeit in der abendländischen Literatur* (Bern, 1946), pp. 399, 458; Georg Lukács, *Deutsche Realisten des 19. Jahrhunderts* (Berlin, 1951), p. 5; Robert Minder, *Der Dichter in der Gesellschaft* (Frankfurt a/M, 1966), pp. 145 ff.

[4] Lukács, *Deutsche Realisten des 19. Jahrhunderts*, pp. 5–6, 13.

[5] "Briefwechsel zwischen Theodor Storm und Emil Kuh," ed. Paul R. Kuh, *Westermanns Monatshefte*, LXVII (1890), pt. 1, p. 107 (September 1872).

⁶ Lukács, *Deutsche Realisten*; Peter Goldammer, *Theodor Storm. Eine Einführung in Leben und Werk* (Leipzig, 1966); Fritz Böttger, *Theodor Storm in seiner Zeit* (Berlin, 1958); H. E. Teitge, *Theodor Storms Briefwechsel mit Theodor Mommsen* (Weimar, 1966).

⁷ To Storm, man's tragic existence is seen essentially in the fact of human suffering and mortality; but it is also seen in man's self-assertion and struggle in the full knowledge of his limitations, thereby implying a higher human potential beyond Storm's own explicit definition of tragedy, which is purely mechanistic. For the latter point, cf. "Was der Tag giebt," unpublished diary (1880–1883), Landesbibliothek Schleswig-Holstein, pp. 2–3.

⁸ Elmer Otto Wooley, "Storm und Bertha von Buchan," *Schriften der Theodor-Storm-Gesellschaft*, II (1953), 20.

⁹ Richard Brinkman, *Wirklichkeit und Illusion. Studien über Gehalt und Grenzen des Begriffes Realismus für die erzählende Dichtung des 19. Jahrhunderts* (Tübingen, 1957).

¹⁰ On the question of Storm's concealment as the author of his prose, cf. Hannelore Faden, *Die Physiognomie des Erzählers bei Storm*, Diss. Frankfurt a/M 1954, pp. 1–10. For a definition of the terms "author" and "narrator," cf. Franz Stanzel, *Narrative Situations in the Novel: Tom Jones, Moby-Dick, The Ambassadors, Ulysses*, trans. James Pusack (Bloomington, 1971), pp. 23–27, and Wayne Booth, *The Rhetoric of Fiction* (Chicago, 1961), pp. 70–73. It should be noted that by the definition of these critics the narrator (whether or not he appears as a figure in a novella) is only one of the masks of the implied author. Also, the authorial narrator (or implied author) is to be distinguished from the private identity of the writer. Within the framework of the various modes of narration then, the authorial presence is always only one of many fictional guises.

¹¹ From an unpublished letter to Wilhelm Petersen. Cf. Clifford Bernd, *Theodor Storm's Craft of Fiction*, 2d ed. (Chapel Hill, 1966), p. 57.

¹² Cf. Storm's unpublished diary, 1 October 1880, pp. 2–3.

¹³ *Sämtliche Werke*, ed. Peter Goldammer, 2d ed. (Berlin, 1967), I, 184. Hereafter, *G*.

¹⁴ *Sämtliche Werke*, ed. Albert Köster (Leipzig, 1920), VIII, 210. Hereafter, *K*.

¹⁵ *G*, I, 771 ff.

¹⁶ *K*, I, 301.

¹⁷ This is one of only 82 proverbs in Storm's works. Storm's use of proverbs, moreover, is atmospheric rather than didactic. Cf. Wolfgang Mieder, "Die Funktion des Sprichwortes in Theodor Storms Werken," *Schriften der Theodor-Storm-Gesellschaft*, 22 (1973), 95–114.

¹⁸ Walter Silz, *Realism and Reality* (Chapel Hill, 1962), p. 128.

¹⁹ *K*, VII, 262.

²⁰ *G*, I, 192. For a close analysis of the poem, especially its prosodic elements, cf. Walter Silz, "Theodor Storm's 'Über die Heide'," *Studies in German Literature of the Nineteenth and Twentieth Centuries: Festschrift for Frederic Coenen*, ed. S. Mews (Chapel Hill, 1970), pp. 105–10.

²¹ *K*, VII, 191. This observation was first made by Hannelore Faden, *Physiognomie des Erzählers*, pp. 115–17.

²² *K*, VI, 123 f.

²³ *K*, VI, 121.

²⁴ *Heyse-Storm Briefwechsel*, ed. Georg Plotke (München, 1918), 29 August 1886.

²⁵ The length, the episodic character, and the undramatic nature of the story justify the term. The last point is supported by the fact that "erzählte Zeit" and "Erzählzeit" are constant, i.e., no particular event is singled out around which everything else is grouped.

²⁶ Silz, *Realism and Reality*, p. 123.

²⁷ Volker Knüfermann, "Realismus. Untersuchungen zur sprachlichen Wirklichkeit der Novellen 'Im Nachbarhause links', 'Hans und Heinz Kirch' und 'Der Schimmelreiter' von Theodor Storm," Diss. Münster 1967, pp. 99–100.

²⁸ Silz, *Realism and Reality*, p. 118.

²⁹ *K*, VII, 264.

³⁰ *K*, VII, 301.

³¹ *K*, VII, 346.

[32] *K*, VII, 372 f.

[33] Jost Hermand, "Hauke Haien, Kritik oder Ideal des gründerzeitlichen Über-
menschen?" *Wirkendes Wort*, 15 (1965), 40–50.

[34] On balance, it can be said that the whole effect, determinism and personal guilt, adds to Hauke's eclectic but impressive stature as a tragic hero—a myth that could signify a spiritual renewal in the sense of Nietzsche's superman. One cannot single out any one element, such as reason or superstition, as representing the true meaning of the novella.

Judith-Aurelie-Seraphine
Zu Arthur Schnitzlers Komödie der Verführung

William H. Rey

Verführer—!
Gibt's denn so was wirklich?

Die folgenden Ausführungen sind veranlaßt durch das im Jahre 1973 erschienene Buch von Ernst L. Offermanns, *Arthur Schnitzler. Das Komödienwerk als Kritik des Impressionismus*, das eine der bedeutsamsten Leistungen der zeitgenössischen Schnitzlerforschung darstellt. Der Verfasser schildert den Weg Schnitzlers von den frühen Vorformen der Komödie (*Reigen, Kakadu, Wurstl*) zu den Komödien des Eros (*Zwischenspiel, Das weite Land*) und schenkt den sozialen und politischen Komödien (*Fink und Fliederbusch, Professor Bernhardi*) besondere Aufmerksamkeit. Denn hier tritt der Gesellschaftskritiker Schnitzler am deutlichsten hervor, der die äußere und innere Korruption seiner Zeit an den Pranger stellt. Das Verdienst Offermanns' besteht darin, mit der Legende von dem Impressionisten Schnitzler endgültig aufgeräumt und die Bedeutung des Komödienwerkes als kritische Auseinandersetzung mit dem impressionistischen Lebensstil erkannt zu haben. Am überzeugendsten wirkt seine Interpretation von *Fink und Fliederbusch* als satirischer Komödie—eine Interpretation, die einfach vorbildlich genannt zu werden verdient. Es erhebt sich jedoch die Frage, ob Offermanns in seinem durchaus berechtigten Bestreben, den Komödienautor soziologisch zu deuten und als Zeitkritiker zu sehen, nicht zu weit gegangen ist. Gewiß findet sich bei Schnitzler die kalte Leidenschaft des öffentlichen Moralisten, des Aufklärers, die ihn mit einem Zeitgenossen wie Karl Kraus verbindet. Aber er ist eine viel komplexere Natur, und sein Verhältnis zum Irrationalen, also zu der romantischen Welt von Traum, Liebe, Spiel und Tod, hat für das Werk eine ebenso große Bedeutung wie sein kritischer Rationalismus. Diese schöpferische Widersprüchlichkeit seines Wesens tritt nach unserer Meinung in Offermanns' Darstellung nicht deutlich genug hervor, und es scheint daher angebracht, einige Betrachtungen anzustellen, die Offermanns' These nicht eigentlich widerlegen, sondern sie vielmehr kritisch ergänzen sollen. Wir haben zu diesem Zweck Schnitzlers letztes großes Komödienwerk, die *Komödie der Verführung* (1924) ausgesucht und wollen unser Augenmerk vor allem auf die drei Frauengestalten (Judith, Aurelie, Seraphine) richten.[1] Zunächst aber müssen die allgemeinen Voraussetzungen von Offermanns' Auslegung geklärt und berichtigt werden.

Offermanns betont mit Recht die Bedeutung der historischen Zeit für die Handlungsführung. Um die Verflechtung der persönlichen Schicksale mit der Dynamik der Geschichte anzuzeigen, hat Schnitzler die Spielzeit der einzelnen Akte genau festgelegt. Der erste Akt spielt am 1. Mai 1914, der zweite Mitte Juni und der dritte am Tage des Kriegsausbruchs, dem 1. August 1914. Dieser 1. August ist nach Offermanns' Auffassung gleichsam der Fluchtpunkt von Schnitzlers Stück. Alle Handlungslinien führen zu ihm hin, alle Handelnden werden so oder so von der Katastrophe betroffen. Die Komödie führt geradewegs in den Weltuntergang.—Hier stutzt der Leser natürlich. Ein solches Thema eignet sich gewiß vorzüglich für eine Tragödie wie etwa *Die letzten Tage der Menschheit* von Karl Kraus. Aber wie in aller Welt läßt sich eine Komödie daraus machen? Es könnte sich nur um eine nihilistische Komödie handeln, die mit zynischem Gelächter die Nichtigkeit alles Lebendigen vor der Übermacht des Todes demonstrierte. In der Tat spricht Offermanns von einem "allgemeinen Tanz in den Abgrund," und er glaubt, daß die Figuren des Stückes "sich in nichts Wesentlichem von einander unterscheiden" (169).[2] Wenn diese Deutung zuträfe, wenn wirklich alles in die "nackte nihilistische Selbstzerstörung" (162) mündete, dann liefe das Formprinzip des Stückes auf ein Paradox hinaus. Der Dichter hätte in den drei Frauengestalten eine "Reihung von Varianten" (173) vorgeführt, nur um zu zeigen, daß alle drei Personen Abwandlungen des gleichen "problematischen Weltverhaltens" darstellen und deshalb der "universellen Destruktion" verfallen. Der eigentliche Zweck der Komödie wäre dann, die Wiener Vorkriegsgesellschaft in den letzten Phasen ihres Untergangs zu schildern. Das Gestaltungsprinzip der Variation diente ironischerweise dazu, die Monotonie der Destruktion noch zu unterstreichen.

Wenn man sich daran erinnert, daß Schnitzler einmal erklärt hat, der Dichter habe nichts zu beweisen als die Vielfalt der Welt, kann man Offermanns nicht ohne weiteres folgen. Es gibt einen Brief, den Schnitzler bald nach dem Erscheinen der *Komödie der Verführung* an Jakob Wassermann gerichtet hat und den Offermanns auch zitiert (176 f.). Dieser Brief erinnert uns an den Umstand, daß das Stück mehr als fünf Jahre nach dem Ende des Krieges abgeschlossen wurde und also im wesentlichen als Rückblick des Verfassers auf die Vorkriegszeit gelten muß. Wenn aber der Briefschreiber Schnitzler die Vorkriegszeit mit der Nachkriegszeit vergleicht, so kommt er zu der bestürzenden Schlußfolgerung, daß sich erstaunlich wenig geändert hat. Die Ambiguität des Krieges geht ihm auf. Einerseits wird immer wieder betont, daß eine Welt in ihm versunken sei. Andererseits ist "die angeblich versunkene und abgetane Welt . . . genauso lebendig und vorhanden als sie jemals war. In den einzelnen Menschen hat sich nicht die geringste Veränderung vollzogen."³ Daher vertritt er die Auffassung, daß die in der *Komödie der Verführung* auftretenden Gestalten kaum etwas von ihrer repräsentativen Bedeutung eingebüßt haben. Es zeigt sich also, daß der Dichter (trotz der genauen Datierung der einzelnen Akte) seine Figuren nicht als historisch gebunden betrachtet, daß er ihnen vielmehr eine überzeitliche Geltung zuspricht und daß infolgedessen sein Stück mehr sein muß als eine vernichtende Satire gegen die Wiener Vorkriegsgesellschaft.

Bei genauerem Zusehen erweist es sich denn auch, daß Schnitzlers Komödie außer der auf die Katastrophe zudrängenden Geschichtsdynamik ein zweites Konzept der Zeit zugrunde liegt, das kein solch apokalyptisches Gefälle kennt, sondern als Kontinuität und Wiederkehr in Erscheinung tritt. Inmitten der im Zeichen der Vernichtung stehenden Vergänglichkeit zeigt uns der Dichter die Dauer verbürgende Lebenskette der Geschlechter. Es ist ja gewiß kein Zufall, daß sich die Gestalten von Schnitzlers Komödie auf mehrere Generationen verteilen und so Vergangenheit, Gegenwart und Zukunft verbinden. Die eigentliche Handlung setzt die Gruppe der Jungen (um 20 Jahre), zu der die drei Mädchen und Max, ihr "Verführer," gehören, mit der Gruppe der Älteren (um 40 Jahre) in Beziehung. Hier finden sich die für das Schicksal Aureliens wichtigen Männergestalten: Falkenir, Arduin, Ambros. Ihnen ist altersmäßig eine Reihe von Figuren zugeordnet, die alle über 40 Jahre alt sind (Gysar, Westerhaus, die Fürstin). Auf sie folgt der "alte" Kammersänger Eligius Fenz, der wohl etwa sechzig Jahre zählt, und am tiefsten zurück in die Dimension der Vergangenheit reichen die beiden Uralten (über 80 Jahre), der pensionierte Kammersänger Meyerhofer und seine Kollegin, die Devona.

Am anderen Ende der Generationskette aber steht Gilda, die Tochter des Hoteldirektors Hansen, die nach den Angaben des Personenverzeichnisses 15 Jahre alt ist. Wenn nun am Schluß des Stückes der dem Alter zusinkende Don Juan-Darsteller Fenz als "Meergott" (D 947) zu der noch halb kindlichen "Nixe" Gilda in eine scherzhaft-erotische Beziehung tritt, so hat diese "vieldeutig-ironische Schlußapotheose" (164) eine tiefere Bedeutung, als Offermanns einzuräumen bereit ist. Sie markiert nämlich nicht nur das "Ende einer Epoche, die nur noch schöne Illusion war," sondern vielmehr die zyklische Kontinuität des Lebens, die sich unter der Oberfläche des historischen Wechsels ereignet. Daß sich Alter und Jugend gerade am Tage des Kriegsausbruchs, dem 1. August 1914, finden, darf als ein Hinweis auf die relative Bedeutung der politischen Katastrophe verstanden werden. Aus der Begegnung des "Nicht mehr" und des "Noch nicht" (164), wie Offermanns sehr richtig sagt, ergibt sich das mythische "Immer wieder"—ein Zeichen des Weltvertrauens, das die Skepsis Schnitzlers in fruchtbarer Widersprüchlichkeit ergänzt. Der stärkste Beleg aber für unsere These, daß sich in Schnitzlers Stück die Leitmotive Weltuntergang und Weltfortgang dialektisch verschränken, ist die Ankündigung des Kindes, das Seraphine von Max erwartet. Die Nachricht von dem Ungeborenen ist in Schnitzlers Stück mit der Nachricht von dem bevorstehenden Totentanz koordiniert. Der Ausblick auf eine noch ungeborene Zukunft jenseits der Katastrophe ist *eine* Rechtfertigung für Schnitzlers Entschluß, sein Stück eine Komödie zu nennen.

Es ist aber nicht eine Komödie schlechthin, sondern eine Komödie der Verführung, d. h. aber doch ein Stück, in dem der Akt der Verführung im Lichte der Komik oder der Ironie gezeigt wird. Dafür hat nun leider Offermanns wenig Verständnis. Über dem rigorosen Zeitkritiker vergißt er den tiefsinnigen Humoristen Schnitzler, und so nimmt er das Thema der Verführung tierisch ernst. Verführen hat für ihn erotische, moralische, intellektuelle und politische Aspekte (vgl. 129 und 165 ff.). Die Verführten fallen zunächst dem depravierten Eros zum Opfer, dessen Reiz ihre rationale Urteilsfähigkeit lähmt. Die Folge ist das Verfehlen ihrer wahren Identität und, dadurch bedingt, eine Tendenz zur Flucht aus der Wirklichkeit ins Irrationale, die zu individueller oder kollektiver Aggressivität und schließlich zur Selbstzerstörung führt. Ich-Zerfall und kollektiver Wahnsinn, die Hinwendung zu Spiel, Tod und Liebe einerseits und andererseits die aktive Provokation des Krieges sind nach Offermanns nur verschiedene Aspekte des gleichen zerstörerischen Vorgangs. Er setzt daher Schnitzler mit Brecht, den Verfasser der *Komödie der Verführung* mit dem der *Hitler-Choräle* in Verbindung und will in dem "Führer" die höchste Verkörperung des Verführers in Schnitzlers Sinn sehen.

Nach unserer Meinung handelt es sich hier um eine zwar höchst geistreiche, aber dennoch fragwürdige Interpretation, die Schnitzlers dichterische Eigenart zugunsten einer allzu großzügigen Generalisierung vernachlässigt. Es ist gewiß ein bestechender Gedanke, die europäische Kulturgeschichte von Lessing (*Emilia Galotti*) über Kierkegaard (*Entweder-Oder*) bis hin zu Brecht im Zeichen der Verführung zu sehen. Aber der Dichter, der aus dem Akt der Verführung eine Komödie macht, will nicht recht in diese Landschaft passen. Und zwar aus einem sehr einfachen Grund: In Schnitzlers Stück *wollen* die Verführten verführt werden, und das führt zur ironischen Selbstaufhebung dieses Motivs. Die vielerfahrene Frau des Bankiers Westerhaus stellt daher mit gutem Grund die Frage, die wir als Motto gewählt haben, ob es denn so etwas wie Verführer überhaupt gebe (D 905).

In seiner ausgezeichneten Analyse des "Verführers" Max von Reisenberg zeigt Offermanns bei allen kritischen Vorbehalten doch Verständnis für die vielfältige ironische Gebrochenheit dieser Figur. Zwar versucht er zunächst, Max als Nachfahren von Mozarts Don Juan darzustellen, der nach Kierkegaard die dämonische Naturmacht des Eros repräsentiert (133). Aber sehr bald räumt er ein, daß dieser erotische Abenteurer, der allen seinen Liebespartnern Heiratsanträge macht und schließlich auch noch als Vater von Seraphines ungeborenem Kind "Zukunft stiftet" (134), gar kein echter Don Juan ist. Anstatt seine Opfer zu zerstören, dient er "als der 'Erwecker' aller drei Frauen, die erst durch ihn auf den Weg zu sich selbst gelangen" (134). Damit ist die Funktion von Max als erotischer Katalysator, die übrigens an manche von Hofmannsthals Abenteurergestalten erinnert, völlig zutreffend charakterisiert. Hier überwindet der feinfühlige Interpret Offermanns seine vorgefaßte Meinung und kommt unserer Schlußfolgerung nahe, daß eine Verführung der Verführten zu sich selbst kaum noch als Verführung zu bezeichnen ist. Vielmehr tritt in diesem Zusammenhang die erzieherische Intention des Komödienautors hervor, der diese paradoxe Verführung zu sich selbst als eine notwendige Phase des menschlichen Reifeprozesses betrachtet und dessen pädagogische Komödie so in die Nähe parodistischer Bildungsromane wie etwa des *Zauberbergs* rückt. (Beide Werke wurden 1924 veröffentlicht.)

Was der "Verführer" Max einleitet, ist ironischerweise ein Prozeß der partiellen Selbstverwirklichung, der zu verschiedenen Ergebnissen führt, je nach den vorgegebenen Veranlagungen und Lebensumständen der einzelnen Partner. Dabei ist zu betonen, daß keine der drei Frauen als dekadentes Produkt einer dekadenten Gesellschaft erscheint. Sie sind ursprünglich keineswegs Repräsentanten des impressionistischen Lebensstils, dürfen also nicht zu "süßen Mädeln" degradiert werden. Vielmehr sind sie alle potentiell auf eine volle Selbstverwirklichung angelegt, in der sich Trieb und Gesetz, Eros und Ethos verbinden. Die Desintegration der in den Krieg taumelnden Gesellschaft schließt aber eine solche Versöhnung von Es und Über-Ich im Sinne des klassisch-humanistischen Ideals aus. In seinem Stück stellt Schnitzler die Frage, ob und wie der einzelnen Frau angesichts der hereinbrechenden Katastrophe eine ihr gemäße Teilerfüllung möglich sei. Die Entscheidungen der drei Frauen sind also nach unserer Meinung nicht Symptome der allgemeinen Destruktion, sondern sie stellen mehr oder weniger überzeugende persönliche Alternativen zum Sturz in den Weltuntergang dar. Die Aktualität dieser Komödie beruht auf dem Umstand, daß sich unsere Situation, bei allen zeit- und raumbedingten Unterschieden, seit 1914 grundsätzlich kaum geändert hat. Unter der Drohung einer neuen Weltkatastrophe, angesichts des Zerfalls der sozialen Ordnung und der moralischen Werte gewinnt heute die Frage nach der Möglichkeit menschlicher Selbstverfügung erhöhte Bedeutung.

Im Gegensatz zu den Mädchengestalten des Frühwerks (Christine in *Liebelei*) sind die drei "Verführten" in Schnitzlers später Komödie nicht mehr naiv. (Darum können sie auch gar nicht verführt werden!) Sie sind vielmehr durch die Erfahrung der modernen Skepsis hindurchgegangen und wissen also all das, was Christine nicht begreifen konnte: daß die schönen Gefühle nicht dauern, daß Leidenschaft zerstörerisch wirkt, daß in der modernen Gesellschaft die klassische Versöhnung von Eros und Ethos nicht zu erwarten ist. Durch die Krise ihrer Zeit von sozialer Selbstverwirklichung ausgeschlossen, wenden sie sich den drei Zonen zu, die schon immer in Schnitzlers Werk von entscheidender Bedeutung waren, die aber nun als Alternativen zu dem Wahnsinn der Wirklichkeit dienen, dem Spiel, dem Tod und der nicht-legitimierten Liebe.

Nach Offermanns' Auffassung ist dies Eskapismus. Wir meinen einen Akt der Freiheit darin erblicken zu dürfen, das mutige Ergreifen einer individuellen Form des Lebens oder Sterbens, das zugleich einen Protest gegen fragwürdige gesellschaftliche Klischees, wie etwa die konventionelle Ehe, bedeutet. Bei Judith ist dieser Zusammenhang ganz offenkundig, denn sie hat die Hölle einer modernen Ehe, nämlich die ihrer Schwester Julia mit dem Bankier Westerhaus, aus nächster Nähe miterlebt. Ihr Ekel, ihr moralischer Abscheu gegen eine solche legalisierte Form gegenseitiger Zerstörung ist so stark, daß sie darauf verzichtet, Westerhaus für sich selbst zu "erobern" (D 907)—obwohl sie ihn liebt. Sie, die "ein armes, kleines, verwundetes Herz [hat]" wie eine Nähmamsell" (D 907), verbringt ihre erste Liebesnacht an der Bahre des von seiner Frau in den Tod Getriebenen. In der Einsamkeit der Totenkammer wird sie "wissend" (D 930), hier erlebt sie im voraus alle "Wunder, alles Grauen des Daseins"—sogar ihren eigenen Tod. So erfährt sie die Tragik menschlicher Existenz in einer antizipierenden Vision und kann daher sagen, daß ihr Dasein "eigentlich schon hinter mir liegt" (D 930) und daß alles Kommende "nur wie ein Traum" sein wird. Diese Lebensform des quasi Gestorbenseins erlaubt ihr, die Last des Wirklichen abzuwerfen. Indem sie den Lebensstil der erotischen

Abenteurerin wählt, die nur das Glück des Moments anerkennt, verzichtet sie zwar auf die echte menschliche Erfüllung in Liebe, Leid und Schicksal, aber sie tut dies in dem Wissen, daß unter den gegebenen Umständen eine solche Erfüllung für sie zur Illusion geworden ist. Und sie gewinnt eine beachtliche Autonomie gegenüber den demütigenden Zwangsläufigkeiten einer auch die "Liebe" verdinglichenden Gesellschaft. Offermanns setzt ihre "impressionistisch-fiktive Lebensform" (144) mit Recht als "durchaus sentimentalisch" gegen die Naivität des erotischen Abenteurers Max ab. Dies bedeutet aber, daß der dekadente Impressionismus Anatols hier eine überraschende Relevanz gewinnt— und zwar als kritische Reaktion gegen die Versklavung des Menschen durch den spät-kapitalistischen Materialismus.

Die Analyse der Gestalten Falkenirs und Aureliens gehört zu den glänzendsten Partien von Offermanns' Buch (148–59). Er schildert überzeugend, wie Aurelie, beseelt von dem Drang nach echter Selbstverwirklichung, in der Bindung an den geliebten Falkenir Erfüllung zu finden hofft. Der Erwählte aber, gequält von der Angst vor den dämonischen Triebmächten, die er in Aurelie wirksam sieht, weigert sich, diese Bindung einzugehen, und legt ihr nahe, ihr wahres Ich durch die völlige Preisgabe an den dionysischen Lebensrausch zu finden. (Schnitzler nimmt hier ein Motiv aus der Erzählung *Die Hirtenflöte* wieder auf.) Falkenirs Schuld gegenüber Aurelie besteht darin, daß sie, seinem Rat folgend, die Integration von Trieb und Geist verfehlt und stattdessen von einem Extrem zum anderen taumelt: Aus der prä-existentiellen "Märchenfee" (151) wird durch die Vermittlung Maxens die "Mänade." Es versteht sich von selbst, daß die wahre Aurelie in keinem dieser Extreme zu finden ist. Aber ironischerweise glaubt sie, in der "Mänade" ihr wirkliches Ich entdeckt zu haben. Dagegen sinke ihre vorherige Existenz zu "Maske und Lüge" (D 962) herab. Einerseits ist sie also durch Verführung und Selbsthingabe nach ihrer Meinung zur Wahrheit über sich selbst durchgebrochen, und Offermanns spricht mit Recht von ihrer "forcierten Gebärde des Triumphs über ihre Selbstbefreiung" (154). Andererseits aber besitzt sie genug sittliche Substanz, um ihre "Selbstfindung als Verworfenheit" zu sehen. Damit erreicht der schon vorher potentiell in ihr angelegte Konflikt zwischen Eros und Ethos seinen Höhepunkt. Die ursprünglich auf Selbstintegration ausgerichtete Aurelie tritt uns im dritten Akt im Zustand der Selbstzerrissenheit entgegen, und das große Thema ihrer Gespräche mit Falkenir, der nunmehr seine Fehlentscheidung bereut, ist die Frage, ob und wie die Spaltung ihres Wesens geheilt werden könne.

Wieder also geht es um das Problem der Selbstverwirklichung—wie bei der Begegnung der Beiden im ersten Akt. Aber unterdessen hat sich das Verhältnis der Dialogpartner gewandelt. Nun ist es Falkenir, der um Aurelie wirbt und ihr mit seiner Liebe Sicherheit, Zuflucht, Heimat und Frieden bietet (D 951 f.). Es ist leicht zu sehen, daß in seinem Angebot gerade die Macht fehlt, deren überwältigende Dämonie Aurelie mittlerweise erfahren hat—der Eros. Falkenirs Konzept einer auf Verstehen, Verzicht, Vergeben begründeten Ehe (D 964 f.) ist einseitig ethisch orientiert und setzt, wie Offermanns richtig erkennt (156), die Verdrängung der elementaren Sexualität voraus. Aurelie ahnt, daß in einer solchen Ehe die erotischen Triebe, die Falkenir als "Gespenster der Vergangenheit" (D 953) bezeichnet, wieder empordrängen und sie beide in "Scham und Verzweiflung" (D 965) stürzen werden. Trotz ihrer Liebe zu Falkenir scheint ihr die Gewalt des Triebhaften so groß, daß sie eine echte Versöhnung von Eros und Ethos in der Ehe ausschließt. Da die Treue keinen Ort in dem triebbeherrschten Leben hat, bietet sich den Liebenden als letzte Zuflucht—der Tod. Es ist bedeutsam, daß die Nachricht vom Kriegsausbruch ihr Gespräch an entscheidender Stelle unterbricht (D 954). Für Aurelie kann sie nur als eine Bestätigung ihrer These von der Übermacht der Triebe erscheinen. Daher hat es also einen tiefen Sinn, daß sie ihren Entschluß zum gemeinsamen Selbstmord mit Falkenir am 1. August 1914 faßt und ausführt. Im gleichen Augenblick, in dem Europa dem Wahnsinn der Aggression verfällt, finden die Liebenden den Frieden, den ihnen das Leben versagt hat, im Meer. Wie schon angedeutet, interpretiert Offermanns die zeitliche Koinzidenz dieser Ereignisse als sachliche Analogie. Unter Berufung auf Freud bezeichnet er Kriegsausbruch und Selbstmord, Sadismus und Masochismus, als "Äußerungsformen des *einen* Spannungszustandes, der in der Unaufhebbarkeit des Antagonismus von 'Es' und 'Über-Ich'" besteht (161). Ja, die Selbstzerstörung der Liebenden schließt nach seiner Meinung eine versteckte Bejahung des Weltuntergangs durch die gegenseitige Zerstörung der Hassenden ein, und so zögert er nicht, Schnitzlers Aurelie mit Wagners Brünhilde und deren Verlangen nach der "Götterdämm'rung" in Verbindung zu bringen (161).

Träfe dieser Vergleich zu, so müßte in der Tat das gemeinsame Ende von Aurelie und Falkenir im Meer als "Ausdruck eines völligen Determinismus und völliger Hoffnungslosigkeit" (161) gelten. Wir weigern uns jedoch zu glauben, daß Schnitzler seine beiden Charaktere als unbewußte Komplizen der für den Krieg verantwortlichen Massenmörder konzipiert habe. Im Gegensatz zu deren Sadismus ist der "Masochismus" der Liebenden durchaus ethisch motiviert. Letzten Endes geht es ihnen um die Rettung der Treue, der wahren Liebe und damit der menschlichen Würde vor den elementaren Lebensmächten.[4] In diesem Sinn kann ihr gemeinsames Sterben als Selbstopfer betrachtet werden, das im äußersten Gegensatz zu dem im Kriege ausbrechenden Willen zur Macht steht. Gewiß sind sie zu einer "rationale[n] Bewältigung" (162) des Gegensatzes von Trieb und Geist nicht imstande, aber dies ist bedingt durch ihr Schicksal, in einer Epoche der katastrophalen Triebentladungen geboren zu sein. Eine Versöhnung von Es und Über-Ich durch den Einzelnen zu erwarten in dem Augenblick, in dem sich die Vater-Länder der Gewalt des Es in die Arme werfen, wäre völlig unrealistisch. Die einzige Freiheit, die dem Individuum unter diesen Umständen gegeben ist, ist die Freiheit zum Tode.

Nach unserer Meinung kommt diesem Motiv der Freiheit, das in der deutschen Literatur bis hin zu Schiller und Lessing immer wieder auftritt, eine entscheidende Bedeutung für Schnitzlers Stück zu, wenn es seinen Titel, *Komödie der Verführung*, zu Recht tragen soll. Ohne die lächelnden Augen der sterbenden Aurelie ("Ganz glückselig lächelten sie," D 973) verwandelt sich die Komödie in eine nihilistische Orgie der Selbstzerstörung, als die sie Offermanns auch tatsächlich darstellt. Um seiner vorgefaßten Meinung willen muß er darauf verzichten, dieses glückselige Lächeln zur Kenntnis zu nehmen. Für ihn handelt es sich um "das resignierende Lächeln" (164) Aureliens, und das Ergebnis ihres letzten Gespräches mit Falkenir ist "eine aus völliger Ungeklärtheit und hoffnungslosem Einander-nicht-verstehen herrührende stumme Resignation" (171). Demgegenüber ist festzuhalten, daß Schnitzler in dem Lächeln Aureliens die paradoxe Einheit von Selbstgewinnung und Selbstverlust angedeutet hat, die ein verklärendes Licht über den Gemeinschaftstod im Meer wirft. Daß die "Nixe" Gilda (nach Offermanns Repräsentantin einer "verspätete[n] Nixenromantik," 160) den Bericht über diesen Tod erstattet, kann dessen Sinn nicht beeinträchtigen. Ja, der Titel des Stückes gewinnt hier noch eine tiefere Bedeutung als im Zusammenhang mit Judith. Denn Aurelie provoziert nicht nur ihre "Verführung" durch Max—sie will den Weg der Leidenschaft zu Ende gehen; sie meint, ihr wahres Selbst in der Hingabe an den Lebensrausch zu finden und muß erfahren, daß es schließlich der Tod ist, der ihr das Lächeln der Erfüllung schenkt. Ihr Liebestod ist als Komödienthema nur möglich aufgrund der Einsicht des Autors in das uralte Mysterium, das Eros und Thanatos verbindet.

Es ist sehr begreiflich, daß Offermanns nicht zu viel über die dritte Frauengestalt, Seraphine, zu sagen hat, denn sie steht im stärksten Widerspruch zu seiner Deutung des Stücks als Darstellung der "universellen Destruktion" (173). Er ist zwar durchaus bereit, ihr eine Ausnahmestellung einzuräumen, aber der Leser soll den Eindruck gewinnen, daß diese Ausnahme eher die Regel bestätigt, als daß sie sie aufhebt. Er gibt jedoch zu, daß Seraphine "eine Art von 'impressionistischer Sittlichkeit' als Vorstufe zu neuer Kontinuität" (163) verwirklicht, ohne uns allerdings im einzelnen zu erklären, wie sie das eigentlich macht. So sei also zunächst einmal festgestellt, daß in Seraphine eine der lebendigsten Frauengestalten erscheint, die dem späten Dramatiker Schnitzler geglückt sind. Ihre einfache Natürlichkeit liefert einen Farbton in der Konfiguration des Stückes, der sich wohltuend von der melancholischen Frivolität Judiths und der zuweilen etwas schwülen Melodramatik Aureliens abhebt. Obwohl ihr der Autor einen schmaleren Raum zugewiesen hat als der hochproblematischen Aurelie, kommt ihr doch eine einzigartige Bedeutung zu: Mitten im Weltuntergang hält sie, die werdende Mutter, die Dimension der Zukunft (und damit der Hoffnung) offen.

Daß Schnitzler in seiner Komödie das Motiv der Verführung ironisch behandelt, zeigt sich ganz deutlich bei ihr. Denn die engelgleiche, ewig-reine Seraphine demonstriert ihren Willen zur "Verführung" am auffälligsten. Auf dem Maskenfest im ersten Akt wirft sie ihrem ahnungslosen "Verführer" gleich drei Rosen vor die Füße, damit er sie nur ja nicht ignoriert, und sie bietet ihm auch eine passende Gelegenheit, indem sie ihn in ihr Haus einlädt. Ihr Benehmen müßte als aufdringlich gelten, wenn es nicht legitimiert wäre durch den natürlichsten Wunsch, den eine Frau haben kann. Seraphine will mit dem geliebten Mann glücklich sein und ein Kind von ihm empfangen. Das darf sie ihm allerdings erst sagen, als alles vorbei ist, und der erstaunte Vater in den Krieg ziehen muß (D 970 f.). Denn der von ihr erwählte Vater ihres Kindes ist ja Max, der Prototyp des erotischen Abenteurers, und Seraphine kennt diesen Typ ganz genau. Sie weiß, was man von ihm erwarten darf—und was man nicht von ihm erwarten darf, und sie liebt ihn auf die einzige Art, auf die er geliebt werden kann: als der, der er nun eben ist. Noch einmal tritt so in Schnitzlers dramatischem Werk das reine Mädchen dem Abenteurer entgegen, aber diesmal ist sie bewaffnet mit dem skeptischen Wissen ihrer Zeit. Dies erlaubt ihr, nicht nur den erotischen Glanz, sondern auch die menschlichen Schwächen ihres Partners zu sehen. Sie durchschaut ihn als einen eitlen, treulosen, leichtsinnigen Menschen (D 878), dem man seines Charmes wegen doch nicht böse sein kann. Sie spielt die Strenge, sie erweist ihre Überlegenheit, indem sie ihm zu verstehen gibt, daß sie sich über ihn lustig macht (D 881). Wie schade, daß Offermanns den eigenartigen Reiz dieses Dialogs nicht sieht und von einer "Plauderei im besten Anatol-Stil" (135) spricht.

Allerdings, die Überlegenheit Seraphines ist erkauft durch den bewußten Verzicht auf die volle Selbstverwirklichung als Frau und Mutter in der Ehe. Es genügt nicht zu sagen, sie suche "der Illusion auszuweichen" (136)—Seraphine *hat* keine Illusionen. Wie Judith und Aurelie weiß sie, daß unter den gegebenen Zeitumständen die Liebe nicht dauern kann. Das subjektive Gefühl hat in der zusammenbrechenden Gesellschaftsordnung kein objektives soziales Äquivalent. Aber anders als Judith und Aurelie entscheidet sich Seraphine gegen das Glück des Moments und gegen den Frieden des Todes. Mit einer rührenden Tapferkeit nimmt sie den überzeitlichen Lebensauftrag auf sich, Mutter zu sein—ohne Mann und ohne legalen Schutz. Von Anfang an geht es ihr darum "zu ihrem Kind den richtigen Vater zu finden" (D 863), und dies Ziel erreicht sie mit dem, was man die List der weiblichen Vernunft nennen könnte. Was Offermanns "impressionistische Sittlichkeit" nennt, ist also eigentlich die Überwindung des Impressionismus durch das Ethos opferbereiter Mütterlichkeit.

Als das Erstaunlichste an diesem Vorgang muß die Wiedergewinnung des echten Seelentones in Wort und Gebärde gelten. Der Zauber der Liebesszene zwischen Seraphine und Max im zweiten Akt (der einzigen des ganzen Stückes!) beruht darauf, daß hier von Täuschung und Betrug keine Rede sein kann. Nüchtern und herb spricht Seraphine die Wahrheit aus: "Daß dies ein schöner Abend ist—der niemals wiederkehrt" (D 928). Aber das Wissen um die Flüchtigkeit des Glücks, um die Unzuverlässigkeit des Liebespartners führt bei Seraphine nicht zu der melancholischen Frivolität des impressionistischen Menschentyps, sondern zu vertiefter Empfindung. Die Wärme des echten Gefühls wird wieder möglich, weil sie gleichsam durch die Kälte der Skepsis und des Verzichts hindurchgegangen ist. So kann Seraphine dem Abenteurer Max am Anfang der Szene von ihrer verstorbenen Mutter erzählen, so gewinnen konventionelle Gesten (ihr Kuß auf sein Haar, sein Kuß auf ihre Stirne) neue Bedeutung. Im Rückblick will es Seraphine sogar so scheinen, als ob das Wissen um die Einmaligkeit ihrer Liebesnacht "vielleicht das Allerschönste dran" (D 971) sei. Das Unwiederholbare des Glückes ist für sie kein Anlaß zur Trauer—sie sieht darin vielmehr das Signum echter Liebe.

Zum Schluß sei wenigstens noch ein Hinweis auf den sorgfältig angelegten Aufbau des Stückes, vor allem des dritten Aktes, gegeben. Schnitzler hat offenbar Wert darauf gelegt, Todes- und Lebensmotiv so miteinander zu verschränken, daß der Untergang Aureliens und Falkenirs im Meer gleichsam eingebettet ist in die zukunftsweisenden Gespräche zwischen Seraphine und Max. Wir hören zunächst von Gilda, daß Aurelie ein Boot bestiegen hat und im Begriff steht, hinauszurudern. Ergriffen von einer angstvollen Ahnung, stürzt Falkenir zum Strand, der auf der Bühne nicht sichtbar ist (D 968). Aber dann bricht der Autor diese Szenenfolge ab und schaltet das Hauptgespräch zwischen Seraphine und Max ein, in dem Max von seiner Vaterschaft erfährt (D 969–71). Dieses Gespräch hinwieder wird abgelöst von dem Bericht Gildas über den Liebestod Aureliens und Falkenirs (D 972–73). Darauf folgt der Abschied Maxens von Seraphine. (Sie "nimmt seinen Kopf in ihre Hände, küßt ihn auf die Lippen," D 974). Und wir erfahren von ihrem Entschluß, am Ort zu bleiben, um die Toten zu erwarten. Sie, die werdende Mutter, wird bereit sein "zum Empfang, wenn sie nachts ans Ufer treiben" (D 974).

ANMERKUNGEN

[1] Alle Zitate sind dem zweiten Band der *Dramatischen Werke* (Frankfurt am Main, 1962) entnommen und mit dem Zeichen D und Seitenzahlen in Klammern versehen.

[2] Ernst L. Offermanns. *Arthur Schnitzler. Das Komödienwerk als Kritik des Impressionismus* (München, 1973). Alle Zitate mit Seitenzahlen in Klammern.

[3] Schnitzlers Brief wurde veröffentlicht in der *Neuen Rundschau*, LXVIII (1957), 98 f.

[4] Wenn das Motiv des Liebestodes in Schnitzlers Komödie mit Wagners Werk in Verbindung gebracht werden soll, dann ist weder an Siegfried und Brünhilde, noch an Tristan und Isolde zu denken. Vielmehr ergibt sich eine gewisse Analogie zu Senta und dem Holländer, auf die Andreas Török in seinem Aufsatz "Der Liebestod bei Arthur Schnitzler: Eine Entlehnung von Richard Wagner," *Modern Austrian Literature*, IV/1 (1971), 57–59, hingewiesen hat. Offermanns zitiert diesen Artikel (231).

Hadrian, Antinous, and a Rilke Poem

George C. Schoolfield

I

The Emperor Hadrian, who is the speaker of Rilke's "Klage um Antinous," has enjoyed considerable popularity among poets, not least because he belongs to their guild: "Fuit enim poematum et litterarum nimium studiosissimus." One of his own poems, from the tiny corpus of imperial verse accepted as authentic,[1] has been frequently anthologized and as frequently translated. The famous poem, of course, is Hadrian's "address to his soul," the "animula vagula blandula," the companion and guest of the body, the soul, which now is about to go off to some unknown place, all wan and numb and naked, "pallidula rigida nudula," unable, as of old, to jest, "nec ut soles dabis jocos." The translators have been many, some of them distinguished, all of them longer-winded than was the dying emperor: Ronsard ("Amelette Ronsardelette,/ Mignonnelette, doucelette"), Prior ("Poor little pretty fluttering thing"), Herder ("Ach Seelchen, armes Seelchen!"), Byron ("Oh gentle, fleeting, wav'ring sprite"), and, in distant Finland, Frans Michael Franzén ("Själ lilla!/ Stilla! Fladdrerska,/ Pladdrerska./ Än en minut,/ Flämtande,/ Skämtande,/ Njut!"). The poem has been paraphrased, too. Jakob Bidermann had his actor Philemon, in the seventeenth-century Jesuit martyr-play, sing a parody on it before his assumption of a Christian role and a Christian martyrdom.[2] Turning the pagan master of the world into a pious communicant, Pope threw out the diminutives, expanded the five short lines into three six-line strophes, and ended with a climax that would become familiar to all of us:

> O Grave, where is thy victory?
> O Death, where is thy sting?

And Richard Le Gallienne, changing Pope's title, *A Dying Christian to His Soul* to the—for the 1890s—more topical *The Décadent to His Soul*, did not remove himself as far from Pope's Christian standpoint as the new title would make us think:

. . . the soul wept with hollow hectic face,
Captive in that lupanar of a man.
And I who passed by heard and wept for both,—
The man was once an apple-cheek dear lad,
The soul was once an angel up in heaven.

II

Apart from being a poet, Hadrian had a second sort of reputation that also attracted literary attention: his affection for beauty. He loved handsome things, and among these handsome things was the Bithynian boy, Antinous, whom he made his favorite during one of those incessant imperial journeyings of his: accompanying his master to Egypt, the boy was drowned while the imperial barge was sailing up the Nile. The loss of Antinous caused Hadrian exquisite pain. According to the *Vita Hadriani* of Aelius Spartianus, the emperor wept for him like a woman: "quem muliebriter flevit." Spartianus, who appears to have flourished toward the end of the third century, regarded these events of 130 A.D. with some distaste—that is, if any emotion at all can be detected in his dull accountings. "According to some," Spartianus says, Antinous killed himself "out of devotion to Hadrian," and, "according to others, on that account which both his beauty and Hadrian's excessive sensuality ['nimia voluptas Hadriani'] suggest. However this may be, the Greeks deified him at Hadrian's request."

The other historian to whom we owe our main knowledge of Hadrian's reign, Dio Cassius, stood a good deal closer to Hadrian's time than did Aelius Spartianus; Hadrian died in 138, and Dio Cassius was born in 150—in Bithynia, by the way, the homeland of the sorely lamented favorite. In book 69 (or, rather, Xiphilinus' surviving epitome of it) Dio Cassius tells how Antinous dies: "either by falling into the Nile, as Hadrian writes in his autobiography [which has been lost], or, as the truth is, by being offered in sacrifice." The latter phrase is less terrifying than it sounds; Antinous had "voluntarily undertaken to die (it being necessary that a life should be surrendered freely for the accomplishment of the ends Hadrian had in view)." (Another chronicler, the fourth-century Aurelius Victor, puts the cause of the sacrifice more clearly: "When Hadrian wished his life lengthened, but the mages declared that another must sacrifice himself in his place, all the others refused, but Antinous offered to die.") The lost youth was handsomely rewarded for his sacrifice by his bereaved master; Hadrian had a city built—Antinoë or Antinoöpolis—at the spot where Antinous had so devotedly done away with himself; he set up statues, or rather sacred images, of the boy "practically all over the world," and "finally, he declared that he had seen a star which he took to be that of Antinous, and gladly lent an ear to the fictitious tales woven by his associates to the effect that the star had really come into being from the spirit of Antinous and had then appeared for the first time. . . . On this account, then, he became the object of some ridicule."

But not just ridicule: the Antinous cult flourished, poets wrote verse in Antinous' praise, verse now, to our good fortune, mostly lost; and, as Pausanias (himself a contemporary of the dark events on the Nile) writes in his description of the art treasures of the ancient world, "I have not seen Antinous alive, but I have admired his portraits and his statues." It was an admiration that would be shared, understandably enough, by future connoisseurs of ancient art and fair boys: Winckelmann describes some of the Antinous statues he had seen in the *Geschichte der Kunst des Altertums* (XII, 1, 17). On the other hand, Antinous and his cult, with its "Antinous games," provided water on the scandalized mill of the Christian fathers. The words of one, Prudentius, may stand for the indignant arguments of many: "What shall I say of Antinous now placed in a celestial seat,/ Antinous, the delight ["delicias"] of a divine prince,/ Antinous despoiled of a masculine fate in an imperial embrace." The relationship between Hadrian and his young friend was culpable first of all because emperor and favorite were of the same sex, and then because Hadrian had deified his lover—a savior-youth, having sacrificed himself for the sake of another and having been placed among the stars, could make even triumphant Christianity uncomfortable.[3] The very thought made Tertullian rage: "Quo decorior Ganymedes aut carior suo amatori? . . . Passim scorta ascendunt," he wrote in *Ad nationes*. "Everywhere, the whores are going up to heaven." It was from this Christian tradition of hatred for Antinous that the Jesuit Bidermann took some details of his play *Philemon*, mentioned in connection with Hadrian's poem above; Bidermann locates the action in Antinoë, the city of paganism at its worst.

III

The tale of Hadrian and Antinous experienced a new popularity during the second half of the nineteenth century. In 1851, before going off to Rome, the young Ferdinand Gregorovius had been encouraged by his teacher Wilhelm Drumann to publish a little book about the life and times of Hadrian. In 1883, Gregorovius, now world-famous, decided to issue a revised version of his book, in part, he says in his introduction, because no one else had written a scholarly work about this "merk-würdigen Kaiser," in part because new material, mainly in the form of inscriptions, had come to light during the last thirty years. Yet there was also publisher's wisdom behind the republication; Hadrian, *cum Antinoo*, had become a popular item in the world of fiction. In 1881, the Egyptologist and historical novelist, Georg Ebers ("dieser liebevolle Gelehrte," as the young Rilke once called him) published still another of his successful historical fictions, this one called *Der Kaiser* (in two volumes): the book dealt with Hadrian and closed with the death of Antinous. The relationship between master and favorite, it should be added (Ebers was not the man to fly directly in convention's face), is depicted in what may be called a "respectable" light; the couple engages in lengthy conversations and naught else. The suicide of Antinous is brought about by a number of causes: a Christian girl, upon whom Antinous' eye has fallen with normal (if well-controlled) emotions, has been slain after her refusal to worship the emperor's graven image; Antinous is likewise upset because Hadrian entertains plans of adopting him and thus making him a successor to the imperial throne, a post for which he—"der nicht von heute auf morgen zu denken vermochte"—has small qualifications; and finally (the story of the self-sacrifice) Antinous means to protect his master from a horrible fate predicted by an Egyptian prophetess. In short, Antinous is a deeply disturbed youth: "Schmerz, Unruhe, Un-glück starrten ihn an, wohin er auch schaute." A solution, or an escape, lies close at hand: "Da lag der Nil, da war ein Kahn," and, after some powerful oarstrokes have put Antinous in midstream, he slips over the side and goes gurgling to the bottom. Learning of the youth's death, Hadrian refuses to see anyone, not even his wife Sabine, who has come along for the Nile excursion; he vents his emotions in a somewhat complicated monologue. First, in order to calm any fears on the gentle reader's part, Ebers injects a flat contradiction of Spartianus' "quem muliebriter flevit," and then takes care to have Hadrian make it clear that he loved Antinous as a father would: "Könnte ich nur weinen wie die Weiber, oder wie andere Väter, denen der Tod ihre Söhne entreißt; das wäre meine beste Arznei." Having thus made his bow in the direction of nineteenth-century moral convention, Hadrian is free to behave like a pagan emperor, and he does, threatening his retinue ("Ihr Armen werdet es nun schlecht haben, denn die Sonne meines Lebens hat ihren Glanz verloren"), and then telling the whole of humanity that it will have to partake in his laments: "Die ganze Menschheit soll mit mir klagen," because it has lost, in "der treue Geselle" (a phrase somewhat out of place: another sop to the century?), an example of "die Schönheit der Götter," and of "übermenschliche, göttliche Treue."[4]

Ebers is not the only scholar-author who found Antinous attractive. At the beginning of the 1880s, Professor Adolf Hausrath of the University of Heidelberg fell prey to an eye-ailment that forced him to spend three months in a darkened room. During this time, he composed a novel, called *Antinous*, in his mind; released from confinement, he put it down on paper, and published it in 1881, using the pseudonym George Taylor. It was a measured critical success, in both its original German and the English translation (1882); as for Hausrath, he went on to other glories and became rector of the university in 1882. The book of Hausrath-Taylor, coming out the same year as *Der Kaiser*, readily bears comparison with the better-known work: it is much shorter and comes considerably closer to frankness about the relationship between the emperor and the boy. The friendship was, in Hausrath's view, a seduction, the story, to quote the English translation, of "how a healthy nature was ruined by companionship with a diseased one." Thus the expression of melancholy, so often seen in the representations of Antinous,[5] is accounted for. The motives of Antinous, who ties his own hands in order to prevent himself from swimming, are mixed, as in *Der Kaiser*; but here the mixture is subtler and more believable. He is oppressed by a feeling of guilt at the affair with Hadrian; he has found Christian associates whose faith may have rubbed off on him, for all his opposition to it; he is directly unhappy because the girls laugh at him as "Hadrian's handsome peacock"; he is convinced that if Hadrian dies he will be cast out of the imperial household; and he thinks, finally, that he can prolong the life of Hadrian, to whom he—despite all—is devoted. Still more interesting than the emotional confusion of Antinous, however, is the portrait of Hadrian: an egoist, something of a bully, something of an opportunist, who seizes upon the death of Antinous as a means of controlling "the millions of souls entrusted" to his care. He tells the Christian Phlegon, "When I see how Antinous' image appeals to the heart, I believe that I have found the right means. In a century, Antinous will be a god like Mithras, while no one will speak of your crucified Jew." Hadrian, to be sure, has a moment of insight, in the midst of his somewhat gruesome statesmanship, when he remarks, "My love has brought a curse on everyone. My own Person was my god, and now I am left alone with myself."

For at least two German authors of the turn of the century, Antinous' homosexuality need not be muted, or ignored, in order that the Bithynian youth might become a figure of essential goodness, richly devoted to a demanding master. In *Die Bücher der Hirten und Preisgedichte* (1895),

Stefan George entitled a poem, addressed to the young Belgian Edmond Rassenfosse, "An Antinous"; in it, he thanked "Antinous" for the latter's well-meant attempts to console the bard in his sadness at having to leave Rassenfosse behind in Brussels. Then, in the *Fünfte Folge* of *Blätter für die Kunst* (1900–1901), George's disciple, Friedrich Gundolf, published *Antinous: Dramatisches Gedicht in drei Teilen*; we must assume that the publication had the master's approval.[6] In Gundolf's *Antinous*—which, for the rest, makes us glad that Gundolf forsook George's circle and creative writing for creative literary history—Hadrian, burdened with care, is charmed by the flute-playing youth whom pirates have carried away from Bithynia. After having ascertained that Antinous is uninterested in "der reiz der frauen"—"Zum reigen trieb die breite lust die anderen/ Mir blieb die flöte"—Hadrian invites the flutist to forget that the careworn gentleman addressing him is an emperor, and Antinous does his level best to oblige:

> Ich habe begriffen was uns beiden geschah
> Ich küsse das siegel auf deine verlangende seele
> Ich fühle dein siegel auf meinem brennenden auge
> Laß mich in Dir vergehn! dein bin ich. nimm mich hin!

After an interlude comprised of an *andante amoroso*, Hadrian decides in the third and concluding part that Antinous does not love him for himself alone. "Zermalmt doch nimmer entsagend," Antinous decides to throw himself into the Nile, trusting that his act will restore Hadrian's faith in him, and that he, indeed, will become a part of Hadrian's somewhat nebulous religion:

> Empfangt mich ihr heiligen wasser und werdet schwer
> Von meinem schmerz! vor meinem kaiser heilt ihr mich
> Zum elemente werd ich das er gläubig ehrt.

There is, then, a sympathetic literary attitude toward Antinous, which tries to find the cause, or causes, of the melancholy expression that he was customarily given in antique statuary. Having called attention, in an essay from 1874, to Rafael's effort to "Christianize" Antinous in the Jonah-fresco of the Chigi chapel,[7] the Swedish author Victor Rydberg, in a poem, conjectured that Antinous' melancholy resulted from the deified boy's contemplation of the "mysteries of being":

> Hvad ser han då, som fängslar så hans syn?
> Hvad bådar under kransen vemodsskyn?
> O, om hans sorgset blida anlet är
> en spegel för det varandes mystèr![8]

On the other hand, five years later, the Dane, Herman Bang, in his first novel, *Haabløse Slægter*, saw Antinous not as a handsomer and not necessarily soteriological version of the sorrowing Christ, but rather as a pathetic human being. The hero of Bang's novel, young William Høg, has become the friend and adept of Bernhard Hoff, an elegant and apparently blasé man of letters. On the mantel in Hoff's living room there are three busts, of Venus, Niobe, and Antinous; the last is given a full interpretation by Hoff: "the bust is that of a poor child, given more to bear than he was able, an early sorrow, an all too early experience, a great secret or something of the sort. No matter what it was—his shoulders could not bear its weight, and so he closed his mouth upon his own outcries, and let the waters of the Nile and Acheron come between the world and himself!"[9] Subsequently, the Swedish admirer of Bang, Ola Hansson, wrote, in *Tidens kvinnor* (1891), about the two aspects of love, the one "physical, full of blood," the other milder and gentler, a "moonlit Antinous-face." The heroine of Hansson's novella "Gallblomma" ("Gall Flower") is revolted by the first (copulation) and yearns to find the second, to her mind a mixture of spirituality and what Hansson calls "epidermal sensuality," a sensuality of touch and no more.[10]

Opposed to this "good" Antinous of German and Scandinavian authors, an Antinous always self-sacrificing, always gentle, sometimes nearly divine, sometimes pathetically human, there appears, in other literatures of the *fin-de-siècle*, an Antinous who stands for a perverse sexual allure or even cruelty: indeed, he can become a topical figure, reduced from a portrait to a reference. This Antinous is the seducer or the seducer's talisman, not the seduced; Hadrian either vanishes or becomes Antinous' victim. In *The Romantic Agony*,[11] Mario Praz has cataloged a good many of the Antinouses of the French authors of the *décadence*, or of its forerunners: Barbey d'Aurevilly's Major Ydow in "À un dîner d'athées" in *Les Diaboliques* (1874), wreaking unspeakable sexual vengeance upon his unfaithful wife; Verlaine's "Hercule à vingt ans, Antinous à trente" in "Extrêmes-onctions" (1890), slain by a girl as he forces her to commit an unnatural act; Rachilde's (Marguerite Eymery's) *Monsieur Vénus* (1889), a woman who whips herself into a frenzy of lust (for young men whose "maleness" is less pronounced than hers) by keeping a bust of Antinous in her boudoir; the Princess d'Este in Sar Péladan's *Le Vice suprême* (1884), who likes boys reminiscent of "l'affranchi d'Hadrien"; the main figure of Jean Lorrain's (Paul Duval's) *Monsieur de Phocas* (1901), who, inspired by the Antinouses of the Louvre and Naples's Museo Nazionale, makes an erotomaniac search for human

beings with eyes like those that, he imagines, these statues should possess ("Si ce buste m'appartenait, je ferais incruster des émeraudes dans
ses yeux"). Amusingly, the authors of French *décadence* are in a position
much like that of the Christian fathers; they imply that they are shocked at
the very rottenness of the youth, or at the rottenness that his images (or
living reproductions) arouse in their viewer. Also, they are more diplo-
matic in sexual matters than might have been expected, for they attempt
to keep the love in which Antinous is involved "heterosexual," mean-
while never abandoning the suggestion of perversion.[12] Only Jean Lorrain is frank about the homosexuality of Antinous, as is apparent not
only in *Monsieur de Phocas,* but also in *Le Vice errant* (1902), where two
traveling Englishmen, Lord Feredith and Sir Algernon Filde, own a
private yacht called *Edward III:* we are told that the ship might have been
called the *Cydnus,* after Hadrian's Nile barge, since Algernon himself is
the author of a book called *Hadrien sur le Cydnus.* Before issuing these
novels, Lorrain had already included a poem about Antinous in the
series on "Les éphèbes" in his collection, *L'ombre ardente* (1897),[13] a
poem that says that, after "siècles méconnus," the boy—or rather his
"handsome, transparent feet," which Hadrian massages with his "mains
avares"—will walk in triumph anew: "Et font revivre, hélas! mille ans
après ta mort,/ l'ère auguste des dieux et des amours bizarres."[14] Lorrain's Lord Feredith had been suggested by Lord Alfred Douglas, and
his Algernon Filde, it goes almost without saying, by Oscar Wilde.[15]

    Wilde, of course, had himself not let slip the opportunity of using
the Antinous reference as a code for the beauty that is evil and destroys.
As the painter Basil Hallward tries to confess his love to Dorian Gray,
and to tell the handsome youth that he has painted his portrait, he
says, in somewhat ominous praise of Dorian's spiritual lineage:
"Crowned with heavy lotus blossoms you had sat on the prow of Ad-
rian's barge, gazing across the green turbid Nile." Poor Basil does not
heed the warning signal he himself has sent, or has not read enough of
recent French literature to know how dangerous loving an Antinous
may be; he becomes one of Dorian's victims.[16] In Wilde's literary opinion, Antinous was, in fact, alluring enough to move inscrutability's very
statue; in Wilde's poem, "The Sphinx," the stone creature is addressed:

> You heard from Adrian's golden barge the laughter of Antinous
> And lapped the stream and fed your drouth and watched with
>   hot and hungry stare
> The ivory body of that rare young slave with his
>   pomegranate mouth!

The rare young slave of this French-English line is quite a different sort, it is plain, from the pensive melancholiacs of the German-Scandinavian tradition.[17]

IV

When Rilke wrote his *Klage um Antinous*, then, the name of the imperial favorite meant various things to various readers: the beautiful boy long appreciated by readers of Winckelmann, the sad self-prober and, perhaps, savior, the often dangerous object—or perpetrator—of "amours bizarres." What Rilke intended to say with his title, and, more important, with the text subjoined to it, provides one of the countless riddles of Rilke-scholarship—or, if the term will be allowed, of Rilke-philology.

It is a riddle that no one has made a serious effort to solve. The most extensive discussion of the poem is to be found in Hans Berendt's *Rilkes Neue Gedichte* (1957), a discussion that, despite certain insights, to which we shall return later on, offers still another example of Berendt's obstinate wrong-headedness.[18] In her excellent book on *Der Neuen Gedichte anderer Teil*, Brigitte L. Bradley brings up the poem in passing.[19] (Two other recent reflections on the *Neue Gedichte* do not mention it at all.)[20] It might be expected that some words on the poem could be found in the several considerations of "Rilke und die Antike": but Harry Mielert,[21] who wrote first on this altogether interesting topic, does not mention Antinous, nor does Zinn,[22] in his fine and detailed treatment of the theme, nor do Werner Kohlschmidt[23] and Katherina Kippenberg.[24] The suspicion crosses our minds: perhaps the poem does not fit under the rubric of "antiquity" at all—evidently it does not for these scholars, of whom at least two were trained classicists. Perhaps the very topic smacked too much of decay, of that Roman decay that, we know, the decadents (permanent or temporary) of the nineteenth century, and beyond, found so attractive: remember Gautier's famous musings on the gaminess of the Latin of the later Empire, "la langue marbrée déjà des verdeurs de la décomposition et comme faisandée," Des Esseintes' quite unclassical passions in Latin literature (of which we get a sweetened echo in Le Gallienne's *Book-Bills of Narcissus*), even the fascination which Heliogabalus had for Poe, Jean Lombard, Stefan George, Louis Couperus.[25] A discussion of the *Klage um Antinous* does turn up, in passing, in a monograph devoted to Rilke's views of a sometime outpost of empire; in *Rilkes ägyptische Gesichte*, Alfred Hermann includes the poem because of its Egyptian locale, offering a somewhat condescending summary of what is taken—perhaps rightly—to be the poem's main thought: "[die Klage] wendet die Sache so, daß schuldhafte Ursache für die Entrückung des Geliebten die mangelnde Liebeskraft des Kaisers gewesen sei."[26] In truth, Hermann is mainly interested in making an impressive religious-historical point in connection with the poem's second line: that Rilke knew the story, told in the Westcar papyrus, of a magician who bent back the waters of the Nile at the behest of King Snofru, in order that a piece of jewelry, lost in the depths by a rowing-girl, could be found. To those who admire Rilke's inventiveness, it seems not unlikely that the image of seizing the waters was Rilke's own. To be sure, it can readily be shown that the poet may have known the story from Gressmann-Ungnad-Ranke's *Altorientalische Bilder und Texte zum alten Testament*, but the book appeared in 1909, a year after the publication of the second part of the *Neue Gedichte*.

A first question to be asked about the *Klage um Antinous* concerns the date of its composition. Berendt gives the date 1903–04, on the grounds that Rilke probably saw the famous Antinous-relief in Winckelmann's Villa Albani during his Roman winter. Here, Berendt leaves two facts out of account: 1) that the directly datable material in the second part of *Neue Gedichte*—the vast majority of the poems, in other words—all comes from 1907 or 1908; 2) that the Rilke of the middle period did not customarily compose directly after "inspiration"—a time span of some months often came between impetus (if the impetus can be identified) and production. Ernst Zinn's approximate dating of the poem (made, we must guess, on the basis of notebooks in the Rilke-archive) is a better one than Berendt's: Zinn says "Herbst 1907, Paris, oder Frühling, 1908, Capri."[27] Thus, the *Klage* was written either after Rilke's first stay on Capri (from December 1906 to May 1907) or during his second one (from the end of February to the middle of May 1908). If we are to believe, with Berendt, that the *Klage*'s composition was prompted by the contemplation of a piece of antique art—and certainly there are plenty of examples of this sort of thing in the *Neue Gedichte*—then a dating in connection with Rilke's South Italian days has much to be said for it.

The traveler to Capri has to approach the island, unless he is a yacht-owner, like the Krupps, by way of Naples, and Naples was a city Rilke enjoyed—and in which he found certain art-collections of great appeal to him. He had gone there first, with Clara, in June of 1904, just before leaving Italy for Scandinavia. "Neapel war viel," he told Lou Andreas-Salomé from Castle Borgeby;[28] too much, indeed, to cram into the four days he was able to stay. The focus of his attention must have been the Museo Nazionale; at least, the Museum is what he mentioned to Clara when, alone, he passed through Naples again in late November 1906, on his way to shelter in the Villa Discopoli of Alice Faehndrich: "War heute endlich im Museum. Habe vieles wiedergesehen . . . Kleine Fragmente, einzelne Bronzen, Orpheus, Eurydike, Hermes; sehr viel Bestätigendes, Hilfreiches . . ."²⁹ His passion for the Museum did not abate. When Clara stopped off to see him on her way to Egypt, a month or so later, it was included in the Naples tour once more. Going into town that May, on his way back to Paris, he—aided by his hostesses—gave the Museum a farewell look;³⁰ and, a year later, again departing after his second Capri winter, he told Manon zu Solms-Laubach, one of the younger and lovelier Discopoli friends, that, "Ich trenne mich wieder so schwer . . . soll jeden Tag weiter und komme doch immer wieder ins Museum, zu den antiken Bildern vor allem, die von Jahr zu Jahr immer stärker, eigener, einziger auf mich wirken."³¹

The Museo Nazionale enjoyed a special reputation, in the literature of decadence, because of one of its treasures, or one of its collections. In Lorrain's *Le Vice errant*, Wladimir Noronsoff knows the places to appeal to his traveling English exquisites, Lord Feredith and Sir Algernon: "Le Musée de Naples, les fouilles et les fresques de Pompeii, voilá ce qu'il faut à ces Anglais." The Pompeii reference will be readily understood by us all, but what about the National Museum? A passage from a German novel, *Prinz Kuckuck* (1906–1907) of Otto Julius Bierbaum, will help. In its third part, "Der Hofmeister," the young and handsome hero, Henry Felix, goes to Naples in the doubtful companionship of his mentor, the homosexual Karl, elsewhere described in the novel as "weibisch und schleimig." Karl has had bad luck in the past; following wealthy Henry to London, he joined the Club of the Green Carnation, where most of the boys who provided the entertainment were a good-hearted and devoted sort, living up to the best British traditions of service. But Karl fell into the clutches of a by now familiar topical figure: Fred, the circus-boy, "sein Antinous," who turned out to be the sole blackmailer amongst all the club's artistic staff. Naples revives Karl's spirits: "Das Museo Nazionale machte seine Einbildungskraft von gewaltigen Vorstellungen strotzen." What attracts British travelers and German tutors is, we fear, the nude male statuary of the collection—the Sleeping Satyr, the Drunken Faun, and, above all, the Naples-Antinous, the statue of the emperor's favorite, which has become such a crowd-pleaser that the corridor where it stands has been named for it.³²

The drift of our argument should not be misunderstood: Rilke did not visit the Museum for the reasons attributed to fiction's late-born decadents. His interest, as can be ascertained from his letters, lay primarily with the reliefs, the antique gravestones, and the antique paintings. Nevertheless, he cannot very well have avoided taking the Antinous statue, and its remarkable vogue, into his cognizance. It could be argued, by those who are students of Rilke's creative practices, that the statue's very popularity would have been a deterrent to his poetic im-

156   *George C. Schoolfield*

pulse. And it could be rejoined that the contemporary popularity of an artistic work, or a figure in art's annals, did not drive Rilke away, if he believed that the popularity rested on a misconception, or a misunderstanding: witness the apostrophes to Beethoven and Ibsen in *Malte Laurids Brigge*, or the alternate, Tolstoy-ending to that novel; witness, in *Neue Gedichte*, "San Marco" and "L'Ange du Méridien." Getting ahead of ourselves, we might say that Rilke may have felt that the peculiar popularity of Antinous needed a corrective. It may be important in this connection that Capri, which Rilke disliked at first ("Dieser Ort hat sein Gepräge durch recht übel ausgeübte Begeisterung bekommen"),[33] had a reputation of its own for decadent erotic practices,[34] thanks not least to the efforts of Friedrich Alfred Krupp to behave like the Tiberius described by Suetonius. If we give credence to Leopold von Schlözer, who—a short-run Eckermann—set down a series of conversations he had with Rilke during the first Capri winter and spring, a leading topic of Rilke's talk was a parallel study of Roman and contemporary degeneration[35]—in short, he mused on a favorite theme of decadent literature.

Still another factor, perhaps preparatory to the composition of the Antinous poem, should also be listed. During the Capri spring, Rilke was reading—and reading aloud to his hostesses—the lecture of Hugo von Hofmannsthal, "Der Dichter und diese Zeit," published in the *Neue Rundschau* for March 1907. On 21 March 1907, Rilke thanked the author for having written it: "Ich hatte mich in den letzten Tagen immer wieder mit Ihrem Vortrag . . . beschäftigt."[36] Hofmannsthal defines the poet, it will be remembered, as a kind of secular saint, a Johannes Calybita—a beggar who dwells beneath the stairs of his own house, in the dark, unknown, unnoticed, but open to all things: "Er ist da und wechselt lautlos seine Stelle und ist nichts als Auge und Ohr und nimmt seine Farbe von den Dingen, auf denen er ruht"—the observer, no, the hidden comrade, the soundless brother of all things. These words must have struck home to Rilke who, in the *Neue Gedichte*, was making the attempt to include the largest scale of subjects in his new collection, an attempt, that, after publication, cost him some of his readership and earned him hard words, even though politely couched, from previous admirers of his art. To Jakob Uexküll, Rilke made the well-known defense of the "Häßlichkeit oder Verworfenheit" of some of his subjects: he has learned, he says, "die Kunst nicht für eine Auswahl aus der Welt zu halten, sondern für deren restlose Verwandlung ins Herrliche hinein."[37] This openness, being preached by Hofmannsthal and practiced by Rilke, was in contradiction to the priestly exclusivity of a third poet and colleague—the third man would not have liked the word "colleague"—on the German Parnassus, Stefan George, who had had small personal contact with Rilke and (in retrospect) still less regard for him. As for Rilke himself, he may have wondered what George would think of the lecture by Hofmannsthal, if George deigned to read it; in it, George is expressly praised, and yet much of it can be read as a direct criticism of George.[38] And Rilke shortly got another reason to have George on his mind. In May 1907, Friedrich von Oppeln-Bronikowski (a precursor of the scholars who, in the 1920s, pestered Rilke with questions about "influences") wrote to Capri, asking Rilke about George's impact on his work. For his trouble Oppeln-Bronikowski got a curt and testy answer, in which Rilke said that he admired George's poems, that he had met George nine years before, and that he did not believe the "influence of works of art" could be measured.[39] Considering the courtesy and circumspection of Rilke's usual epistolary tone, it was a letter friendly neither to Oppeln-Bronikowski nor to George.

Here we come upon a matter that has been brought up once before by Eudo C. Mason in his essay on Rilke and George, first published in the *Korff-Festschrift* in 1957.[40] Mason's remarks, though brief, are almost the only useful statement made by scholarship about the *Klage um Antinous*. He suggests that the poem might be "so etwas wie eine bewußte Auseinandersetzung mit dem Maximin-Kult." Such would be possible, Mason reasons, if Rilke had been acquainted with the privately printed *Maximin: Ein Gedenkbuch* and the privately printed edition of *Der Siebente Ring*, both from 1907; otherwise, the poem is a comment on the Maximin-cult, "as it were *a priori*, in an uncanny fashion." According to Salis (Mason mentions the passage), Rilke told him during the Swiss years that he could not understand *Der Siebente Ring*, that it was evidently written for the adepts of the cult alone; Baladine wrote to Mason in 1957 that Rilke had shown her a copy of the *Maximin: Ein Gedenkbuch* at Muzot in 1921, remarking, in a mysterious tone, that the boy had died "den Opfertod." Still more circumstantial and external evidence could have been introduced in support of Professor Mason's proposal. For one thing, Rilke's brief period of direct interest in George's work came in 1897, when George's poem to "Antinous" was available to every reader of *Blätter für die Kunst*, in which Gundolf's *Antinous* appeared three years later. For another thing, Rilke need not have read the Maximin-book and *Der Siebente Ring* in order to have found out something about the story of George and Maximilian Kronberger: the Austrian had keen ears for literary gossip, and he had been in Munich (where the Maximin drama had recently taken place) in late November 1906, on the eve of his departure for Naples and Capri, and again in February 1908, as he started out for his second springtime in the south of Italy. Next, if Rilke *did* get his hands on the *Gedenkbuch*, then he read a sentence in its foreword that was particularly suggestive of the Hadrian-Antinous story: "Gemäß einem frühen vertrag den er geschlossen wurde er auf einen andren stern gehoben," a phrase that makes us think both of Antinous' appearance as a star in Dio Cassius' account, and of the climax of Rilke's poem, in lines 9–10. The conclusion of the foreword likewise recalls the Antinous-cult established by Hadrian and foreshadowed the demands that George would make upon the members of his circle—demands that they believe in the "divinity" of Maximin: "Wir können nun gierig nach leidenschaftlichen verehrungen in unsren weiheräumen seine säule aufstellen uns vor ihm niederwerfen und ihm huldigen." (It goes almost without saying that the "Opfertod" mentioned by Rilke in 1921 affords still another parallel to the Hadrian-Antinous story: Professor Mason remarks that Rilke may have heard such rumors from members of the Alfred Schuler–Ludwig Klages group during World War I in Munich.)

An argument of some significance that could be advanced against Mason's conjecture is that Rilke seems not to have used his works for literary polemics; his *oeuvre* contains nothing, evidently, like Thomas Mann's Gerhart Hauptmann portrait in Pieter Peeperkorn, or the possible Ludwig Derleth portrait in Daniel zur Höhe. Such portraiture, to be sure, lies closer at hand for a novelist than a lyricist, whose best weapon in this line may be the parody—and Rilke was not a parodist. Yet a rejoinder could be made to this objection: in March 1907, Ellen Key—by this time, Rilke had grown quite tired of her and the hopelessly amorphous optimism she espoused—came up to Naples from Syracuse, intending to pay a visit to Rilke on Capri. At the same time, she was the guest of the Duke of Cajanello, the widower of Charlotte Leffler, a Swedish woman's-rights authoress to whom she had once devoted a baddish book. The upshot of this unwelcome visit[41] (and of Rilke's failing affection for "die gute Ellen") was the Schulin episode in *Malte Laurids Brigge*, with the setting taken from an experience Rilke had had in Sweden in November 1904, but including, in its very characters, a not altogether flattering portrait of "die Allerweltstante" Ellen (as Wjera Schulin) and of the subjects of two of her works, Charlotte Leffler (who becomes the oldest Schulin sister, "die an einen Marchese in Neapel verheiratet gewesen war, von dem sie sich nun langsam unter vielen Prozessen schied"), and Charlotte's friend, the mathematician, physicist, and novelist Sonja Kovalevsky, who becomes the Schulin-sister called Zoé, "von der es hieß, daß es nichts gab, von dem sie nichts wußte." (In his Capri letters from this time, Rilke mentions both Charlotte Leffler and Sonja Kovalevsky.) If, in 1907 or 1908, Rilke could make literary fun of his old friend, Ellen Key, in a hidden manner, why could he not—a little less discreetly—criticize Stefan George, a man who, Rilke knew, entertained a low opinion of him?

V

Yet the question remains: if the *Klage um Antinous* is a comment upon George and Maximin, what sort of comment is it? And is the comment the single intention of the poem? Does it intend to make an observation about the topical figure of Antinous as well, recently so very popular in European letters? Does it belong to either of the two "Antinous-traditions" mentioned above? Here, at last, it is time to turn our attention to the text of Rilke's contribution to the literature on the emperor and his favorite:

KLAGE UM ANTINOUS

Keiner begriff mir von euch den bithynischen Knaben
(daß ihr den Strom anfaßtet und von ihm hübt . . .).
Ich verwöhnte ihn zwar. Und dennoch: wir haben
ihn nur mit Schwere erfüllt und für immer getrübt.

Wer vermag denn zu lieben? Wer kann es? —Noch keiner.
Und so hab ich unendliches Weh getan—.
Nun ist er am Nil der stillenden Götter einer,
und ich weiß kaum welcher und kann ihm nicht nahn.

Und ihr warfet ihn noch, Wahnsinnige, bis in die Sterne,
damit ich euch rufe und dränge: meint ihr den?
Was ist er nicht einfach ein Toter. Er wäre es gerne.
Und vielleicht wäre ihm nichts geschehn.

Looking at the poem on the printed page, we may be struck, initially, by a simple physical fact: its lines are *longer* than those of the other poems in *Neue Gedichte*. In the Zinn edition, the typesetter has had to put the left-hand margin very close to the edge of the page, and, even so, has been forced to drop the last word of line 5, preceded by a bracket, down to the empty space left at the end of line 6. The lines are long because, in contrast to the other poems in *Neue Gedichte* (which stick close to iambic or trochaic patterns), they contain dactyls ("Keiner begriff mir von euch den bithynischen Knaben") or "false spondees" and dactyls ("Ich verwöhnte ihn zwar. Und dennoch: wir haben . . . "), or dactyls again ("ihn nur mit Schwere erfüllt und für immer getrübt").

Also, the longer lines (within the poem) come first in their pairs, in the cases of ll. 1–2, 5–6, 9–10, 11–12; with 14 syllables as opposed to 11, 13 to 11, 15 to 12, and 15 to 9. In the case of ll. 7–8, the second line emerges as the longer in the line of print, but, in fact, again has the fewer syllables: line 7 has 13 syllables, line 8 only 11. Only in ll. 3–4 of the first strophe is the second line of the pair longer, by one syllable: 1.3 has 12, 1.4 has 13. We wonder what Rilke is up to: it appears that he is playing a metrical trick on the reader, creating a predecessor to the "imitation hexameters" of the *Duino Elegies*. Without lacing himself into a tight metrical corset (as, for example, his fellow Austrians did, Ferdinand von Saar in the *Wiener Elegien* [1893], and Hofmannsthal in such poems as "Unendliche Zeit" and "Südliche Mondnacht"), he tries to give the *impression* of writing elegiac couplets, distichs, long lines alternating with slightly shorter ones. The clearly marked caesuras contribute to the creation of the effect of the elegiac couplet; we are lured into believing that we read dactylic hexameters and "dactylic pentameters" (two-part lines, each half of which contains two dactyls—or, in the first half, spondees—followed by a long syllable), although every line in the poem, with the exception of the last, is a true pentameter.[42] (Lines 8 and 10 can, straining, be read as hexameters.) In other words, Rilke affects to employ the kind of verse-form that Hadrian—*nota bene*, the poet Hadrian—would have used, had he written a lament for the lost youth. At the same time, Rilke has, as it were, left his metrical hands quite free for other purposes, perhaps of a dramatic nature; once upon a time, as a *Privatist* in Prague, Rilke had tried to write elegiacs, and knew how constraining they were:

> Schauderst du, teueres Kind, gar wohl vor der düsteren Schwelle,
> die auch dein lieblicher Fuß einstens so willig betritt?

The imitation distichs of *Klage um Antinous* are a device to be compared with another elementary but effective trick Rilke plays on the reader at the end of *Sappho an Alkaios*, again with the intent of creating a kind of "antique verisimilitude." There the poem—as though found incomplete in a papyrus—breaks off after two lines of the final strophe.

Otherwise, in the language of the poem, we may detect a few quasi-antique elements, but only a few. One is the ethical dative—or dative of feeling, as some grammars more accurately call it—in the first line: "Keiner begriff *mir* von euch den bithynischen Knaben." It has a "classical" sound to those who once laboriously memorized such grammatical patterns as "Quid *mihi* Celsus agit?" Likewise, the second line has the "utinam" plus optative-subjunctive forms we learned: "utinam ne natus essem." It is noteworthy that these reminiscences of the basics of Latin grammar (a language in which Rilke's training had been late and hasty) come near the beginning of the poem, an indication that they may be used in order to create a certain "antique" linguistic mood. The curious verb form at the end of the second line: "daß ihr den Strom anfaßtet und von ihm *hübt*," is attributable to the same end. Here, it is surely not an attempt at dialect coloring (in the 1790s, Adelung had stamped the form as "oberdeutsch"), but rather a bit of intentional old-fashionedness: Goethe, Schiller, Stolberg, Uhland employed it, and, in Rilke's own day, it was taken out of the poet's supply-box by Otto Julius Bierbaum for those poems in *Irrgarten der Liebe* to which he wished to give a quaint or stilted tone.[43] But at the same time, in addition to their apparent Latinizing and their antique verb, the opening lines tell much about their speaker, who is self-centered, self-righteous, scolding, and clearly not an easy man to work for.

The form of Hadrian's lament is descended from a mixed lyric-dramatic genre that the young Rilke had once cultivated under a high-sounding name, "the psychodrama"; the English and American poetic tradition calls it, more simply, the dramatic monologue, a favorite nineteenth-century form, in which the poet, without having to construct a whole drama, writes the great verbal aria in which the hero, often inadvertently, tells much about what is going on inside him, and, at the same time, populates the stage with the other imaginary characters of the imaginary play. Rilke's Hadrian of 1907–08 possesses a good many of the same verbal habits as his Murillo, in the psychodrama by that name, of 1895: aposiopesis, rhetorical question, the brachylogy of abrupt and breathless sentences; yet Hadrian owns a virtue given neither to Murillo nor to Browning's Mr. Sludge the Medium: he is brief. The dramatic monologue has become remarkably compressed, put into the shape of a short elegy—or is threnody a better word?

Surely, the cast is not small. Although Hadrian is the only speaker, we know that he is surrounded by a group of scared courtiers and mages, trembling (the emperor browbeats them even as Philipp in Verdi's *Don Carlo* browbeats his chorus), but still ready to take the main chance: to get back the emperor's favor in any way they can; and both emperor and retinue are aware of a second leading actor in the drama, now missing from the stage, like Ibsen's Fru Rosmer. Antinous is gone, but present. Similarly, there is a compression of time in the poem. The body of Antinous lies in the muddy depths, but the courtiers have already enrolled him among the gods, and named a constellation after him, events that, according to historical accounts, stretched over several days. Yet, for all its abbreviation of characters and events, the poem, syntactically, seems not to be tightly made, a point that bothered

Berendt, who speaks of *disjecta membra*. Certainly, the poem's lack of straightforward development, and of clearly discernible connections between lines, seems not to be "classical," a reason, perhaps, for Rilke's care to set up the signposts of antiquity mentioned above. The mind and tongue of Hadrian, as he berates his counsellors on board the *Cygnus*, do not advance reasonably from point to point; they careen from notion to notion. For this reason, threnody might seem a better appellation than elegy, where the speaker has had time to think the loss over. Hadrian's breathlessness, and disorganization, are to be found in the great threnodies of Herakles in Euripides' play, after he has murdered wife and children, and in Seneca's imitation; but, in the classical threnodies just adduced, the chaotic aria of woe is only a part of the drama. In Rilke, the brief poem is both threnody *and* drama, expressing wild grief, and telling of the past, telling of the future.

Hadrian begins his threnody by shoving the blame for what has happened off onto the courtiers: "Keiner begriff mir von euch den bithynischen Knaben." At the same time, he willy-nilly lets the cat out of the bag about the real source of the tragedy by his "dative of feeling," discussed above, and the rather impersonal and condescending way he refers to the dead boy—"den bithynischen Knaben." (May we guess that he uses the very phrase about Antinous that the courtiers were wont to use behind the emperor's back?) Then, in an aside (are the parentheses to indicate his awareness of the impossibility of his demand? is it said under his breath? or are they there to guide the reader through the swervings of Hadrian's thought from the live Antinous to the dead one?), Hadrian asks for the *adynaton*, something that cannot be done, only to break the idea off quickly. The practical Roman, even in his grief, knows enough not to spin the impossible wish out too far, and besides, its expression has served a purpose. The courtiers have been told what he thinks of them: *you* have caused all the trouble, and now *you* must repair it—but you cannot. Then, however, a first drop of self-cognition seeps into his outward-directed fury: "*Ich* verwöhnte ihn zwar," but the burden is too much to bear; someone else has to share the blame with him, and the handy courtiers, once again, are there: "Und dennoch: wir haben." Hadrian's argument and implications may be paraphrased thus: I spoiled him, you spoiled him to please me; in doing so, and in seducing him (in the broader sense of that verb), we made him heavy, literally, muddied him, sent him to the bottom.

In the fourth line, with its "mit Schwere erfüllt" and "für immer getrübt," Berendt (who puts the matter so discreetly that the thrust of his suggestion is obscured) believes he has discovered a personal lament by Rilke about a chapter in his life that the poet often discussed in general terms, rarely in specific ones: the nature of the ill treatment he received in military school.[44] Some circumstantial evidence supports Berendt's proposal, whether we agree with it or not. Rilke never broached the matter of homosexuality in his letters, not even those to Lou, although he is frank enough about other delicate themes in the erotic sphere. The account that Musil gives, in *Törless*, of conditions at Mährisch-Weißkirchen, a school that the novelist attended some ten years after Rilke fled from it, tells us what we need to know about practices that must have been common. Certainly, the violence of Rilke's reaction to the polite inquiry by his old teacher Sedlakowitz, with the poet's striking (but quite unspecific) reiteration of how he had been "geistig und körperlich mißhandelt," cannot be dismissed as sheer exaggeration, or an attempt to maintain one of his life's leading legends.[45] Still another factor to be noted in this puzzle (and a puzzle it will probably remain, for lack of real evidence) is the sudden and almost inexplicable enthusiasm that Rilke expressed—near the end of his life, when he was trying to make some sense of all that had gone before—for the works of Hans Blüher on *Die Rolle der Erotik in der männlichen Gesellschaft*, works that deal, among other things, with the brutal homosexuality practiced in preparatory and military schools.[46] In truth, we know all too little about this most secret part of Rilke's personality for us to make a connection—let alone an identification—between Rilke's Antinous and the poet himself, as Berendt seems to do; it may, or may not, be the case that the story of Antinous' ancient fate (and of Maximin's contemporary one) touched an old and awful wound in Rilke, a wound dealt him when, as a boy, he went through a hell he likened in the Sedlakowitz letter to what Dostoyevsky, a young man and a little better able to defend himself, had endured in a Siberian prison camp. (It may be worth noting that Rilke repeated the image, and the verbiage, of the fourth line in an obscure poem from *Aus dem Nachlaß des Grafen C.W.*: "Ach, was bin ich kaum geübter/ zu begreifen, was es meint,—/ hat mich ein im Tod getrübter/ Knabe nahe angeweint?"; the poem in question was written in November 1920, the letter to Sedlakowitz on the ninth of the next month.) Autobiographical considerations aside, what we must do with the fourth line on a textual level is to admire the very wealth of its overtones and implications: the story of the drowning in the Nile, into whose mud the boy—"weighted" with the seductive affection of older men—sinks; the hint, again in "Schwere," of that "Schwermut" that all observers have detected in the countenance of the Antinous statues (Gundolf catches it as his Antinous tells the Nile's waters to become "schwer" from his pain); and, finally, the permanence of what has happened. A life misused so badly is a life misused "für immer": in the case of Antinous the misuse has gone on beyond death, to be recorded in the melancholy statues, and, caricatured, in the *topos* of decadence.

Having taken the blame, partially, the emperor—come down for the nonce off his imperial high horse—tries to find the excuse, to make the apologia for himself. The fifth line is often quoted out of context, in the course of discussions of that well-known Rilkean theme of the difficulties of loving, and, in particular, of the perils of possessive love. In Hadrian's case, loving has become particularly and cruelly possessive, not only because of the homosexual nature of the affair, which, as it were, robbed Antinous of his gender; but because Hadrian, as emperor, could smother his beloved in endless and overwhelming signs of his love, and, quite literally, allow his favorite no other life than what he had as a bearer of Hadrian's passion. (It is a credit to Hausrath-Taylor's forgotten novel that, in his Antinous, he anticipates what Rilke says.) Alive, Antinous had no existence save with Caesar, and dead, he continues in the same subjugation, enrolled among the gods, made the object of a cult, but all at Hadrian's behest, Hadrian's creature forever: "Und so hab *ich* unendliches Weh getan." Seeing what he has done, Hadrian is more pathetic, and more sympathetic, than ever he has been before in the poem. (These lines, by the way, will call to mind some other famous expressions about the difficulty of loving by writers a little older than Rilke, and usually classified among the decadents: Oscar Wilde's "Yet each man kills the thing he loves" and Herman Bang's "Vi lider og bereder Lidelser—mere véd vi ikke" ["We suffer and cause suffering—we do not know more"] from *Det hvide Hus*, a novel that Rilke much admired. The sentiment lay in the literary air.)

The enrollment of Antinous among the gods, whether it has taken place officially as yet or not, is one of the results of Hadrian's imperial affection. The city on the Nile named after him, the temples of the Antinous cult: all this will come along shortly; but Antinous has already become one of those pacifying gods (and we may think here of the political import of the Antinous cult, a pacifier, like so much else in the welter of religions of the empire). Nonetheless, Antinous can no longer pacify the man who made him a god. Rendered an institution for all, he is out of the reach of the bereaved man. The ruler of the world is shut out, and complains about it: "und ich weiß kaum welcher und kann ihm nicht nahn." The repetition of the first-person pronoun, coming close after the confession of guilt just above ("Und so hab *ich* unendliches Weh getan"), sounds quite plaintive in the last line of the strophe: "und *ich* weiß kaum welcher." Hadrian is so much in doubt that his very syntax becomes doubtful: is "welcher" a partitive plural genitive, or a nominative singular with verb unexpressed? In creating this grammatical amphiboly, Rilke knew very well what he was doing.

The complaint is the coupling to the next stage of Hadrian's threnody: having belatedly looked into himself, accused himself, excused himself, he returns (as thoughts circle in times of bereavement) to the place where he had started: the blame again goes onto the members of the retinue, called insulting names this time. Having failed to perform the one task, of bringing Antinous back to life from the depth of the Nile, they have performed another in its stead:

> Und ihr warfet ihn noch, Wahnsinnige, bis in die Sterne,
> damit ich euch rufe und dränge: meint ihr den?

The courtiers cast the dead boy to his place among the stars in an effort to please their master and to obtain more control over him: they have the special, if specious, knowledge that Hadrian does not, just as we suspect that they will use the cult itself, about which Hadrian knows so little (the amphiboly of "welcher" again) in order to insinuate themselves into his favor. He will need them, he realizes, to bolster his own faith in the new cult (and here we might guess that Rilke thinks of the rather ludicrous demands George made upon his followers as he instructed them to *believe* in the divine Maximin). Hadrian's disgust at what has happened, and at what is to come, is too much for him to bear; he turns into himself, and the poem ends with remarks which seem not to make any sense at all, or to make sense only to their speaker. "Was ist er nicht einfach ein Toter": what does it mean? We are worried about the meaning of "Was" and the absence of a question mark; Berendt repunctuates the sentence for us: "Was, ist er nicht einfach ein Toter?" But the line does not need a mark of interrogation at its end, for it is a statement, and the initial *was* is not an outcry nor an interrogative word, but an intensifier, of the kind Rilke uses elsewhere in the *Neue Gedichte*, in "Die Liebende":

> *Was* bin ich unter diese
> Unendlichkeit gelegt,
> duftend wie eine Wiese,
> hin und her bewegt.

and in the *Sonette an Orpheus* (II,2):

> *Was* haben Augen einst ins umrußte
> lange Verglühn der Kamine geschaut:
> Blicke des Lebens, für immer verlorne.

These are not questions; in the former instance, the "was" is neither expletive, again, nor substitute for "warum," in the latter not an interrogative pronoun. In all three cases it emphasizes what follows: "How simply he is a dead person," perhaps, not "Why isn't he just one dead?", as J. B. Leishman translates.[47] Hadrian has come to the insight, the final one, that Antinous is simply a dead being, as, in life, he was simply a human being; both there and here, Hadrian has betrayed him, misused him, "für immer getrübt." The last two sentences of the poem, the falling-away after the statement of the insight, are homely, colloquial, altogether unimperial, even to the syncope in the final word: "Er wäre es gerne./ Und vielleicht wäre ihm nichts geschehn." They are contradictions, of course, and impossibilities: the earlier *adynata*, the impossibilities of resurrection and deification, are supplanted by the very human and impossible desire of Hadrian to make wrong things right. The last line is built on omissions—the omission of an unhappy man whose thoughts have become ever more stuttering, ever more incomplete. Hadrian says: Antinous would like to be what he in fact *is*, simply a dead person, and what now, after his bogus transfiguration, he cannot be. And then, if he were simply a dead person, he would, just as simply, have been a simple live person, too, one whom Hadrian—the man, not the emperor—would have treated as such. "Und vielleicht wäre ihm nichts geschehn" is a line that can be read to mean: "if he were regarded only as an ordinary dead person, then he would not have had these misuses befall him after death" (J. A. Symonds refers to the "gimcrack quality of the new god"); but it is better taken in an expanded sense, as the bitterest self-accusation and statement of tragic paradox: "if I could only have left him as an ordinary human being, a boy in Bithynia, then nothing at all would have befallen him." Yet here, we come back to an impossibility again, the last one in the poem: for Hadrian *was*, after all, the Emperor of Rome, who had gone to Bithynia, where he found Antinous, the boy whose beauty (meeting the emperor's power and weakness) then led to wretched death and silly cultic transformation. If the essence of tragedy is inevitability, this is a tragedy.

The poem can and should be read with an eye to its literary-historical aspects: its title must surely have caught the eye—and aroused certain expectations—on the part of the reader who was familiar with the literature of decadence, and the *topos* of the vicious Antinous. Rilke's poem, in effect, rehumanizes the figure after two decades of sensational literary abuse. Thus it belongs to the "sympathetic" German-Scandinavian current, and is, probably, that current's best-known representative. As for the problem of George's connection with the poem, it should be obvious by this time that Rilke's Hadrian has several Georgian characteristics, but possesses greater self-knowledge and greater compassion.

Indeed, the poem could be read as a sermon to George: after his "Georgian" behavior, Hadrian's final reactions show a sensitivity of which the "Meister" has proved himself to be quite incapable. But, beyond these factors, one more must be remembered: the poem's quality as a handsomely made work of art—how much is said and implied, and how skillfully, within a very small space.[48] It is the kind of transformation of the sordid into the splendid that Rilke mentions in his apologia to Jakob Uexküll.

NOTES

[1] Paul Bourget, in "Un césar voyageur," *Études et portraits* (Paris, 1888), p. 319, detects "un style mièvre et contourné de décadence" in Hadrian's Latin. Hadrian, for the rest, is particularly the Roman emperor of decadence for Bourget; cf. his theory of decadence in "Charles Baudelaire," *Essais de psychologie contemporaine* (Paris, 1883), p. 17. For Bourget, of course, decadence is not a pejorative term; Hadrian represents "un plus riche trésor d'acquisition humaine" than does "un chef germain du IIe siècle." (See also Raymond Pouilliart, "Paul Bourget et l'esprit de décadence," *Les lettres romanes* (Paris, 1951), pp. 199–223, esp. 208–11.)

[2] *Philemon* I:4: "Ades bona, ô bona cithara,/ Suavicula, blandula, tinnula,/ In ventre sunt jejunia,/ O, affer, affer pabula,/ Improbulâ, querulâ, durulâ,/ Siti cremantur guttura,/ Ades bona, ô bona cithara,/ Philemoni fer pocula."

[3] J. A. Symonds, "Antinous," *Sketches and Studies in Italy and Greece* (London, 1874), II: 220: "A parody dangerous to the pure form of Christ."

[4] In America, with the blank-verse tragedy *Antinous* (1891), the poetess Abbie Carter Goodloe followed the same respectable line, but added a dash of romantic interest. Hadrian's wife, Sabina, falls in love with Antinous, who rejects her advances. She confesses her guilt to Hadrian and then kills herself, eventually to be followed into death by Antinous, whose suicide results, it appears, from filial embarrassment. Goodloe's Hadrian is both fatherly and elderly; having heard Sabina's confession, he remarks to Antinous: "A rude day this has been, Antinous!/ Such shocks become too much for mine old age."

[5] As Herder says, discussing the "Genien der Jünglingschaft," *Sämtliche Werke* (Leipzig, 1877–1913), XVIII, 347, "Die Antinous haben freilich einen düstern Zug, wie sie auch, ihrem Urbilde nach, haben sollten."

[6] Probably because it showed the disciple ready to make any sacrifice for the master, and because of its "Georgian" language. Neither George nor Gundolf scholarship has attempted to analyze the nuances—biographical, autobiographical, and artistic—of the little play.

[7] Viktor Rydberg, "Antinous," *Skrifter* (Stockholm, 1896–99), IX: 213–34; p. 232: Rafael's intention was to "christianize Antinous, to make his beauty holy, and to give the self-sacrificing youth a place in the reverence of those persons who adore the mystery of self-renunciation and the mystery of eternal life, won by self-renunciation."

[8] Ibid., p. 233: "What does he see there, which thus captures his vision?/ What does the melancholy cloud beneath the wreath portend?/ Oh, [I wonder] if his sadly serene countenance is/ a mirror of the mysteries of being?"

[9] Herman Bang, *Haabløse Slægter* (Copenhagen, 1965), pp. 243–44. Hoff, for the rest, has been called a "modern edition of a Heliogabalus *manqué*" by one of his several

detractors (p. 221)—a phrase reminiscent of Barbey d'Aurevilly's description of the poet of *Les fleurs du mal* as "un Héliogabale artificiel."

¹⁰ Ola Hansson, *Samlade skrifter* (Stockholm, 1917–22), V, 18. The collection was published in German by S. Fischer as *Alltagsfrauen*; because of its daring nature, it could not find a Swedish publisher until 1914. In her repressed eroticism, Hansson's "Stella" comes the closest to perversity of all the "ideal" figures associated with Antinous.

¹¹ Mario Praz, *The Romantic Agony*, 2d ed. (London, 1951), pp. 314 ff.

¹² Gabriele d'Annunzio used Antinous "heterosexually" to tell one of his early mistresses, Barbara Leoni, what he thought of her charms. Describing a statue of Antinous that he kept in his workroom, he wrote: "L'Antinoo ha la tua bocca, pura ma triste, voluttuosa ma con non so che di amaro, ardente ma crudele. Io mi alzo, per un desiderio folle e puerile; e vado a baciare l'Antinoo in bocca." (*Lettere a Barbara Leoni* [Milano, 1957], p. 52: May 1888).

¹³ A notice in the magazine of Anatole Baju, *Le Décadent* (15 November 1888), had already called for poetry about Bathyllus, Antinous, Alexis, the famous youths of antiquity, "les spatalocinèdes," the "exciters to wantonness." Cf. A. E. Carter, *The Idea of Decadence in French Literature* (Toronto, 1958), p. 110.

¹⁴ Antinous comes as the last in Lorrain's series of eight youths, the others being Ganymede, Alexis, Narcissus, Hylas, Bacchus, Bathyllus, and Athys. Lorrain's "hélas!" in the penultimate line laments the thousand years of scorn Antinous has endured, not the renaissance of the "ère auguste."

¹⁵ Praz, pondering Lorrain's substitution of "Filde" for "Wilde," says in *The Romantic Agony*, p. 433: "Lorrain's favorite system seems to be to change slightly certain well-known names by altering the initial letter, without bothering about the linguistic absurdity that results." However, an argument could be made for a learned cunning in Lorrain's hermetic naval nomenclature: *Edward III* combines the name of one homosexual monarch (England's Edward II) with the number of another (France's Henri III)—after all, Lord Feredith and Sir Algernon have Nice as their main *escale*. Also, Lorrain substitutes *Cydnus* for *Cygnus* ("The Swan," the name tradition has assigned to Hadrian's Nile vessel) because, we assume, of the special erotic connotations of the former name: it was up the river Cydnus in Cilicia that Cleopatra sailed to seduce Antony (according to Plutarch, in Dryden's translation: "She herself lay all alone under a canopy of cloth of gold, dressed as Venus in a picture, and beautiful young boys, like painted Cupids, stood on each side to fan her"). The river's name was then transferred to the barge itself.

¹⁶ Four years before the publication of *The Picture of Dorian Gray* (1891), Lionel Johnson—who, for the rest, had introduced Douglas to Wilde—wrote a dramatic monologue, "Julian at Eleusis," in which the doomed aesthete and emperor worships Antinous instead of Christ: "Wondrous Antinous! Oh, fairer thou/ Than the dim beauty of Christ crucified/ . . . Beneath the vast night in old Egypt thou/ Gavest thyself for Hadrian: neither foul,/ Nor any slave's death, was thy death; for Nile / Took thee. Then in the heavens burned one more star,/ And earth reddened with unknown lily flowers,/ O consecrate and fair! for joy of thee!"

¹⁷ A systematic study of the figures of Hadrian and Antinous, and of Antinous as a *topos*, in the literature of the nineteenth and early twentieth centuries would be a rewarding task for a comparatist; the above survey pretends to be neither exhaustive nor nuanced. The scholar who undertook the job might find an early example of the evil Antinous as simple *topos* in the "Danse macabre" (*Tableaux parisiens*) of *Les fleurs du mal*: "Fiers mignons, malgré l'art des poudres et du rouge,/ Vous sentez tous la mort! O squelettes musqués,/ Antinoüs flétris, dandys à face glabre," and, under the same rubric, he would want to follow down the several leads given for French narrative prose by Praz and for verse by Carter. He would find an interesting blending of the "good" and "evil" Antinouses, seen full length, in the novel (*Antinous*, 1903) of the Finnish neo-romantic, Volter Kilpi (1874–1939). Finally, his task would be complicated by the use of Antinous as a simple signal-word for male beauty, as in the case of the altogether heterosexual and quite middle-aged Italian lover of the singer, Ottilie Pauws, in Louis Couperus's *Van oude*

menschen, de dingen die vorbijgaan (1906)—a surprisingly unresonant employment of "Antinous" on the part of an author whose works are, otherwise, a treasure trove of decadent *topoi* tellingly placed. The whole Antinous-craze in letters may be seen as simply one aspect of the later nineteenth century's fascination with what the catch of Esmé Amarinth (Oscar Wilde) in Robert Hichen's *The Green Carnation* calls (to the tune of "Three blind mice"), "Rose-white youth,/ Pas-sionate, pale./ Ah! there's nothing in life so finely frail/ As rose-white youth." Yet the proposed systematic study should certainly not neglect Hadrian, Bourget's admirably decadent emperor, enormously powerful yet vulnerable, because of his refinement, the nature of his passion, and his age: if the period liked youthful love objects, it also liked lovers well on in years.

[18] Hans Berendt, *Rainer Maria Rilkes Neue Gedichte* (Bonn, 1957), pp. 202–5.

[19] Brigitte L. Bradley, *Rainer Maria Rilkes Der Neuen Gedichte anderer Teil: Entwicklungsstufen seiner Pariser Lyrik* (Bern and München, 1976): she connects it with the "Klage um Jonathan," calling attention to the "Doppelmotiv von Liebe und Tod" and "der homoerotische Aspekt" (pp. 50, 51).

[20] Wolfgang Müller, *Rainer Maria Rilkes 'Neue Gedichte': Vielfältigkeit eines Gedichttypus* (Meisenheim am Glan, 1971), and Hartmut Engelhardt, *Der Versuch wirklich zu sein: Zu Rilkes sachlichem Sagen* (Frankfurt a.M., 1973).

[21] Harry Mielert, "Rilke und die Antike," *Die Antike*, XVI (1940), 51–62.

[22] Ernst Zinn, "Rainer Maria Rilke und die Antike," *Antike und Abendland*, III (1949), 201–50.

[23] Werner Kohlschmidt, "Rilke und die Antike," in Kohlschmidt, *Rilke-Interpretationen* (Lahr, 1948), pp. 37–38.

[24] Katharina Kippenberg, "Verhältnis zur Antike," in Kippenberg, *Rainer Maria Rilke: Ein Beitrag* (Wiesbaden, 1948), pp. 298–304.

[25] In *Four Beasts in One: The Homo-Cameleopard* (translated by Baudelaire in the *Nouvelles histoires extraordinaires*), *L'Agonie* (1888), *Algabal* (1892), and *De berg van licht* (1905–6): a study of the Heliogabalus in literature, from de Sade past Poe and Gautier to the turn of the century, would be as rewarding as a monograph on Hadrian and Antinous, although the findings might show less variety in the treatment of the boy-emperor's figure.

[26] Alfred Hermann, *Rilkes ägyptische Gesichte: Ein Versuch wechselseitiger Erhellung von Dichtung und Altkultur* (Freiburg-München, [1955]). (Reprinted from *Symposion* IV [1955], 371–461.) See in particular p. 394 (p. 28).

[27] *Sämtliche Werke*, I (Wiesbaden, 1955), p. 865.

[28] Rainer Maria Rilke and Lou Andreas-Salomé, *Briefwechsel* (Zürich-Wiesbaden, 1952), p. 179 (3 July 1904).

[29] To Clara: *Briefe 1906–1907* (Leipzig, 1930), p. 107; *Briefe 1904–1907* (Leipzig, 1939), p. 197 (2 December 1906).

[30] To Clara: *Briefe 1906–1907*, p. 278; *Briefe 1904–1907*, p. 334 (21 June 1907).

[31] Quoted in Helmut Wocke, *Rilke und Italien* (Giessen, 1940), p. 53.

[32] Francisco de la Maza, *Antinoo: El último dios del mundo clásico* (Mexico, 1966), p. 212, calls the statue "la plenitud de Antinoo," and takes his predecessor, the Norwegian Lorentz Henrik Dietrichson, (*Antinous* [Kristiania, 1884]), in the study of statues of Antinous to task for having dared to vitiate the Naples statue's force by calling it "Antinous-Adonis."

[33] To Elisabeth and Karl von der Heydt: *Briefe 1906–1907*, p. 118, *Briefe 1904–1907*, p. 209.

[34] When Bierbaum's wretched Karl grows tired of the "Roman baths" of Naples, he sails over to Capri, there to refresh himself in an affair with a fisherman, aptly named Tiberio. (He then hires Tiberio to murder Henry in the Blue Grotto, but the planned assassination turns into mutual seduction—at least, this is Henry's version of how he escaped.)

[35] Leopold von Schlözer, *Rainer Maria Rilke auf Capri: Gespräche* (Dresden, 1931), esp. pp. 25–30.

[36] *Briefe 1906–1907*, p. 231; *Briefe 1904–1907*, pp. 294–95 (21 March 1907).

[37] *Briefe 1897–1914* (Wiesbaden, 1950), p. 263 (19 August 1909).

[38] For example, Hofmannsthal says of "poets of the time": "das unscheinbarste Dasein, die dürftigste Situation wird ihren immer schärferen Sinnen seelenhaft; wo nur aus fast Wesenlosem die schwächste Flamme eines eigenen Daseins, eines besonderen Leidens schlägt, sind sie nahe."

[39] *Briefe 1906–1907*, pp. 255–56, *Briefe 1904–1907*, pp. 316–17 (29 May 1907: Rilke replied from a hotel in Rome).

[40] Eudo C. Mason, "Rilke und Stefan George" in *Gestaltung und Umgestaltung: Festschrift Hermann August Korff* (Leipzig, 1957), pp. 248–78, reprinted in Eudo C. Mason, *Exzentrische Bahnen: Studien zum Dichterbewußtsein der Neuzeit* (Göttingen, 1963), pp. 208–49; reprinted, but with the final section (including the discussion of "Klage um Antinous") omitted, in Käte Hamburger, *Rilke in neuer Sicht* (Stuttgart, 1971), pp. 9–37.

[41] For an account of it, see G. C. Schoolfield, "Rilke, Gorki, and Others; A Biographical Diversion," in Karl S. Weimar, ed., *Views and Reviews of Modern German Literature: Festschrift for Adolf D. Klarmann* (München, 1974), pp. 105–20.

[42] In the third of her observations on the poems, Bradley says: "Die ungewöhnliche Sprachführung in 'Klage um Antinous' hängt übrigens mit einem Metrum zusammen, das zwar fünfhebig ist, im Takt aber an den Hexameter anklingt." Bradley, *Der Neuen Gedichte anderer Teil*, p. 52.

[43] Bierbaum, however, employs only the indicative, "hub." Rilke had some fondness for the subjunctive form, using it in still another poem of the *Neue Gedichte*, "Josuas Landtag" ("als hübe sich der Lärm von dreißig Schlachten/ in einem Mund"), in the "Requiem for Wolf Graf von Kalckreuth" ("daß du ihn hübest"), in the "Improvisationen aus dem Capreser Winter" ("und hübe es hinaus aus mir"), in the "Skizze zu einem Sankt Georg" ("Während, silberner über dem silbernen Tier,/ unberührt von der Kühle und Trübe,/ sich der Helm, vergittert und spiegelnd, hübe"), in a sketch from Capri, dated 1907 ("Wie wenn ich jeden Morgen mich erhübe"), in the "Gedichte für Lulu Albert-Lasard, X" ("und er hübe sie in seine Hände"), and in the poem for Nanny Wunderly-Volkart, "Valangin" ("war er manchmal so bewegt, als hüb er selbst ein namenloses Gesicht"). It is interesting that of these appearances of the form, all save two are clustered in the years 1906–1908, and three (in the "Improvisationen," the "Skizze," and the nameless sketch) are from 1907, the year of the composition of "Klage um Antinous." Rilke not only liked the antique effect (which he employs in the "Klage" and "Sankt Georg," where the rhyme words, "getrübt" and "trübe," have the same stem), but, evidently, the very sound. (I am indebted to Professor Ulrich Goldsmith, who is preparing a much-needed word index of Rilke's lyrics, for all the instances above save that in "Josuas Landtag"; I am likewise indebted to Ms. Liselotte Davis and Professor Hermann J. Weigand for having approached Professor Goldsmith on my behalf.)

[44] Berendt, *Rilkes Neue Gedichte*, pp. 203–4.

[45] It was, to be sure, first printed in an "official" partial biography by a member of the family, Carl Sieber, *René Rilke* (Leipzig, 1932), pp. 161–68.

[46] See the letter to Lou Andreas-Salomé of 21 February 1919 (*Briefwechsel*, p. 412) and the letter to Katharina Kippenberg of 24 February 1919 (*Briefwechsel* [Wiesbaden, 1954], p. 333).

[47] *New Poems* (London, 1964), p. 171. The French translation by Jacques Legrand (Rainer Maria Rilke, *Oeuvres 2: Poésie*, ed. Paul de Man [Paris, 1972], p. 231) says: "Que n'est-il donc le simple mort qu'il eût tant aimé être."

[48] Even the immediately following poems in *Neue Gedichte*, "Der Tod der Geliebten" and "Klage um Jonatan," provide a contribution to the meaning of "Klage um Antinous," as it does to theirs. Certainly, the very title of the second poem requires the reader to make a comparison between David, the passionate and straightforward friend of Jonathan, and Hadrian, the overbearing and culpable lover of Antinous.

The Publications of Herman Salinger

Compiled by A. Tilo Alt

A. Books

1942   1. *An Index to the Poems of Rainer Maria Rilke*. Madison, Wis.: The University of Wisconsin Press, 1942. 32 pp.

1944   2. (Trans.). Heinrich Heine. *Germany: A Winter's Tale, 1844*. Introduction by Hermann Kesten. New York: L. B. Fischer, 1944. XIX, 156 pp.

1950   3. *Angel of our Thirst*. Poems. Prairie City, Ill.: Grinnell College Press, The Decker Press, 1950. 54 pp.

1952   4. (Trans. & ed.). *Twentieth Century German Verse: A Selection*. Princeton: Princeton University Press, 1952. XXIII, 93 pp.
        a. Reprint. Freeport, N.Y.: Books for Libraries Press, 1968.

1960   5. (Ed. with Haskell Block). *The Creative Vision: Modern European Writers on Their Art*. New York: Grove Press, 1960. 197 pp.
        a. Reprint. Gloucester, Mass.: Peter Smith, 1968.

1962   6. (Trans.). Rudolf Hagelstange. *Ballad of the Buried Life*. Introduction by Charles W. Hoffmann. Chapel Hill: The University of North Carolina Press, 1962. XXII, 105 pp.
        a. Reprint. New York: AMS Press, n.d.

1962/63   7. *A Sigh is the Sword*. Poems. Introduction by Wylie Sypher. Charlotte, N.C. and Santa Barbara, Calif.: McNally & Loftin, 1962/63. XII, 68 pp.

1963   8. (Ed. with Herbert Reichert). *Studies in Arthur Schnitzler*. Chapel Hill: The University of North Carolina Press, 1963. 163 pp.
        a. Reprint. New York: AMS Press, 1966.

1969   9. (Trans.). Karl Krolow. *Poems Against Death*. Washington, D. C.: Charioteer Press, 1969. XI, 42 pp.

B. Articles

1938   1. "Some Heine Notes," *Modern Language Notes*, 53 (1938), 430–33.

1939   2. "Housman's *Last Poems*, XXX and Heine's *Lyrisches Intermezzo*, 62," *Modern Language Notes*, 54 (1939), 288–90.

3. "Shakespeare's Tyranny over Grillparzer," *Monatshefte für deutschen Unterricht*, 31 (1939), 222–29.

1940   4. "Der Arme Spielmann aus Wien," *American-German Review*, 6 (Feb., 1940), 26–27.

5. "The 'Gartensaal' in Storm's *Immensee*: An Interpretation," *German Quarterly*, 13 (1940), 149–50.

1941   6. "Heine's 'Rote Pantoffeln': Wit and Autobiography," *Monatshefte für deutschen Unterricht*, 33 (1941), 213–16.

1942   7. "Rilke's Opening Lines," *Modern Language Notes*, 57 (1942), 1–9.

8. "The Riddle of the 'Kinderball' in Heine's *Bäder von Lucca*," *Monatshefte für deutschen Unterricht*, 34 (1942), 145–52.

1948   9. "Confessions of a Translator," *Books Abroad*, 22 (1948), 352–56.

1949   10. "Mathilde Heine's Album," *Modern Language Notes*, 64 (1949), 387–91.

1951   11. (Co-author), "What's Wrong with the Nobel Prize? A Symposium," *Books Abroad*, 25 (1951), 215–16.

1953   12. "Hans Egon Holthusen: The Panther and the Prophet," *Poetry*, 82 (1953), 335–41.

1955   13. "More Light on Rilke's *Requiem auf den Tod eines Knaben*: A Comparative Approach," *Monatshefte für deutschen Unterricht*, 47 (1955), 81–88.

14. "Heinrich Heine's Stature after a Century," *Monatshefte für deutschen Unterricht*, 48 (1956), 309–16.

1961   15. "More Light on Kafka's Landarzt," *Monatshefte für deutschen Unterricht*, 53 (1961), 97–104.

1963   16. "On Translating Lyrical Poetry," *Reality and Creative Vision in German Lyrical Poetry*, ed. A. Closs. London: Butterworths, 1963, pp. 14–29.

17. "Helping Heinrich Heine Explain His Archetypal 'Night Journey' Poem," *Literature and Psychology*, 13 (Spring, 1963), 30–36.

18. "Rebellion and Reconciliation," *South Atlantic Quarterly*, 62 (1963), 355–76.

1965   19. "Arthur Schnitzler's Influence as an Historian of Contemporary Society," *Journal of the International Arthur Schnitzler Research Association*, 4 (Spring, 1965), 17–19.

1967   20. "Ernst Waldinger: Austro-American Poet," *Journal of the International Arthur Schnitzler Research Association*, 6 (Spring, 1967), 45–46.

21. "Heinrich von Kleist's Penthesilea: Amazon or Bluestocking," *Comparative Drama*, 1 (Spring, 1967), 49–55.

22. "Hans Carossa," *Encyclopedia of World Literature in the 20th Century*, ed. W. B. Fleischmann. New York: Frederick Ungar, 1967, pp. 205–6.

1970   23. "Time in the Lyric," *Studies in German Literature of the Nineteenth and Twentieth Centuries: Festschrift for Frederic Coenen*, ed. S. Mews. Chapel Hill: The University of North Carolina Press, 1970, pp. 157–73.

1972   24. (With Alois Arnoldner), Introduction to Ernst Elster, *Prinzipien der Literaturwissenschaft*, reprint of the 1897–1911 eds. New York, London: Johnson Reprint Company, 1972, pp. V–X.

1975   25. "Heine's 'Valkyren' Reexamined," *Modern Language Notes*, 90 (1975), 673–77.

n.d.   26. "Heinrich Heine, The Child in the Man," *Festschrift for Helmut Rehder* (forthcoming).

C. Translations

1928/29   1. "Rondel" by Charles d'Orleans, *Poet Lore*, 39 (1928/29), 595.

1939   2. "A Child Cried at Night" by Ernst Wiechert, *Poet Lore*, 45 (Summer-Autumn, 1939), 352.

1945   3. "It Is Going To Snow" by Francis Jammes, *Poet Lore*, 51 (Winter, 1945), 290.

1947   4. "Winter Landscapes: I. Road; II. Tree; III. River; IV. Thaw" by Alfredo Ortiz-Vargas, *The University of Kansas City Review*, 13 (Spring, 1947), 198–99.

1949   5. "Eva" and "I was a Child" by Rainer Maria Rilke, *Accent*, 9 (1949), 171.

1951   6. "Death is Great" by Rainer Maria Rilke, *Poet Lore*, 56 (Summer, 1951), 173.

1952   7. "Carnet de Poche: 'Solitude,' 'Doubt,' 'Divine Disgrace,' 'Growing Old'" by Rainer Maria Rilke, *The Poetry Review* (London), 43 (October–December, 1952), 221–22.

1953   8. "Man of Action"; "My Life, My Death"; "With Roses in Raron"; "The Panther and the Prophet" by Hans Egon Holthusen, *Poetry*, 82 (1953), 330–41.

1954   9. "Birth of Venus" by Paul Valéry, *Western Review*, 18 (Spring, 1954), 210.

1956   10. "Sombre Landscape" by Kurt Loup, *The Carolina Quarterly*, 9 (Fall, 1956), 55.

1956/57 11. "Landschaft aus Schreien" by Nelly Sachs, *The Beloit Poetry Journal*, 7 (1956/57), 26–29.

1959   12. "Ballade vom verschütteten Leben" and "Der siebente Gesang" by Rudolf Hagelstange, *Insel Almanach auf das Jahr 1959*, pp. 108–12.

          13. "Brigitta" by Adalbert Stifter, *Nineteenth Century German Tales*, ed. A. Flores. New York: Doubleday, 1959, pp. 251–301.

1960   14. Poems by six authors, *An Anthology of German Poetry from Hölderlin to Rilke*, ed. A. Flores. New York: Doubleday, 1960.

          a. "I See Thee in a Thousand Pictures" by Novalis, p. 87.

          b. "Serenade" and "Cradlesong" by Clemens Brentano, pp. 95–97.

          c. "Nocturne" and "Conversation in the Forest" by Joseph von Eichendorff, pp. 111, 123.

          d. "The Pond"; "The Reflection in the Mirror"; "Sleepless Night"; "Moonrise" by Annette von Droste-Hülshoff, pp. 153, 158–59, 160–62, 166–67.

          e. "I Dreamt the Old, Old Dream Anew"; "I Love a Flower . . ."; "Babylonian Sorrows"; "Affinities"; "Death is at Hand" by Heinrich Heine, pp. 176, 186, 202–5, 210.

          f. "Evanescence" by Hugo von Hofmannsthal, p. 331.

1962   15. Poems from Old High and Middle High German, *An Anthology of Medieval Lyrics*, ed. A. Flores. New York: The Modern Library, 1962.

          a. "The Lay of the Hildebrand," pp. 400–1.

          b. "Lady, Wilt Thou Heal My Smart?" by Heinrich von Mohrungen, pp. 426–27.

1963   16. "Liebeslied" and "Song" by Rainer Maria Rilke, *Approach,
        A Literary Quarterly*, 48 (Summer, 1963), 33.

1964   17. "Song of the Harpplayer" by Joh. Wolfg. von Goethe, *An-
        thology German Poetry*, ed. A. Gode and F. Ungar. New
        York: Ungar, 1964, pp. 100–1.

1965   18. "Flower, Tree, and Bird" by Hermann Hesse, *The Tree and
        the Master*. New York: Random House, 1965, pp. 148–49.

        19. "Valvins" by Paul Valéry, *Hartwick Review*, 1 (October,
        1965), 17.

1966   20. Poems by four authors, *Modern European Poetry*, ed. W.
        Barnstone. New York: Bantam Books, 1966.

        a. "Eva" and "Walk" by Rainer Maria Rilke, pp. 112–13, 115.

        b. "Nocturne" by Georg Trakl, pp. 127–28.

        c. "Dead Season"; "Walk"; "Poems Against Death" by Karl
        Krolow, pp. 156, 158–61.

        d. "Eye of Time" by Paul Celan, p. 163.

        21. "Schumann" by Marcel Proust; "Secret Ode" and "Lost
        Wine" by Paul Valéry, *Hartwick Review*, 2 (1966), 36–37.

        22. "Rain" by Paul Verlaine, *Poet Lore*, 61 (1966), 169.

        23. "Hyacinths" by Theodor Storm, *Lyrica Germanica*, 1 (May,
        1966), 1.

1967   24. "Ballad after Shakespeare" by Hans Egon Holthusen,
        Hartwick Review, 3 (Spring, 1967), 16.

        25. "The Bridegroom" by Joh. Wolfg. von Goethe, *Lyrica
        Germanica*, 2 (May, 1967), 1.

1968   26. "Tristan" by August von Platen; "Was will die einsame
        Träne?" by Heinrich Heine, *Lyrica Germanica*, 3 (Sep-
        tember, 1968), 5, 8.

        a. "Was will die einsame Träne?" by H. Heine. Reprint.
        Death and Empress, a play by Edward J. Meyers, Duke
        University Library, pp. 31–32.

        27. "Orpheus in der Mittelwelt" by Wolfgang Weyrauch; "Im
        Fortgehen und andere Gedichte" by Karl Krolow, *Dimen-
        sion*, 1 (1968), 168–75, 320–27.

1969   28. "Finding Words" by Cyrus Atabay; "Life Itself" and
        "Forces That Build Society" by Karl Krolow, *Dimension*, 2
        (1969), 440–51, 686–89.

        29. "Late Summer" by Hermann Hesse; "In the Warm Noon"
        by Karl Krolow, *The Above Ground Review*, 1 (Winter,
        1969), 2–3.

        30. "The Murderer"; "Portrait of a Hand"; "Magician"; "In-

sect Season"; "Before Mowing" by Karl Krolow, *Café Solo*, 1 (Summer, 1969), 52–61.

1970   31. "Alone" by Hermann Hesse, *Adventures in World Literature*, ed. J. Applegate et al. New York: Harcourt, Brace & World, 1970, p. 918.

32. "Suspicion"; "Daybreak"; "Blood of Night"; "Sunday Weather" by Karl Krolow, *The Archive*, 83 (Autumn, 1970), 43–44.

1971   33. "Protective Coloration" and other poems by Cyrus Atabay, *Dimension*, 4 (1971), 16–25.

1973   34. Six poems by Karl Krolow, *Mundus Artium*, 6 (1973), 124–32.

35. "Gespräch über Bäume" by Rudolf Hagelstange, *Dimension*, 6 (1973), 106–31.

1974   36. "Happiness"; "When Day Comes"; "Remembering Prussia" by Karl Krolow, *The Literary Review*, 17 (Summer, 1974), 501–3.

1974/75   37. (With Harriet Dishmann) "The Bread of Early Years" and "Metaphysical" by Martien de Jong, *New Collage Magazine*, 6 (1974/75), 3, 24.

1975   38. "Greek Impressions" by Erich Fitzbauer, *Dimension*, 8 (1975), 463–65.

1976   39. (With Harriet Dishmann) "Vegetation" and "Paradise (once again) Regained" by Martien de Jong, *Grilled Flowers*, 1 (Spring, 1976), 11.

40. "Adagio" and "Memento" by Rudolf Hagelstange, *International Poetry Review*, 2 (Spring, 1976), 32–33.

41. "Without Knowledge" by Attila Jozsef, *The Archive*, 89 (Fall, 1976), 79.

D. Poems

1936   1. "Vine," *Poetry*, 47 (February, 1936), 254–55.

1937   2. "Brahms Trio," *Deutsches Dichten in Amerika*, 1 (April, 1937), 29.

1942   3. "Thunderbreak"; "Idiot Boy in the Snakehouse"; "Vision," *Princeton Verse between Two Wars*, ed. A. Tate. Princeton: Princeton University Press, 1942, pp. 79–80.

1943   4. "Voices from a Polish Village: 'Rabbi,' 'Baby,' 'Actor,' 'Boy,'" *Fantasy*, 27 (1943), 28.

1944   5. "Lines in Bivouac"; "Vulgar Word"; "Simple Dialogue,"
        Poetry, 65 (1944), 14–17.

1946   6. "Army of Occupation, I: Soliloquy at Verdun, II: Ger-
        many 1945," *Poetry*, 67 (1946), 190–91.

        7. "Army of Occupation II: 'Roses for Defeat,' 'Abstinence,'
        'Sunday,' 'Nocturne by the Rhine,'" *Poetry*, 68 (1946),
        79–81.

        8. "Be Weather"; "Recognition"; "Refuge"; "Sleep Darkens
        You"; "Antidote for Death"; "Dear-like, You More . . .";
        "Psychology No. 1: Inspiration," *The University of Kansas
        City Review*, 13 (Autumn, 1946), 72–74.

        9. "Mariana Beata Mea," *The University of Kansas City Review*,
        13 (Winter, 1946), 96.

1947   10. "Requiem for Pan" and "Morning Visit," *Poetry*, 70 (1947),
        21–22.

       11. "Brief Legend"; "World's Rose"; "To One Who Mostly
        Died Young"; "Inventory and Invocation"; "Rex Regnat
        Sed Non Gubernat"; "City Walk: November"; "Colloquy
        from 'Gallery for my Daughter'"; "Psychology No. 2:
        Themes and Recapitulation," *The University of Kansas City
        Review*, 13 (Spring, 1947), 193–97.

       12. "Stanzas for Commencement 1947," *The University of Kan-
        sas City Review*, 13 (Summer, 1947), 332–33.

1948   13. "Self Portrait, I–II," *Poetry*, 72 (1948), 254–55.

       14. "Vanishing Eden"; "Last Day on the Island"; "Inland Is-
        land," *The New Mexico Quarterly Review*, 18 (Summer,
        1948), 228, 340.

1949   15. "Faust Returns from the Mothers," *Wake*, 8 (Autumn,
        1949), 98.

       16. "Sultry Morning: Rural," *Poetry*, 75 (1949), 14.

       17. "Creed: Central," *Prairie Schooner*, 23 (1949), 272.

1950   18. "Souvenir of Dresden" and "There Was a Crooked Man,"
        Poetry, 77 (1950), 74–75.

1951   19. "Now the Names are Little," *Prairie Schooner*, 25 (1951),
        76.

1952   20. "The Knee"; "Mortal Melodies, No. 1"; "Mortal Melo-
        dies, No. 2"; "Mortal Melodies, No. 3," *Poetry*, 80 (1952),
        22–25.

1953   21. "Paternal Ashes," *Poetry*, 81 (1953), 226.

       22. "Recollections of . . . I: Beard, II: White Nights, III: Ser-
        vants, IV: Never Owned," *The Beloit Poetry Journal*, 3
        (Spring, 1953), 24–25.

178 *Herman Salinger*

1954 23. "Spectator" and "Nursery Ceiling," *Poetry*, 84 (1954), 216–18.
24. "Lines Before the Decapitation of the Statue of Liberty," *The Beloit Poetry Journal: Walt Whitman Centennial Issue*, 5/1 (1954), 16.
25. "Three Deaths," *Poetry*, 85 (1954), 27.
1955 26. "Traumatic Circus," *The Beloit Poetry Journal*, 5 (Spring, 1955), 26–27.
1956 27. "Cocktails," *Saturday Review*, 1 September 1956, p. 32.
28. "Old Professor Q.," *AAUP Bulletin*, 42 (Winter, 1956), 661.
1957 29. "Green Evening," *Prairie Schooner*, 31 (Fall, 1957), 195.
30. "Portrait H. J. W.," *Festschrift for Hermann J. Weigand*, ed. K. von Faber-du Faur, K. Reichardt, H. Blum. New Haven: Yale University Press, 1957, p. 14.
1959 31. "God is not an Analyst," *The Beloit Poetry Journal*, 9 (Spring, 1959), 27.
32. "In Laws and Lust," *Saturday Review*, 18 April 1959, p. 14.
1960 33. "Correction," *Prairie Schooner*, 34 (Summer, 1960), 142.
34. "Sonntag," *The American-German Review*, 26 (April–May, 1960), 34.
1962 35. "Hotel Porter: Old Style (Nollendorff Platz)" and "Mystic Reverse," *Elizabeth*, 3 (March, 1962), 27–28.
1966 36. "Lullaby to a Monster," *The Archive*, 78 (1966), 34.
37. "Myth-History Mélange" and "Connections Breakdown," *Hartwick Review*, 2 (1966), 36, 41.
38. "Experience," *Approach: A Literary Quarterly*, 59 (1966), 23.
1967 39. "August Moon," *Hartwick Review*, 3 (Spring, 1967), 83.
1968 40. "Abendtisch im Freien," *Lyrica Germanica*, 3 (May, 1968), 1.
1969 41. "The World is Full/ the Air is filled," *The Above Ground Review*, 1 (Winter, 1969), 2.
42. "Woods," *Café Solo*, 1 (Summer, 1969), 51.
1972 43. "In the . . ."; "Jetsam"; "Sphinx-Anima"; "Barred Owl"; "Solomon," *The Archive*, 84 (Spring, 1972), 98–102.
44. "Ein Habsburger," *Lyrica Germanica*, 7 (September, 1972), 1.
1973 45. "Epic Elegy," *The Archive*, 85 (Winter, 1973), BA.
1974 46. "Mahler Tenth," *The Archive*, 86 (Spring, 1974), 6.
1975 47. "Ancient Round"; "Coda in August"; "Epiphany No. 8," *The Archive*, 88 (Fall, 1975), 42–44.
1976 48. "Self-Sonnet" and "Conflict," *The Archive*, 88 (Spring, 1976), 65–66.

49. "Mirror: Two Sides," *Mundus Artium*, 9 (1976), 75.

1977   50. "Song for my Daughters"; "If you read this . . ."; "Joys," *The Archive*, 90 (Spring, 1977), 81–83.

E. Book Reviews

Numerous book reviews appeared in the following journals:
Books Abroad
French Review
Journal of English and Germanic Philology
Monatshefte für deutschen Unterricht
Poetry
Yearbook of Comparative Literature

UNIVERSITY OF NORTH CAROLINA
STUDIES IN THE GERMANIC LANGUAGES
AND LITERATURES

45. Phillip H. Rhein. THE URGE TO LIVE. A Comparative Study of Franz Kafka's *Der Prozess* and Albert Camus' *L'Etranger*. 2nd printing. 1966. Pp. xii, 124. Cloth $6.00.
50. Randolph J. Klawiter. STEFAN ZWEIG. A BIBLIOGRAPHY. 1965. Pp. xxxviii, 191. Cloth $7,50.
51. John T. Krumpelmann. SOUTHERN SCHOLARS IN GOETHE'S GERMANY. 1965. Pp. xii, 200. Cloth $7.50.
52. Mariana Scott. THE HELIAND. Translated into English from the Old Saxon. 1966. Pp. x, 206. Cloth $7.50
53. A. E. Zucker. GENERAL DE KALB. LAFAYETTE'S MENTOR. Illustrated. 1966. Pp. x, 252. Cloth $7.50.
54. R. M. Longyear. SCHILLER AND MUSIC. 1966. Pp. x, 202. Cloth $7.50.
55. Clifford A. Bernd. THEODOR STORM'S CRAFT OF FICTION. The Torment of a Narrator. 2nd aug. ed. 1966. Pp. xvi, 141. Cloth 6.00.
56. Richard H. Allen. AN ANNOTATED ARTHUR SCHNITZLER BIBLIOGRAPHY. 1966. Pp. xiv, 151. Cloth $6.00.
57. Edwin H. Zeydel, Percy Matenko, Bertha M. Masche, eds. LETTERS TO AND FROM LUDWIG TIECK AND HIS CIRCLE. 1967. Pp. xxiv, 395. Cloth $12.50.
58. STUDIES IN HISTORICAL LINGUISTICS. FESTSCHRIFT FOR GEORGE S. LANE. Eighteen Essays. 1967. Pp. xx, 241. Cloth $7.50.
59. Wesley Thomas and Barbara G. Seagrave. THE SONGS OF THE MINNESINGER, PRINCE WIZLAW OF RÜGEN. Illustrated. 1967. Pp. x, 157. Cloth $6.00.
60. J. W. Thomas. MEDIEVAL GERMAN LYRIC VERSE. In English Translation. 1968. Pp. x, 252. Cloth $7.50.
61. Thomas W. Best. THE HUMANIST ULRICH VON HUTTEN. A Reappraisal of His Humor. 1969. Pp. x, 105. Cloth $6.00.
62. Lieselotte E. Kurth. DIE ZWEITE WIRKLICHKEIT. Studien zum Roman des achtzehnten Jahrhunderts. 1969. Pp. x, 273. Cloth $8.00.
63. J. W. Thomas. ULRICH VON LIECHTENSTEIN'S *SERVICE OF LADIES*. 1969. Pp. x, 229. Cloth $8.00.
64. Charlotte Craig. CHRISTOPH MARTIN WIELAND AS THE ORIGINATOR OF THE MODERN TRAVESTY IN GERMAN LITERATURE. 1970. Pp. xii, 147. Cloth $7.00.
65. Wolfgang W. Moelleken. LIEBE UND EHE, LEHRGEDICHTE VON DEM STRICKER. 1970. Pp. xxxviii, 72. Cloth $6.50.
66. Alan P. Cottrell. WILHELM MÜLLER'S LYRICAL SONG-CYCLES. Interpretation and Texts. 1970. Pp. x, 172. Cloth $7.00.
67. Siegfried Mews, ed. STUDIES IN GERMAN LITERATURE OF THE NINETEENTH AND TWENTIETH CENTURIES. FESTSCHRIFT FOR FREDERIC E. COENEN. Foreword by Werner P. Friederich. 1970. 2nd ed. 1972. Pp. xx, 251. Cloth $9.75.
68. John Neubauer. BIFOCAL VISION. NOVALIS' PHILOSOPHY OF NATURE AND DISEASE. 1971. Pp. x, 196. Cloth $7.75.
69. Victor Anthony Rudowski. LESSING'S *AESTHETICA IN NUCE*. An Analysis of the May 26, 1769, Letter to Nicolai. 1971. Pp. xii, 146. Cloth $6.70.
70. Donald F. Nelson. PORTRAIT OF THE ARTIST AS HERMES. A Study of Myth and Psychology in Thomas Mann's *Felix Krull*. 1971. Pp. xvi, 160. $6.75.
71. Murray A. and Marian L. Cowie, eds. THE WORKS OF PETER SCHOTT (1460–1490). Volume II: Commentary. Pp. xxix, 534. Paper $13.00. (See also volume 41.)

For other volumes in the "Studies" see page ii and following page.

Send orders to: (U.S. and Canada)
The University of North Carolina Press, P.O. Box 2288
Chapel Hill, N.C. 27514
(All other countries) Feffer and Simons, Inc., 31 Union Square, New York, N.Y. 10003

UNIVERSITY OF NORTH CAROLINA
STUDIES IN THE GERMANIC LANGUAGES
AND LITERATURES

72. Christine Oertel Sjögren. THE MARBLE STATUE AS IDEA: COLLECTED ESSAYS ON ADALBERT STIFTER'S *DER NACHSOMMER*. 1972. Pp. xiv, 121. Cloth $7.00.
73. Donald G. Daviau and Jorun B. Johns, eds. THE CORRESPONDENCE OF ARTHUR SCHNITZLER AND RAOUL AUERNHEIMER WITH RAOUL AUERNHEIMER'S APHORISMS. 1972. Pp. xii, 161. Cloth $7.50.
74. A. Margaret Arent Madelung. THE LAXDOELA SAGA: ITS STRUCTURAL PATTERNS. 1972. Pp. xiv, 261. Cloth $9.25.
75. Jeffrey L. Sammons. SIX ESSAYS ON THE YOUNG GERMAN NOVEL. 1972. Pp. xiv, 187. Cloth $7.75.
76. Donald H. Crosby and George C. Schoolfield, eds. STUDIES IN THE GERMAN DRAMA. A *FESTSCHRIFT* IN HONOR OF WALTER SILZ. 1974. Pp. xxvi, 255. Cloth $10.75.
77. J. W. Thomas. TANNHÄUSER: POET AND LEGEND. With Texts and Translations of his Works. 1974. Pp. x, 202. Cloth $10.75.
78. Olga Marx and Ernst Morwitz, trans. THE WORKS OF STEFAN GEORGE. 1974. 2nd, rev. and enl. ed. Pp. xxviii, 431. Cloth. $12.90.
79. Siegfried Mews and Herbert Knust, eds. ESSAYS ON BRECHT: THEATER AND POLITICS. 1974. Pp. xiv, 241. Cloth $11.95.

For other volumes in the "Studies" see preceding page and p. ii.

Send orders to: (U.S. and Canada)
The University of North Carolina Press, P. O. Box 2288
Chapel Hill, N.C. 27514
(All other countries) Feffer and Simons, Inc., 31 Union Square, New York, N.Y. 10003

Volumes 1–44 and 46–49 of the "Studies" have been reprinted.
They may be ordered from:
AMS Press, Inc., 56 E. 13th Street, New York, N.Y. 10003
For a complete list of reprinted titles write to:
Editor, UNCSGL&L, 442 Dey Hall, 014A, UNC, Chapel Hill, N.C. 27514